**COLLECTION MANAGEMENT**

|  |  |  |
|---|---|---|
|  |  |  |
|  |  |  |
|  |  |  |
|  |  |  |
|  |  |  |
|  |  |  |
|  |  |  |

family table

# family table

## Favorite Staff Meals from Our Restaurants to Your Home

**MICHAEL ROMANO & KAREN STABINER**

*Foreword by Danny Meyer*

PHOTOGRAPHS BY MARCUS NILSSON

A Rux Martin Book
Houghton Mifflin Harcourt
Boston  New York  2013

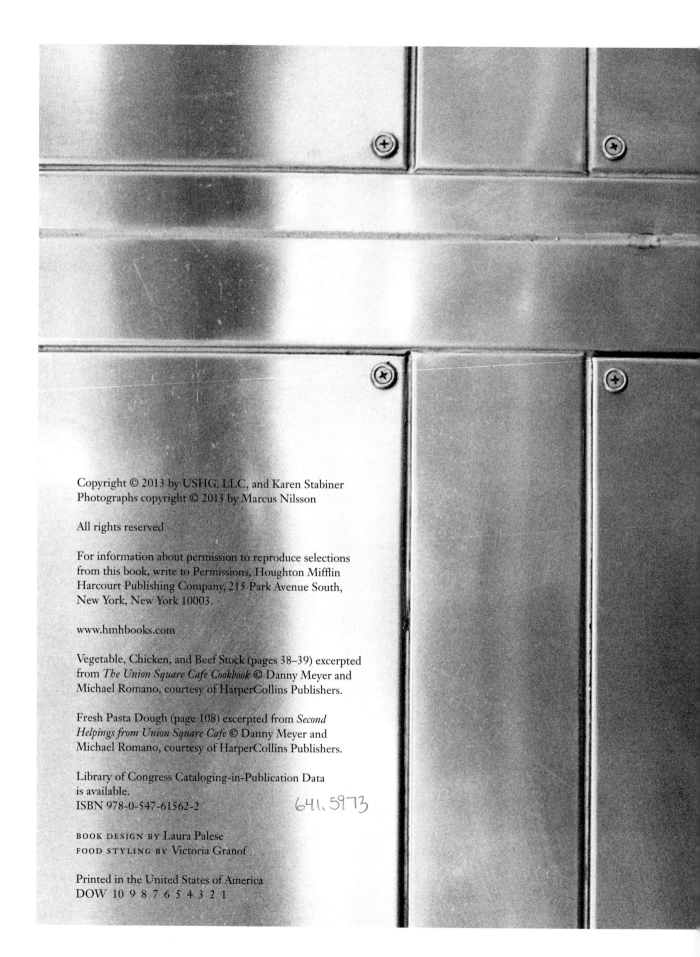

Vegetable, Chicken, and Beef Stock (pages 38–39) excerpted
from *The Union Square Cafe Cookbook* © Danny Meyer and
Michael Romano, courtesy of HarperCollins Publishers.

Fresh Pasta Dough (page 108) excerpted from *Second
Helpings from Union Square Cafe* © Danny Meyer and
Michael Romano, courtesy of HarperCollins Publishers.

Library of Congress Cataloging-in-Publication Data
is available.
ISBN 978-0-547-61562-2

641.5973

BOOK DESIGN BY Laura Palese
FOOD STYLING BY Victoria Granof

Printed in the United States of America
DOW 10 9 8 7 6 5 4 3 2 1

To Danny Meyer, with gratitude for your
enlightened leadership and unflagging
friendship these past twenty-five years—M.R.

For my father, Ira Stabiner, who told me his
own restaurant stories first—K.S.

### RESTAURANTS CREATED BY
### UNION SQUARE HOSPITALITY GROUP

Union Square Cafe
Gramercy Tavern
Eleven Madison Park
Tabla
Blue Smoke
The Modern
The Museum of Modern Art cafes
Union Square Tokyo
Maialino
Untitled at the Whitney
North End Grill

# Acknowledgments

I would like to extend my sincere thanks and appreciation to the following people, without whose help and support this book would not have been possible.

TO ALL OUR RESTAURANT AND CATERING STAFF MEMBERS—those who prepare the meals for the family table and those who just enjoy them—thank you for your patience and for sharing your skills. You are the inspiration for this book, and I am very grateful.

TO KAREN STABINER, whose passion for and belief in this book helped carry it through both the good moments and the challenging ones to its happy completion.

TO DAVID BLACK, whose clear thinking, unwavering support, trust, and friendship mean the world to me.

TO MARCUS NILSSON, who was a delight to work with and who gave us wonderful photographs that really capture the spirit of the book.

TO NICK FAUCHALD, whose tireless and expert testing helped me perfect and transform the recipes from rough sketches to kitchen-ready for your home.

TO DANNY MEYER, whose support and advice were, as always, invaluable.

TO MY EDITOR, RUX MARTIN, whose keen eye, sharp pencil, and confidence in the book helped create the polished work of which I am very proud.

AND TO MY MOTHER, GRANDMOTHER, AND AUNTS, whose loving touch with food taught me to appreciate the family table.—M.R.

A very large family made this book happen, and I'm grateful to many more people than I can list here. My thanks to:

DANNY MEYER, for saying yes to a writer who wanted to spend time in all of his restaurants, day and night.

MICHAEL ROMANO, who is demanding in the best way, inspiring, and very, very funny. It was a privilege to work with him.

RUX MARTIN, OUR EDITOR, who encouraged and challenged us and was always open to discussion.

JANIS DONNAUD, who helped shepherd the project along, and Lynn Nesbit, who set it in motion.

THE FAMILY WITHIN THE FAMILY, people who got more involved than they had time for—Jean-Paul Bourgeois, Terry Coughlin, Geoff Lazlo, Dino Lavorini, Nancy Olson, and Sandro Romano.

MODESTO BATISTA, whom I met early in the process. It's worth getting up early on a Saturday just to bump into him at the farmers' market.

FRIENDS who made and/or ate versions of these recipes as they took shape. In California, Marcie Rothman, notable for Mondays at Marcie's dinners; Cassidy Freeman and Justin Carpenter; Megan and Clark Freeman; and Annette Duffy and David Odell. In New York City, Ginger Curwen (with a nod to Jack), Paula Span, Laura Muha, Lisa Belkin and Bruce Gelb, and every one of my students who showed up for class hungry.

CAROLYN SEE, who is essential to any truly great meal.

MY MOTHER, NORMA, AND MY HUSBAND, LARRY, for two generations of family meals and all the attendant memories.

MY DAUGHTER, SARAH, who equates good food with a good time. One of my favorite texts from her is simply, "What're you doing?" which could mean we're about to bake a pie.—K.S.

# Contents

# Foreword by Danny Meyer

*I was fortunate enough to grow up eating one or two meals a day with my family: breakfast at 7:15 each morning and dinner at 7:00 each night.*

It was a good day when my mom poached or scrambled eggs for us, and an exceptional one when she served fried eggs along with toasted Jewish rye with "corn tzitzel"—a specialty of St. Louis delicatessens, in which the bread crust is dusted with coarse cornmeal. And it was a perfect day when she buttered our toast with butter, not margarine. Cereal days meant my mom didn't feel like cooking, or that she didn't think we should eat so many eggs in one week. Fresh doughnut and bagel runs were generally reserved for weekends.

Even in that simpler era, breakfast was a hurried affair. We fed the dog, pored over the sports section, and watched the *Today* show—the scant twenty minutes allocated to breakfast meant that not much was discussed. Everyone was on a slightly different biorhythm at that hour. Some of us were wide-eyed and ready to grab the world, some were tired and closemouthed. Yet even on those days when scarcely a word was spoken, we affirmed our "family-ness" simply by following the ritual of sitting around the same table.

Evening meals were different. The moment we came home from school, the first question invariably was, "What's for dinner?" Learning that it would be something good helped provide the impetus to get cracking on our homework. Most of our family dinners were cooked by my mom. Most were delicious and varied, and I can't recall a meal when I didn't ask for seconds—except on those (fortunately) rare occasions when she served calves' liver or fish sticks. Mom had a fairly broad rotation of dishes that were drawn from those she had eaten at her own family dinners in suburban Chicago, others were picked up along the way from my St. Louis grandmother and friends, and some were from her travels with my dad in France, where they'd lived for the first two years of their marriage and often dined in family homes.

The family meal was where my brother and sister and I learned to cook. When we reached a certain age, we were expected to contribute something to the dinner. We developed our own specialties. My brother and I loved making Tupperware salads, prepared and shaken in the containers; grilling burgers and ribs on our outdoor pit, often with our father; stirring up chili; and preparing homemade pizza and tacos. My sister became an accomplished baker, turning out quiches, bread, cookies, and cakes.

But it's the conversations at the dinner table I remember more than anything else. We discussed and debated the issues of the day (often with more heat than light, since we were all at different points along the political spectrum). We talked about our accomplishments (or lack thereof) at school, my dad's business, and our favorite sports teams. We decided where to go on our next vacation, caught up on news of our relatives, updated one another on the activities of our friends, and occasionally discussed ethics and values. Often our family meal was joyous with laughter.

When I went away to college, I joined a fraternity my sophomore year—not the kind for sleeping in but, rather, one that was primarily a social and eating club. Though we never called them "family meals," the "brothers" got together for a special dinner each Thursday night and for brunch every Saturday.

Most everything we ate seemed to be stuffed. Our favorite dinner was roasted Rock Cornish game hen with store-bought stovetop stuffing. For brunch, we devoured omelets filled with every anti-hangover protein known to man. Even our bacon-wrapped hot dogs were stuffed with cheese. The food was the apparent draw, but it was the stitching together of a community that mattered the most. Though I didn't realize it at the time, it's clear to me now that I'd never have joined the fraternity had I not craved that sense of belonging at a family table.

Years later in New York City, on the first day of my first restaurant job at a Flatiron District seafood restaurant called Pesca, I was given succinct instructions on how to ready the restaurant for lunch service. I was to fill (but not overfill) the reservation book; write and type out the daily specials, walk down the street to have them copied, and stuff the lists into Lucite frames; check in the waiters and waitresses; make a seating plan for lunch; and prepare some comments to deliver to the staff during family meal.

All those directives made sense except for the last one: I had never heard the expression "family meal" outside my own home, and it had never occurred to me that a restaurant referred to its staff members as "the family." Nor had I known that it was standard for a restaurant to feed its employees twice a day—once before lunch service and then again before dinner service. I gradually reset my body clock to eat lunch at 10:45 and dinner at 4:45.

It didn't take me long to start looking forward to family meal as one of the highlights of my day. The food was homey, abundant, and generally very good; the conversation (and gossip) fascinating; and, as a bonus, I saved a ton of money by not having to pay for my food.

I was twenty-six years old and living alone, and the restaurant quickly became both the place where I worked and the place where I saw "family." My restaurant family fed me, coached me, and recommended plays, museum exhibits, jazz shows, restaurants, dance clubs, and even wines to taste. I also got advice on whom to date—and one of those suggestions stuck: At one of my final meals, before leaving the restaurant to study cooking in Italy and France, I asked out one of the waitresses, Audrey Heffernan. Our first date was on my last night of work, and today we are married, with four kids.

At one family meal, I was introduced to a new cook who had just returned to New York from stints in important restaurants and private homes in France and Switzerland. He stood out from the other cooks because of his professional demeanor and seriousness of purpose—he was set on becoming a chef, and soon. The two of us hit it off, and we spent lots of time discussing food and wine. That young cook was Michael Romano, and some four years later, we reconnected as colleagues at Union Square Cafe. Neither of us could have predicted at that first family meal that we'd still be in culinary partnership nearly thirty years later!

In late 1984, in preparation for opening my first restaurant, Union Square Cafe, I began a cook's *stage*—a kitchen apprenticeship—at La Réserve, a lovely small hotel restaurant in Pessac, France, just outside Bordeaux. I was to live with the chef and accompany him on his daily trip to the morning market. My introduction to the restaurant was at an evening family meal, where the cooking staff was still dealing with something serious: the devastating recent loss of the restaurant's second Michelin star. Morale was low. A couple of cooks had departed, concerned about their résumés. I felt like an interloper.

I was assigned five jobs by the chef, tasks he felt I could accomplish without risking the restaurant's reputation. I was to pluck feathers from birds, chop shallots, carve lemons into crowns, open oysters, and cook family meal three times a week. I made my first meal on my second day at work. The chef had given me a budget and asked for my shopping list the day before. I made St. Louis–style ribs, using my grandmother's recipe for the barbecue sauce and roasting them in the

oven, as well as an eggplant pasta I'd learned in Rome and a salad I'd often made back in St. Louis that included sliced salami and provolone.

I had picked wisely: No one could compare my spareribs with any others, because none of the cooks had ever heard of pork ribs with barbecue sauce. I tried not to feel offended when they poured ketchup all over the pasta. The next time, I made it with a legitimate tomato sauce. Despite the profusion of pork and cheese, that first meal was a big hit, and it served as my initiation into my new French family. I was invited to accompany *l'équipe* (the family "team") at every post-service and weekend activity, and they embraced me to the point of teaching me an adequate level of kitchen French. I had a new family, thanks to family meal.

• • •

I realized how formative those meals could be in my early days. A delicious meal cooked by a colleague for many others nourishes not only the body but also the soul, sending out a message of "one for all, all for one." A staff that takes care of itself even before the guests arrive is likely to display real hospitality to its guests.

Conversely, I learned that a poor meal can put the family in a foul mood that affects the quality of the service. Serving scorched scrambled eggs or a leftover, too garlicky pasta sends a message that the cook doesn't care about making fellow workers happy. They will be tolerant to a point, but if the pattern persists, morale sags and the "siblings" predictably act out—not a good thing for a restaurant or its guests.

Family meal is usually cooked by the sous chef or more junior cooks, often on a rotating basis. At its best, the meal gives cooks the joy of stepping out of their normal routine to prepare favorite personal recipes, or improvised dishes, often reflecting their ethnic backgrounds. Generally the meal is pulled together from ingredients already stocked in the restaurant but bears little resemblance to what guests will see on the menu. The walk-in refrigerator is the market basket.

Family meals are used to welcome new members of the team and to say good-bye to veterans who are leaving. They are occasions for celebrating birthdays, restaurant anniversaries, promotions, and maternity leaves, as well as for reading poetry, singing songs, and, mostly, for bonding.

The conversation at the lunch or dinner table can be scintillating some days and less so on others, just as it is for families at home. And, just as in a real family, each staff member takes on an archetypal role: Every restaurant has its mother hen, stern father, comedian, storyteller, wise guy, golden child, mother's helper, straight-A student, and dilettante.

At each of our restaurants, a satisfying family meal is crucial to the philosophy that we call "enlightened hospitality." That is how we intentionally blur the lines between work and home so that we can make our guests' experience of going out feel like coming home. Providing a delicious, nutritious, nurturing experience at family meal is a pretty good indicator that we can accomplish that.

This book is a peek behind the scenes and a look at what our family of staff members cooks for one another before they cook for you. It's also a celebration of the remarkable people who make up our restaurant families—people who spend more time at the table with one another than with their own families.

Most of these recipes won't break the bank, and they are all eminently doable. They are cooked in family-sized batches, with family-style presentations. Have fun, and thanks for welcoming our family into your home.

# Introduction

*When I was growing up, it was hard to see where family life left off and meals began—my best memories include both. My mother had six brothers and sisters, my father had four siblings, and I had a sister and lots of cousins.*

My grandparents lived upstairs from us in our East Harlem tenement, and almost everyone in the extended family lived in the neighborhood. I don't remember a Sunday without a festive meal or without relatives.

And what food! Some Sundays when I was little, I'd be sent off to an aunt or upstairs to my grandmother, and over time I got to see how every component of those endless dinners was made. The aunt who made ravioli had no room in her kitchen, so she opened up the ironing board, spread a tablecloth on it, and used it as extra counter space. I was just about as tall as that ironing board, and I stood there as she filled the ravioli, sealed the edges, and lined them up, counting off how many I was going to eat.

They were all so good, but my favorites were the pillowy ones filled with creamy fresh ricotta. My interest in her food was rewarded when my aunt appointed me to test the spaghetti to see whether it was done. She taught me how to bite into a strand and know, right then, yes or no. Looking back, I guess I was setting my feet on the path to a food career without even realizing it.

When I was thirteen, our family began to migrate to the Bronx—first an aunt and uncle, then my grandparents, and then us—and the weekly Sunday family meals continued until I went to college. Even then, food was as central as it can be to three roommates who suddenly have no parents around to feed them. I moved in with two high school buddies, one of them the local butcher's son, and while we didn't put in the kind of time my mother did, we ate well.

I started college without much of a sense of where I was headed, but to help make ends meet, I worked as the frozen drink man at Serendipity, an Upper East Side restaurant where frozen hot chocolate, my primary responsibility, was the

most famous item on the menu. There was no official family meal, no time when we sat down together to eat; we grabbed food on the run whenever we had the chance. But the family feeling was certainly there. The owners of Serendipity saw potential in me that I hadn't yet seen myself—a genuine love of food, and no fear of hard work—and they arranged a meeting with James Beard for me. It was just the sort of life-changing event you might imagine. I arrived at his townhouse not knowing what to expect, and I left with an impatient passion. Thanks to his encouragement, I knew I had to get started on my life in food, and fast.

I dropped out of college and enrolled in a two-year food program at New York City College of Technology. A year later, I was on my way to three months of study in Bournemouth, England—and some of the worst food I'd ever eaten. If I hadn't fully appreciated the joys of a great homemade meal with family and friends, I certainly did after three months of deprivation. At school, we worked with beautiful ingredients—grouse, Dover sole—but the professors ate the dishes we made, while we had to settle for the staff cafeteria, which specialized in starchy, overcooked, bland food. It was an odd, demoralizing notion, asking people who live to cook wonderful food to eat one bad meal after another, and it unified us only in our desire to get up from the table and go back to work.

As soon as I finished my studies, I headed to Paris—like Moses traveling to the Promised Land—and I landed a *stage*, a kitchen apprenticeship, at the hotel Le Bristol. The food at family meal was the opposite of what I'd had in England—it had to satisfy the demanding sous chef—but the tension that pervaded our twice-daily meals made enjoyment impossible. The chef ate with the other hotel executives, never with us, and the front-of-the-house staff ate by themselves. The kitchen staff sat at a long table, with the sous chef at the head and the rest of us in descending order of importance according to our stations, down to the lowest of the low at the far end.

I still remember the day the sous chef took a bite of cauliflower, hesitated, and spat it out. He glared down the table and asked who had made it. An apprentice, a kid in his teens, said that he had. The sous chef gestured for him to approach. Meekly, the boy made his way to the head of the table—and, just like that, the sous chef punched him in the chest.

The boy just turned and walked back to his seat, which to me was the oddest part of the incident. Nobody made a big deal out of a kid getting punched for a disappointing vegetable. It was business as usual—hardly the most conducive atmosphere for what was supposed to be a break in a long day of work.

After more training and work in Paris, southwestern France, and Zurich, I went home and started working in New York City restaurants. I became the first American executive chef at La Caravelle, a legendary French restaurant in midtown Manhattan, where I supervised a kitchen full of trained chefs who expected the same type of high-quality family meal I'd had at the Bristol—minus the fisticuffs.

When Danny Meyer asked me to run the Union Square Cafe kitchen in 1988, I brought along two traditions that mattered to me: I wore a suit to work, as I had at La Caravelle, a habit no one else was interested in adopting, and I insisted on a sit-down meal twice a day for my restaurant family, one that would bring them together rather than keep them apart. That was a far more popular idea. Some of the staff had come from restaurants where they had just enough time to run out for fast takeout on their breaks. Some had had jobs where they ate out of quart containers at their stations or waited to eat until they had finished their shifts.

The rules for our family meal were simple: It couldn't be fancy or complicated, but it did have to be full of flavor. People had to sit down to eat, with everyone gathered in the same room—front of the house and kitchen staff together. That's how we started, over twenty years ago, and it's what we've done at each of the Union Square Hospitality Group's restaurants ever since, whether it's a meal for fifty at Gramercy Tavern or a meal for ten at Untitled at the Whitney.

To some of the staff, sitting down together seemed a luxury; to me, it was essential. People work better when they take a break. I don't buy the notion that stopping makes it harder to get started again. And I rail against the idea of, "No, I'm too busy, I'll grab something quick in the kitchen." I say, "You think you're saving time and getting more work done, but you're not eating or working as well as you would if you took a break. Sit down and eat. You're going to be more productive. Don't ask your body to multitask."

I think that's true for your family as well. It's always good to take a moment to stop, sit down, and catch your breath over food and conversation, away from your desk, your electronics, your to-do list, everything but what's on your plate and the other people seated at the table. The challenge for the home cook is to keep meals fun when you're strapped for time, on a budget, and in danger of repeating the same familiar dishes again and again. *Family Table* is intended as a happy remedy, offered by cooks who operate under similar constraints but have the benefit of experience in a professional kitchen. We are sharing our family meals and the knowledge that went into creating them in the hope of inspiring and informing yours.

And when I say "we," I mean it: This collection comes from about four dozen contributors, from sous chefs to prep cooks and porters, from cooks with classical training to cooks who learned everything on the job. While our executive chefs aren't usually involved in making daily family meals, they've contributed favorite recipes they enjoy with their own families, in keeping with the spirit of the book.

The only common denominator in all these recipes is enthusiasm and a tasty idea. This is home cooking at its best. Some of the dishes are staffers' personal family favorites, a parent's or grandparent's specialty updated with accessible, market-fresh ingredients and clever techniques. Some are inspired improvisations, the result of a cook's ability to look at a collection of ingredients and figure out how to make them harmonize in a new way. And some are reconsidered classics, a standard preparation made just a little bit better.

The result is a world tour of various cuisines, with some recipes that may be completely new to you and others that may look familiar but come with a twist. And because the original recipes were made to serve dozens of people, all of these adapt easily to home entertaining. To celebrate our family, we also offer stories of life behind the scenes, which Karen Stabiner collected, about chefs whose names you know and about people you never see. Here you'll find great dishes and stories from the whole family, including former members of the group like Eleven Madison Park and Tabla.

Even after all this time, family meal is still a draw for me. Sometimes I walk over to one of the other restaurants in the late afternoon, or I manage to schedule a meeting around the time that the midday meal comes out. It's a chance for me to spend time with my restaurant family, both the people I've grown up with professionally and the next generation we're proud to be bringing along. In a funny way, I've come full circle: Like that little guy counting ravioli and looking forward to dinner with my relatives, I still can't tell where family leaves off and the meal begins, which is just the way I like it.

I hope that these recipes inspire your family as well to sit down together at the table.

# Soups

Chilled Carrot Soup with Frizzled Ginger  26  |  Michael Anthony's Corn Soup  28  |  Pappa al Pomodoro  30  |  Michael Romano's Secret-Ingredient Soup  32  |  Pasta e Fagioli  35  |  Chicken Soup with Pastina & Parmigiano  36  |  Vegetable Stock  38  |  Chicken Stock  39  |  Beef Stock  39

*Raquel Mota presides over an ever-changing menu* at the Museum of Modern Art's staff cafeteria, which serves both museum employees and restaurant staffers who get hungry between family meals. The menu ranges from her own Dominican favorites to an assortment of soups: seasonal specialties, meals-in-a-bowl, steaming-hot comfort soups, and chilled ones for warmer days. This quick and easy carrot soup is spiked with ginger, both in the broth itself and as crunchy little threads floated on top, and it is good hot as well as cold.

# Chilled Carrot Soup with Frizzled Ginger

4 tablespoons (½ stick) unsalted butter

1 small yellow onion, coarsely chopped

2½ pounds carrots, peeled and coarsely chopped

2 tablespoons finely chopped peeled fresh ginger, plus one 2-inch piece fresh ginger, peeled, for garnish

3 quarts Vegetable Stock (page 38)

Kosher salt and freshly ground black pepper

1 cup vegetable oil

**6 to 8 servings**

In a large heavy saucepan, melt the butter over medium heat. Add the onion and cook, stirring, until slightly tender but not browned, about 5 minutes. Add the carrots, chopped ginger, and stock, bring to a simmer, and cook, uncovered, until the carrots are very soft, 30 to 40 minutes. Remove from the heat.

Puree the soup in batches in a blender until very smooth. Add salt and pepper to taste. Refrigerate if you want to serve the soup cold, 3 to 4 hours. (*The soup can be made up to 2 days ahead, covered and refrigerated.*)

When you're ready to serve the soup, slice the remaining piece of ginger into thin strips, then slice lengthwise into strands as thin as possible.

In a small skillet, heat the oil to 350 degrees over medium heat. To test it, add a strand of ginger—if the oil is the right temperature, the ginger will fry to a golden brown in about 30 seconds; if the oil is too hot, the ginger will burn almost immediately. Adjust the heat if necessary, add the remaining ginger, and fry until golden; drain on paper towels.

Reheat the soup if you're serving it hot. Ladle into bowls and garnish each bowl with a few strands of the frizzled ginger.

*Gramercy Tavern chef Michael Anthony* grew up in Cincinnati, but when his parents retired, they moved to a rural area where all roads seem to lead to a farm stand. In high corn season, his family puts every part of an ear to work. For this recipe, the whole kernels go into a silken soup based on a stock that uses the cobs, and then Michael adds an uncommon set of spices to create a symphony of summer flavors.

# Michael Anthony's Corn Soup

### For the corn stock

4–6 ears corn

1 large onion, finely chopped (2 cups)

1 large carrot, thinly sliced (1 cup)

2 garlic cloves, smashed and peeled

Kosher salt

1 fresh thyme sprig

1 small fresh rosemary sprig

### For the soup

6 tablespoons (¾ stick) unsalted butter

1 cup thinly sliced shallots (about 4 medium)

1 large garlic clove, thinly sliced

1 leek, white and light green parts only, halved, thinly sliced, and well washed to remove grit (about 1 cup)

1 star anise

1 teaspoon coriander seeds

1 tablespoon honey

5 large fresh basil leaves

1 fresh tarragon sprig

1 fresh thyme sprig

1 small fresh rosemary sprig

1 teaspoon kosher salt, or more to taste

2 teaspoons fresh lime juice, or more to taste

*4 servings*

TO MAKE THE CORN STOCK: Cut the corn off the cobs; you should have about 3½ cups. Set aside. Cut the cobs into thirds.

Put the cobs, onion, carrot, and garlic in a large saucepan and cover with 8 cups water. Add a pinch of salt, the thyme, and rosemary, bring to a simmer, and cook, uncovered, for 45 minutes.

Strain the stock through a fine-mesh strainer into a bowl; you should have about 5 cups.

TO MAKE THE SOUP: In a medium pot, melt the butter over medium-low heat. Add the shallots and garlic, and cook, stirring, until softened, about 3 minutes. Add the leek and cook for 2 minutes. Add the reserved corn kernels and cook for 2 minutes.

Tie the star anise and coriander seeds up in a cheesecloth packet and add to the pot. Add the honey and 4 cups of the corn stock, raise the heat to medium, and bring the soup to a simmer. Cook, uncovered, for 10 minutes.

Tie the herbs together with kitchen twine. Remove the pot from the heat, add the herbs, and let steep for 5 minutes.

Remove and discard the herbs and spice packet. Puree the soup in batches in a blender, then strain through a fine-mesh strainer into a saucepan, pressing on the solids to release all the liquid. If necessary, thin the soup to the desired consistency with some or all of the remaining corn stock.

Reheat the soup over medium heat. Stir in the salt and lime juice, taste, and adjust the seasonings if needed. Serve.

*Loads of tomatoes, both fresh and canned,* a half loaf of good bread, and fresh basil are the basic elements of this thick Italian soup, which requires only a short prep and an unsupervised simmer.

The fresh tomatoes add their bright acidity to the soup, while the canned tomatoes contribute body and sweetness. Pappa al pomodoro is a great answer to what to do with that irresistible flat of tomatoes you bought with more enthusiasm than strategy at the farmers' market. It is equally good hot or at room temperature.

# Pappa al Pomodoro

3½ pounds ripe tomatoes

¾ cup olive oil, plus more for drizzling

1 tablespoon finely chopped garlic

1 tablespoon kosher salt

½ teaspoon red pepper flakes, or more to taste

1 28-ounce can plum tomatoes, crushed with your hands, with their liquid

1 bay leaf

8 ounces day-old rustic Italian bread, such as ciabatta, crusts removed, cut into ½-inch chunks (about 4 lightly packed cups)

¼ cup finely chopped fresh basil, plus more for garnish

¼ cup grated Parmigiano-Reggiano, plus more for serving

**4 to 6 servings**

To peel the tomatoes, bring a large saucepan of water to a boil. Cut a shallow X in the bottom end of each tomato and plunge them into the boiling water for about 1 minute. As soon as the skins start to curl away at the X, drain the tomatoes and put them in a bowl of cold water to stop the cooking.

Drain the tomatoes again and gently peel off the skins. Core and coarsely chop.

In a 4-quart saucepan, heat ¼ cup of the oil over medium heat. Add the garlic and cook, stirring, until lightly browned, 3 to 4 minutes. Add the salt, red pepper, fresh and canned tomatoes, and the bay leaf. Bring to a simmer and cook, uncovered, for 45 minutes, or until reduced to a stew-like consistency.

Add the bread and simmer for about 5 minutes, until completely soaked through. Add the basil and simmer for 2 minutes.

Remove the soup from the heat and remove and discard the bay leaf. Stir in the cheese and the remaining ½ cup oil. Adjust the salt and red pepper if needed. Serve hot or at room temperature, topped with more grated cheese, basil, and a drizzle of oil.

# Finding the Rhythm

"I am soooooo far in the weeds, yeah," sang a Gramercy Tavern cook who was running down the kitchen aisle with a large tray of chicken, trying to finish his part of the late-morning family meal in addition to his other responsibilities. When he got to the oven, he dropped to a squat, balanced the full tray with one hand while he opened the door with the other, and, in a single motion, shoved the pan into the oven, pivoted to grab another pan from a cabinet on the opposite side of the aisle, straightened up, and walked away.

A half hour of concerted effort later, and he still wasn't quite caught up. "Behind, behind, behind, behind," he called as he headed down the line again, to make sure that no one stepped into his path as he delivered a third tray of chicken to the oven. A moment later, he was off to somewhere else with a tray of pineapple, singing, "Oh, I've got three minutes, oh, I've got three minutes," in a falsetto tinged with urgency. Still, three minutes turned out to be just enough, and his contribution to family meal hit the table in time.

Once lunch service began, the singing stopped and the chat had mostly to do with traffic control: "Hot, hot, hot, hot, hot," at which everyone inhaled slightly and edged a half step closer to the stove, and then relaxed as the cook passed behind them. Or "Corner!" shouted frequently to avoid a collision at the edges of the room.

Hours later, as dinner service began, chef Michael Anthony prowled the kitchen, finally settling in at the front end of the line, tasting spoon at the ready, to monitor and adjust the dishes before they left the kitchen. He watched four sets of hands as they built the components of a single plate, sometimes stepping in to demonstrate how something should be done, or stood next to the harried expediter, a force field of calm.

Sometimes Michael took a moment to survey the scene, the master inventor making sure that all the gears, wheels, and levers were working properly. He enjoyed seeing the singing cook get back in his groove and took pleasure in watching Juan Matias, who has worked the garde-manger station since 1997, turning out cold appetizers, small salads, and other food that doesn't require heat. Juan took one step to the right, then back, turned in place to get something behind him, and turned again.

"That's the slow slide," said Michael, appreciatively. A single step in any direction and the cook had what he needed, with never a second step and never a wasted motion. A kitchen hinges on such small economies.

*The secret ingredient in this satisfying soup* is a small amount of cornmeal (polenta), just enough to thicken the broth slightly. It balances the substantial sausage and greens for a soothing cold-weather dish.

Aleppo pepper comes from the town of Aleppo in northern Syria; the flaky crushed sun-dried pepper has a slightly smoky flavor. It's become easier to find in gourmet markets, but if necessary, you can substitute red pepper flakes.

# Michael Romano's Secret-Ingredient Soup

2 tablespoons olive oil

¾ cup finely chopped onion

¾ cup finely chopped peeled carrot

¾ cup well-washed thinly sliced leeks

1 teaspoon finely chopped garlic

1½ teaspoons kosher salt

¼ teaspoon freshly ground black pepper

¼ teaspoon Aleppo pepper or red pepper flakes

8 ounces Italian fennel sausage (sweet or hot), casings removed

2 tablespoons medium-grind cornmeal (polenta)

5 cups Chicken or Vegetable Stock (page 39 or 38)

4 cups packed stemmed and coarsely chopped kale or chard leaves, or a combination

Grated Parmigiano-Reggiano for serving

**4 to 6 servings**

Heat the oil in a large saucepan over medium heat. Add the onion, carrot, leeks, garlic, salt, black pepper, and Aleppo pepper and cook, stirring, until the onion becomes translucent, 8 to 10 minutes. Add the sausage and cook, breaking it up into small pieces with a wooden spoon, until no longer pink, about 5 minutes.

Drain off the excess fat, leaving about 2 tablespoons in the pan. Stir in the cornmeal. Add the stock, stirring, and bring to a boil, then reduce the heat and simmer, covered, for 30 minutes, stirring occasionally.

Stir in the greens and cook for 15 minutes more, or until tender.

Ladle into bowls and garnish with grated Parmigiano.

*The late-afternoon family meal at the Union Square Cafe* is served in a small, clubby back room, the kind of place a passerby would like to be invited to visit—if only there were a single spare chair.

The restaurant's version of this thick, satisfying pasta-and-bean soup includes some chopped coppa—air-dried pork shoulder—to spice things up a bit. Use an Italian salami such as sopressata if coppa is hard to find. You can replicate the dish in no time.

# Pasta e Fagioli

1 cup shelled fresh cranberry beans or 1 cup canned cannellini beans, with their liquid plus enough water to make 1 cup

Kosher salt

4 ounces (about 1 heaping cup) short dried pasta, such as penne, fusilli, or cavatelli

2 garlic cloves, smashed and thinly sliced

¼ cup olive oil

Pinch of red pepper flakes

1 2-inch fresh rosemary sprig

⅓ cup coarsely chopped spicy coppa (about 12 thin slices; see headnote)

1 large ripe beefsteak tomato, peeled, cored, and coarsely chopped, or 1½ cups coarsely chopped canned tomatoes

1 heaping tablespoon grated Pecorino Romano

1 heaping tablespoon grated Parmigiano-Reggiano or Grana Padano

**4 to 6 servings**

If using cranberry beans, rinse them in cold water. Place them in a saucepan and cover with 3 inches of cold water. Bring to a simmer and cook gently for 20 to 30 minutes, until tender. Remove from the heat, add ½ teaspoon salt, and cool. Set the beans aside in their cooking liquid.

In a large pot, bring 8 cups water to a boil over high heat and add 1½ teaspoons salt. Add the pasta, stir, and cook until al dente; drain.

Meanwhile, in a large saucepan, cook the garlic in 2 tablespoons of the olive oil over medium heat for 2 minutes, or until golden. Remove from the heat, add the red pepper, rosemary, coppa, and tomato, and stir well.

Return the saucepan to the stove and add the cranberry beans and 1 cup of their liquid or the cannellini beans. Increase the heat to high and bring to a boil. Add the pasta, reduce the heat to medium, and gently simmer until the soup thickens, 3 to 5 minutes. Remove and discard the rosemary sprig.

Stir in the cheeses and the remaining 2 tablespoons oil and serve.

*Sometimes the most satisfying dishes are the simplest ones.* Lynn Bound, the chef of the Museum of Modern Art cafes, loves this soup because it's a tasty one-dish meal—and because it's what her waitress mom made ahead to ensure that her three kids always had a home-cooked meal, even when she was working a double shift.

Buying a whole chicken is a better idea than using cut-up pieces, not only because it's cheaper but because the flesh is less exposed, which means it cooks up more tender. A second batch of fresh vegetables added to the finished stock contributes texture and more flavor. You can make the soup in advance, but don't add the pastina until you're ready to serve it so that it will be al dente, not overcooked.

# Chicken Soup with Pastina & Parmigiano

### For the stock

1 3- to 3½-pound chicken

6 celery stalks, coarsely chopped

4 medium carrots, coarsely chopped

1 small onion, coarsely chopped

10 fresh Italian parsley sprigs

1 3-inch Parmigiano-Reggiano rind (optional)

### For the soup

3 carrots, peeled, cut lengthwise in half and crosswise into ½-inch dice (1½ cups)

6 celery stalks, cut into ½-inch dice (2 cups)

1 small onion, cut into ½-inch dice (1 cup)

1 cup pastina

1 tablespoon fresh lemon juice, or more to taste

Kosher salt and freshly ground black pepper

About 1⅓ cups grated Parmigiano-Reggiano

**10 to 12 servings**

TO MAKE THE STOCK: Put all the ingredients in a large pot and cover with 4 quarts water. Bring to a boil over high heat, skimming off any foam on top. Reduce the heat to medium-low and simmer gently, uncovered, for 3 hours, adding water as needed to keep the chicken covered. Remove from the heat.

Ladle the fat off the surface of the stock. Carefully remove the chicken from the pot and let cool.

Strain the stock through a fine-mesh strainer into a bowl. Discard the vegetables and cheese rind, if you used it. Return the stock to the pot (you will have about 4 quarts).

When the chicken is cool, pull the meat from the bones, discarding the skin. Pull the chicken into chunks and set aside, covered.

TO MAKE THE SOUP: Add the carrots, celery, and onion to the stock, bring to a simmer, and cook until the vegetables are crisp-tender, about 10 minutes. Bring the soup to a boil, add the pastina, and cook until al dente, about 5 minutes.

Add the chicken and cook until warmed through. Stir in the lemon juice and season with salt and pepper to taste.

Ladle into individual bowls, top each bowl with about 2 tablespoons grated Parmigiano, and serve.

# The Mentor

Most of the members of chef Lynn Bound's staff at the Museum of Modern Art cafes have not gone to culinary school. For that matter, many of them have never worked in another restaurant. She figures that people with diplomas and experience want to work in kitchens with higher profiles, which is fine with her.

The staff feeds not only visitors to the museum but also the restaurant employees at morning and afternoon family meals and the museum employees at the staff cafeteria. Lynn runs the three large, distinct operations with a harried but determined air, constantly on the lookout for anything that would benefit from her attention.

She values the consistency that comes from building a family from the bottom up, even as she monitors her brood to make sure that they aren't in over their heads. A simple journey from her basement kitchen to the fifth-floor cafe can become a series of zigzags—to send fruit to a couple of diners who look impatient, to taste a new salad, and to exhort everyone to do a bit more, no matter how much they are already doing.

In effect, Lynn runs her own culinary academy. She steps in to help with family meal whenever a teaching moment presents itself. If a cook inherits bits of roasted beets, she does a quick tutorial in how to turn them into a salad with feta cheese and greens. A surplus of carrots leads to a demonstration of how to make a carrot-and-ginger soup.

"It would be nice," she mused, "if someone who worked with me knew what a sweet pea was." But then she stopped herself. "I give them building blocks, I promote porters to kitchen jobs. People like what they do, they're treated like family, and there's room to move up for those who want to."

She tallied her success stories—Little Teresa, who earned her nickname by being the shortest person in the kitchen and advanced from porter to prep; Raquel, whose occasional Dominican specials made the staff cafeteria an even more popular place; José, a newly minted family meal cook. She invests her time in their continuing education, and they repay the favor by sticking around.

# Vegetable Stock

1 tablespoon olive oil

3 cups sliced carrots (about 1 pound)

3 cups sliced onions (about 12 ounces)

2 cups coarsely chopped Savoy cabbage (about 6 ounces)

2 cups well-washed sliced leeks, white and light green parts only (about 5 ounces)

1½ cups sliced celery (about 6 ounces)

1 medium head Bibb lettuce, cored and coarsely chopped

1 cup sliced peeled parsnips

3 garlic cloves, sliced

½ cup coarsely chopped fresh Italian parsley

2 tablespoons finely chopped fresh basil

2 fresh thyme sprigs

1 bay leaf

2 tablespoons kosher salt

1 tablespoon whole black peppercorns

1 russet potato, scrubbed and sliced

2 tomatoes, cored and coarsely chopped

**3 quarts**

Heat the oil in a large saucepan over high heat. Add all the ingredients except the potato and tomatoes and cook, stirring occasionally, until the vegetables soften, about 7 minutes.

Add the potato, tomatoes, and 3 quarts water and bring to a boil. Lower the heat and simmer, covered, for 40 minutes.

Strain the stock through a fine-mesh strainer into a bowl or other container, pressing on the vegetables to extract the maximum amount of stock. (*The stock can be refrigerated, tightly covered, for up to 1 week or frozen for up to 3 months.*)

# Chicken Stock

5 pounds chicken bones, rinsed well under cold water

3 celery stalks, quartered

2 medium carrots, quartered (2½ cups)

1 large onion, coarsely chopped (2½ cups)

1 large parsnip, peeled and coarsely chopped (1½ cups)

¼ cup fresh Italian parsley sprigs

1 teaspoon fresh thyme leaves

1 bay leaf

10 whole black peppercorns

**3 quarts**

Combine all the ingredients in a large pot, add 4 quarts water, and slowly bring to a boil over medium heat. Skim off the foam that rises to the surface. Reduce the heat and simmer very gently, uncovered, for 4 hours, skimming the surface every 30 minutes or so and adding more hot water if the level gets too low.

Strain the stock through a colander and then through a fine-mesh strainer into a bowl or other container. (*The stock can be refrigerated, tightly covered, for up to 2 days or frozen for up to 3 months; remove any hardened fat from the surface before using.*)

# Beef Stock

8 pounds beef bones, preferably meaty

3 cups quartered unpeeled onions

2 cups coarsely chopped carrots

2 cups coarsely chopped celery

2 cups well-washed sliced leeks

2 tablespoons olive oil

3 tablespoons tomato paste

6 fresh Italian parsley sprigs

1 teaspoon dried thyme

1 bay leaf

½ teaspoon whole black peppercorns

**3 quarts**

Preheat the oven to 450 degrees.

Put the bones in a pot and cover with 5 quarts water. Bring to a boil over medium heat, skimming off the foam that rises to the surface. Reduce the heat to low and keep at a simmer.

Meanwhile, put the vegetables in a roasting pan and toss with the oil and tomato paste to coat. Roast for 45 minutes to 1 hour, until the vegetables are well browned.

Transfer the roasted vegetables to the pot and add the remaining ingredients. Pour 1 cup water into the roasting pan, place it on the stove over high heat, and deglaze by stirring to scrape up the browned bits. Pour the water into the pot. Simmer, uncovered, for 5 hours, skimming the surface occasionally and adding more hot water if the level gets too low.

Strain the stock through a colander and then through a fine-mesh strainer into a bowl or other container. (*The stock can be refrigerated, tightly covered, for up to 2 days or frozen for up to 3 months; remove any hardened fat from the surface before using.*)

# Salads

*This bean medley* features flavors and textures on either side of the spectrum—sweet, meaty tomatoes and piquant arugula—tossed with an herb vinaigrette.

Fresh fava beans come dressed in layers: outermost, a plump, dark green pod that holds the beans, which wear a second skin that slips off easily after a brief dip in boiling water. Prepare them often enough, and you'll be able to remove the skin in one quick motion.

# Summer Bean Salad with Tomatoes & Herb Dressing

### For the dressing

¼ cup loosely packed fresh tarragon leaves

¼ cup coarsely chopped fresh Italian parsley

1 teaspoon Dijon mustard

1 large egg yolk

¾ cup extra-virgin olive oil

½ teaspoon kosher salt

¼ teaspoon freshly ground white pepper

4 teaspoons fresh lemon juice

### For the salad

Kosher salt

4 cups total any combination of the following:

Fava beans, removed from the pod

Green beans, trimmed and halved

Yellow beans, trimmed and halved

Romano beans, trimmed and cut into 2-inch pieces

2 cups Sun Gold or cherry tomatoes, halved

4 cups arugula

4 to 6 servings

TO MAKE THE DRESSING: Whir the herbs, mustard, and egg yolk together in a blender. With the motor running, slowly add the oil. Add the salt, pepper, and lemon juice.

TO PREPARE THE BEANS: Bring 8 cups water to a rapid boil in a saucepan and add 2 tablespoons salt. Fill a bowl with ice water.

If using fava beans, add them to the boiling water and blanch for 1 to 2 minutes. Using a slotted spoon, transfer them to the ice water to stop the cooking. Add the remaining beans to the boiling water and cook until tender, about 4 minutes.

Meanwhile, remove the fava beans from the ice water and remove their skins.

Drain the remaining cooked beans and add them to the ice water to cool; drain.

TO MAKE THE SALAD: Combine the beans, tomatoes, and arugula in a serving bowl. Toss with the dressing to taste. Season with salt and serve.

*French Breakfast radishes,* ivory at the tip and deepening to dark pink, contribute a crisp texture, a slightly sweet, peppery flavor, and good looks to this salad. (The more familiar red radishes will work as well.) Chris Bradley, the chef of Untitled at the Whitney, uses flavorful rye and pumpernickel croutons and creates a zesty dressing to complement the lettuce and barely cooked green beans.

# Bibb Salad with Green Beans, Radishes & Rustic Croutons

### For the dressing

⅓ cup red wine vinegar

¼ cup packed light brown sugar

½ cup ketchup

2 tablespoons finely chopped garlic

1 tablespoon paprika

1 tablespoon Worcestershire sauce

1 medium shallot, chopped

½ cup extra-virgin olive oil

2 tablespoons fresh lemon juice

Kosher salt and freshly ground black pepper

### For the salad

Kosher salt

8 ounces green beans, trimmed and cut into 1-inch pieces (about 2 cups)

2 slices day-old rye bread, crusts removed, cut into ¼-inch cubes

2 slices day-old pumpernickel bread, crusts removed, cut into ¼-inch cubes

2 tablespoons olive oil

Freshly ground black pepper

2 heads Bibb lettuce, cored and leaves separated

1 cup thinly sliced (lengthwise) French Breakfast or red radishes

6 servings

TO MAKE THE DRESSING: Place all the ingredients except the olive oil, lemon juice, and salt and pepper in a blender and puree until smooth. With the motor running, slowly drizzle in the olive oil, followed by the lemon juice. Season with salt and pepper and set aside.

TO MAKE THE SALAD: Preheat the oven to 325 degrees.

Bring 8 cups water to a rapid boil in a large saucepan and add 2 tablespoons salt. Prepare a bowl of ice water and set a colander in it.

Drop the green beans into the boiling water and blanch for 1 to 2 minutes, just until crisp-tender. Drain the green beans and place in the colander in the ice water to stop the cooking. Drain the beans again and spread them on a kitchen towel to dry.

Toss the rye and pumpernickel cubes with the olive oil and season with salt and pepper. Spread the bread cubes on a baking sheet and bake until crispy and golden brown, 10 to 15 minutes. Cool to room temperature.

Place the lettuce leaves, beans, radishes, and croutons in a large bowl. Drizzle generously with the dressing and toss well. Season with salt and pepper and serve.

# "I Got a Guy"

At seven o'clock in the morning, before the disappointingly small size of some Asian pears threatened to affect that evening's menu, Modesto Batista strode through Gramercy Tavern's empty front room to survey his domain, steaming coffee mug in hand.

He is the restaurant's chief steward, known for never having met a request he couldn't fill. Coworkers who have known him the longest sometimes call him "Igottaguy," as though that were his name, because he always does, whether it's a source for last-minute fresh water chestnuts or an expert at protecting the floors from wet winter shoes. He would be an imposing figure even if he weren't six foot four and built like a linebacker.

Modesto started working at Gramercy Tavern a month after it opened in 1994, and in the years since, he has supervised the hiring of most of the kitchen employees—those who will never be eligible for a James Beard Award or included on lists of new chefs to watch. The more famous staffers, or the ones who intend to be, wouldn't be in for hours yet. For now, this was Modesto's place.

He came to New York City from his father's farm in the Dominican Republic in 1982, when he was twenty-two, and he turned what he knew—things that grow—into work. Three mornings a week, he shops at the nearby Union Square Greenmarket with three lists in his head: produce for the current menu, produce he has been awaiting for weeks, and produce that may be on the wane, so he can warn chef Michael Anthony of a pending ingredient gap. If Modesto doesn't like what he sees, it doesn't make the plate.

He grabbed an oversized wheelbarrow and rumbled the four blocks to the market forty-five minutes before its official opening. Barring surprises, he knew exactly what he'd be buying and from whom. He walked rapidly along the display at his first stop, nibbling a green bean, breaking a sprig of lemon verbena in two to inhale the scent. He pointed here, there, and at a crate toward the end of the table as the farmer trailed behind him, pen and order form at the ready.

Modesto was about to order green beans when he was distracted by another farmer's better-looking batch; he needed basil but decided after inspecting a bunch that he would buy it at a different stand. He got halfway through the market at warp speed, only to be brought up short by the flat of diminutive Asian pears that were too small to dice properly. His obvious dissatisfaction caught the eye of a farm stand employee, who rushed over to dismantle the stack of flats, arraying them on the ground so that Modesto could see the larger pears. Reaching for an empty flat, Modesto created his own customized batch made up exclusively of the largest fruit.

When he got to the far end of the L-shaped market, he turned and retraced his steps, collecting the most fragile of his purchases to take back in the wheelbarrow.

By nine o'clock, the narrow basement hallway between the restaurant's pastry kitchen and prep area was stacked high with cartons, flats, and bags so that everything could be logged in.

Over the next two hours, Modesto's wife, Iris, and another woman on the prep staff took over the main kitchen upstairs to turn out family meal lunch for forty, as they do every Saturday: marinated Dominican chicken, yuca fritters with anise, rice and beans flavored with more of the marinade, an eggplant and egg stew, fried plantains, and green salad.

Once the food was set out, Modesto did what the spouse of any good cook does: He checked to make sure everyone had what they needed, packed up a plate to take to a fan of Iris's chicken who worked at Maialino, acknowledged compliments on Iris's behalf when she was across the room, and presided over his family's meal.

*This crunchy, tart salad* takes no more than twenty minutes to make. Its flavors work in sets of pleasing contrasts—cabbage and apples, red wine vinegar and honey, golden raisins and scallions—making it a welcome alternative to the predictable green salad.

The crisp ingredients age well; after its debut, the salad can have a happy second life in a lunch box or alongside a main course.

# Cabbage, Carrot & Apple Salad

1 medium head red cabbage (about 2 pounds), quartered, cored, and thinly sliced

3 medium carrots, peeled and coarsely grated (about 2 cups)

2 teaspoons kosher salt

1 cup red wine vinegar

3 tablespoons honey

½ cup extra-virgin olive oil

1 cup golden raisins

3 Granny Smith or other tart, crisp apples, halved, cored, and thinly sliced

1 bunch scallions, thinly sliced (about 1 cup)

**6 to 8 servings**

In a large bowl, toss the cabbage and carrots with 1 teaspoon of the salt. Set aside.

Combine the vinegar, honey, and the remaining 1 teaspoon salt in a medium bowl. Slowly add the oil, whisking constantly. Add the raisins and let soak for 10 minutes.

Add the apples and scallions to the vinaigrette, then add to the cabbage and carrots and stir or toss to coat well. Serve.

*Strained yogurt, even the low-fat type,* has a creamy texture that improves any salad in which it appears. Look for Greek yogurt or labneh in the market, or make your own drained yogurt: Line a sieve with a piece of cheesecloth and set it over a bowl. Pour in 1½ cups regular yogurt, tie the edges of the cheesecloth together, and twist to remove the moisture. Let drain in the refrigerator for 2 to 3 hours.

Persian cucumbers are a more delicate, mildly sweet alternative to the standard supermarket cuke. No peeling required, no need to scoop out the tiny seeds—all the crisp, refreshing benefits of cucumbers with none of the bother, their flavor elevated here by fresh herbs and Middle Eastern spices.

This salad is a perfect accompaniment to Gramercy Tavern's lamb meatballs (page 204).

# Cucumber Salad with Mint & Parsley

6–8 Persian cucumbers (see headnote; about 1 pound), unpeeled, or small pickling cucumbers, peeled

Kosher salt and freshly ground black pepper

1 lemon

½ cup finely chopped red onion

1 teaspoon fennel seeds

1 teaspoon coriander seeds

1 teaspoon cumin seeds

¾ cup regular or low-fat Greek yogurt or labneh (see headnote)

1 teaspoon honey

3 tablespoons extra-virgin olive oil

¼ cup finely chopped fresh mint

¼ cup finely chopped fresh Italian parsley

4 to 6 servings

Slice the cucumbers into thin rounds. Toss with 1 teaspoon salt and ½ teaspoon pepper in a bowl.

Using a Microplane grater, grate the zest from the lemon and toss the zest with the cucumbers, then add the red onion; set aside.

Halve the lemon and juice it; set the juice aside.

In a small dry skillet, toast the spices over medium-low heat until the aroma fills your kitchen, stirring to make sure they don't burn, 4 to 5 minutes. Transfer to a plate and let cool, then grind the spices into a powder in a spice grinder or with a mortar and pestle.

In a medium bowl, whisk together the yogurt, lemon juice, honey, and oil. Thin the mixture with 1 to 2 tablespoons cold water, adding it a bit at a time until you have a mayonnaise-like consistency. Add the ground spice mixture and stir to combine. Stir in the mint and parsley. Taste and add more salt if necessary.

Drain the cucumber mixture, add to the yogurt sauce, and stir well. (*The salad can be made up to 3 hours ahead and refrigerated, covered.*) Serve cold.

*Red cabbage combined with a new set of flavors* turns coleslaw in an Asian direction, redefining it with fresh cilantro and basil, rice wine vinegar, lime juice, sesame oil, and one of the restaurant kitchens' favorite ingredients—Sriracha hot sauce.

# Asian Red Cabbage Slaw

1 medium head red cabbage (about 2 pounds), halved, cored, and thinly sliced

4 celery stalks, thinly sliced

2 medium carrots, peeled and thinly sliced

4 scallions, thinly sliced

⅔ cup rice wine vinegar

⅓ cup honey

⅓ cup fresh lime juice

1–2 teaspoons Sriracha hot sauce

1 teaspoon soy sauce

1 tablespoon toasted sesame oil

1 teaspoon fish sauce (optional)

¾ cup finely chopped fresh cilantro

¼ cup thinly sliced fresh basil leaves

6 to 8 servings

Combine the cabbage, celery, carrots, and scallions in a large serving bowl.

Whisk together the rice wine vinegar, honey, lime juice, Sriracha to taste, soy sauce, sesame oil, and fish sauce, if using, in a small bowl.

Toss the cabbage mixture with the dressing and herbs and serve.

*There is no oil in the dressing for this salad.* Instead, there is maple syrup spiked with smoked paprika, which may make you skeptical. But the allure of the salad lies in its surprising combination of ingredients—and in the simple preparation, which requires only toasting pecans, some chopping and slicing, and mixing the dressing. It will make you wonder, How come I never thought of this?

# Escarole & Apple Salad

1 cup pecans

**For the dressing**

½ cup plain yogurt

1½ tablespoons pure maple syrup

½ teaspoon sherry vinegar

½ teaspoon smoked paprika

½ teaspoon kosher salt

1 head escarole, cored and coarsely chopped

1 Granny Smith apple, halved, cored, and thinly sliced

1 red onion, halved and thinly sliced

⅓ cup finely chopped fresh mint

4 to 6 servings

Spread the pecans in a large dry skillet and toast over medium heat for 5 to 7 minutes, stirring and watching carefully so they do not burn. Transfer to a plate to cool.

TO MAKE THE DRESSING: Combine all the ingredients in a small bowl and mix well.

Combine the escarole, apple, pecans, and onion in a large serving bowl. Toss with the dressing, sprinkle with the mint, and serve.

*Union Square Cafe updates the classic* Italian bread and tomato salad by broiling cubes of fresh bread on just one side instead of using the traditional technique of soaking stale bread in water and then crumbling it. The resulting croutons are both crisp and chewy.

Family meal cooks use tomato trimmings for this, but you'll want a half dozen of your ripest heirlooms. Panzanella is the perfect solution for yesterday's bread and overabundant height-of-summer tomatoes and fresh basil.

# Tomato Panzanella

4 cups cubed (1-inch) rustic bread

¼ cup plus 3 tablespoons extra-virgin olive oil

1 garlic clove, finely chopped

¼ cup torn fresh basil leaves

1 tablespoon red wine vinegar

½ cup thinly sliced red onion

5 cups coarsely chopped cored tomatoes (about 2½ pounds)

Kosher salt and freshly ground black pepper

2 tablespoons grated Pecorino Romano

2 tablespoons grated Parmigiano-Reggiano

**4 to 6 servings**

Preheat the broiler.

Toss the bread cubes with the 3 tablespoons olive oil in a medium bowl. Spread the bread cubes in a single layer on a baking sheet and brown under the broiler for 1 to 3 minutes, without stirring, watching carefully so that they do not burn. Return the toasted bread to the bowl and toss with the garlic and basil.

Pour the vinegar over the onion in a large bowl. Put the tomatoes on top of the onion, season with salt and pepper to taste, and let sit for 5 minutes.

Stir the remaining ¼ cup oil into the tomato and onion mixture. Add the bread cubes and grated cheeses and toss gently once or twice. Serve immediately.

*Lacinato, or Tuscan, kale* is so dark green that it verges on black, with a pebbly surface and long oval leaves. Its strong, slightly sweet flavor requires an equally emphatic dressing, such as this anchovy and mustard version. If you want to add a little bite, use a peppery olive oil instead of vegetable oil.

Charring the kale warms it through without sacrificing crunch.

# Lacinato Kale & Escarole Salad with Anchovy Dressing

### For the dressing

1 tablespoon anchovy paste

1 large egg yolk

1 teaspoon Dijon mustard

Grated zest and juice of 1 lemon

Pinch each of kosher salt and freshly ground black pepper

1 cup vegetable oil

½ head escarole (about 1 pound)

8 ounces lacinato (Tuscan) kale, thick stems removed

2 tablespoons extra-virgin olive oil

Kosher salt and freshly ground black pepper

4 servings

Preheat the oven to 450 degrees. Line a baking sheet with parchment paper.

TO MAKE THE DRESSING: Whisk together all the ingredients except the oil in a small bowl. Slowly drizzle in the oil, whisking constantly. Whisk in 2 tablespoons water. Set aside.

Pull back the leaves of the escarole slightly so that you can add seasoning between them. Drizzle the escarole and the kale with the olive oil and sprinkle with salt and pepper. Put them on the lined baking sheet.

Roast the greens, without stirring, just long enough to get a little charring on the leaves, 4 to 5 minutes—you don't want to really cook the greens, just warm them through and wilt them slightly. Chop the greens into 1-inch pieces.

Transfer the greens to a serving bowl. Add dressing to taste, toss, and serve.

*Gramercy Tavern executive sous chef* Howard Kalachnikoff, confronted with a bunch of yellow bell peppers left over from the restaurant's annual picnic, sliced and slow-cooked them with onions until he had a meek pile of pepper parentheses. He looked around the kitchen for a way to make them memorable, and inspiration struck. Some day-old bread, ten minutes of effort, and the peppers became part of a reinvented panzanella, playing the role that tomatoes usually do and dressed up with capers in addition to the traditional fresh basil.

# Yellow Bell Pepper Panzanella

½ cup olive oil

1 medium onion, halved and thinly sliced

4 yellow bell peppers, cored, seeded, and cut into thin strips

2 garlic cloves, minced

2 cups cut or torn 1-inch chunks day-old bread

2 tablespoons capers, rinsed and drained

2 tablespoons white balsamic vinegar

2 tablespoons red wine vinegar

Kosher salt and freshly ground black pepper

2 cups torn fresh basil leaves

4 to 6 servings

Heat 2 tablespoons of the oil in a large skillet over medium-low heat. Add the onion and cook, stirring occasionally, until translucent and light golden, 10 to 15 minutes.

Add the bell peppers and garlic and cook until very soft, about 30 minutes, stirring occasionally. Remove from the heat and cool to room temperature.

Meanwhile, preheat the oven to 325 degrees.

Toss the bread cubes with 2 tablespoons of the oil and spread on a baking sheet. Toast until light golden, 7 to 10 minutes; check them after 5 minutes to make sure they don't get too dark. Allow to cool.

In a large bowl, combine the pepper mixture and capers and fold in the bread. Add the two vinegars and season with salt and pepper to taste; set aside for about 15 minutes to blend the flavors.

Right before serving, gently mix in the basil leaves and drizzle the salad with the remaining ¼ cup oil.

*Roasting broccoli and fennel until they're tender* and slightly browned brings out a subtle, nutty flavor that plays off the tangy vinaigrette. Prepared this way, broccoli becomes a surprisingly cooperative vegetable, eager to leave its stern reputation behind. All it takes is the creative energy of a cook determined not to be the one who sets out a boring pan of veggies.

# Roasted Broccoli & Fennel Salad with Pickled Onion Vinaigrette

### For the vinaigrette

¼ cup extra-virgin olive oil

Juice of 2 lemons (about ⅓ cup)

¼ cup red wine vinegar

1½ teaspoons sherry vinegar

½ teaspoon kosher salt

Pinch of freshly ground black pepper

¾ cup finely chopped red onion

2 heads broccoli (1½–2 pounds total), cut into bite-sized florets, stems trimmed and thinly sliced

3 tablespoons olive oil

1 fennel bulb, trimmed, cored, and cut crosswise into ¼-inch-thick slices

Kosher salt and freshly ground black pepper

⅓ cup finely chopped fresh basil

⅓ cup finely chopped fresh Italian parsley

6 to 8 servings

Preheat the oven to 375 degrees.

TO MAKE THE VINAIGRETTE: Whisk together the olive oil, lemon juice, red wine vinegar, sherry vinegar, salt, and pepper in a small bowl. Add the onion and whisk well. Set aside.

In a small bowl, toss the broccoli with 2 tablespoons of the oil. Put the fennel in another small bowl and toss with the remaining 1 tablespoon oil. Season both with salt and pepper and spread on separate baking sheets. Roast the broccoli until lightly browned and tender, 15 to 20 minutes. Roast the fennel until tender, 20 to 25 minutes. Remove from the oven.

Combine the vegetables and herbs in a serving bowl and toss with the vinaigrette. Serve warm or at room temperature.

# Beans & Grains

Warm Garbanzo Bean Salad with Fennel, Red Onion & Parsley 60 | White Bean & Tomato Salad 66 | Lentil Salad with Summer Squash & Dried Cherries 69 | Farro & Beans 70 | Risotto with Peas 73 | Couscous with Carrot Juice 74 | Herbed Japanese Eggplant & Bulgur Salad 75 | Corn, Carrot & Wheat Berry "Risotto" 76 | Barley & Spring Vegetables with Pesto 78

*It may be hard to imagine garbanzo beans* as an object of desire until you have tried them in this warm salad with crunchy fennel, red onion, and a smoky vinaigrette. Like any dried beans, garbanzos need to be treated with a little respect, cooked only to the point where they still have some bite. Aim for a slow, consistent simmer, the best way to guarantee that they cook evenly. If the water boils, the beans will end up mushy on the outside and hard in the center.

# Warm Garbanzo Bean Salad with Fennel, Red Onion & Parsley

2 cups dried garbanzo beans or two 15-ounce cans garbanzo beans, drained and rinsed

1½ teaspoons Aleppo pepper or red pepper flakes

4 garlic cloves, smashed and peeled

3 tablespoons kosher salt, or more to taste

2 fresh thyme sprigs

1½ teaspoons Dijon mustard

2 teaspoons smoked paprika

¼ cup fresh lemon juice

2 tablespoons white wine vinegar

1 cup extra-virgin olive oil

1 fennel bulb, trimmed, cut in half, cored, and thinly sliced (about 4 cups)

1 red onion, cut in half and thinly sliced (about 3 cups)

½ cup finely chopped fresh Italian parsley

**6 to 8 servings**

If using dried beans, soak the beans overnight in water to cover, then drain. Or, to quick-soak the beans, rinse them well in cold water, place them in a large pot, and cover with 3 inches of cold water. Bring the water to a simmer, remove from the heat, and let sit for 1 hour; drain.

Rinse the garbanzo beans. Place them in a large saucepan, add ½ teaspoon of the Aleppo pepper and the garlic, and cover with 3 quarts water. Bring to a low simmer and cook, uncovered, for 1 to 1¼ hours, or until tender.

Remove the beans from the heat, add the salt and thyme, and let stand for 15 minutes.

Meanwhile, in a small bowl, whisk together the Dijon mustard, the remaining 1 teaspoon Aleppo pepper, the smoked paprika, lemon juice, and vinegar. Whisking constantly, slowly add the oil. Add salt to taste if necessary.

In a large bowl, toss the fennel and red onion with 3 tablespoons of the vinaigrette.

Drain the beans and discard the thyme and garlic. Toss with the fennel and onion—the heat from the beans will soften the vegetables slightly. Stir in the parsley and toss with the remaining vinaigrette. (*The salad can be made up to 1 day ahead, covered, and refrigerated.*)

Serve warm, at room temperature, or cold.

# The Right Proportions

Zisca Gardner, a single mom and a sous chef at The Modern, likes the small, exacting solution to almost any challenge. Some cooks might feel constrained by the rigors of making artful food, where the exact curve of a swirl of sauce seems to make all the difference. Zisca finds it invigorating.

She faced her first sea change at sixteen, when she immigrated to Brooklyn from Trinidad and had to reinvent herself. First she needed a job, and working in little neighborhood Caribbean restaurants offered a familiar antidote to often overwhelming surroundings. Then it hit her that if she went to culinary school, she might be able to turn food into a career, not just a series of jobs.

The absolute world of teaspoons and half cups—dependable basics—both delighted and reassured her. She was good at this, she learned. When she stepped back into the city with a degree, she was able to find better work. For years she did, though not in jobs that quite fitted her the way she wanted. She racked up experience at a gourmet market and a catering company, only to realize that she wanted something different. "After a while," she said, "'Can you make 200 of these?' was not so exciting."

By then she had a young son, so it wasn't simply a question of finding the right job, but of finding the right job at the right time of day. She started out on the restaurant–interview circuit, looking for a day shift where she could put her increasingly sophisticated skills to better use, and she might have landed somewhere else had she not bumped into a chef she knew from The Modern. The restaurant needed someone for the lunch shift, and Zisca got the job. Five years later, order has replaced the unknown: elegant, architectural food and a dependable schedule that gets her home to spend time with her eleven-year-old son.

Lunch service is an exercise in small adjustments. Before one plate left the kitchen, Zisca stepped in with a pair of long tweezers to nudge a spear of asparagus a quarter of an inch to the left. She raised the tweezers, considered, and then moved the spear less than a quarter of an inch farther. Pleased with the result, she sent the plate out, not dwelling on the fact that within moments a diner would demolish its careful symmetry.

She gestured at the walls with her tweezers. "We're inside MoMA," she said, eyeing the next plate up. "It has to be beautiful."

*The beans get top billing in this salad,* and using dried beans will give it a better flavor, although canned beans are a time-saving alternative. Everything about this dish benefits from some sitting, from the slow-cooked beans to the marinated shallots that flavor the vinaigrette. Make the beans on the weekend and refrigerate them for a busy weekday, when you can easily assemble this quick duet of juicy tomatoes and creamy white cannellini.

# White Bean & Tomato Salad

1½ cups dried cannellini beans or two 15-ounce cans cannellini beans, drained and rinsed

1 small onion, halved (for cooking dried beans)

1 bunch fresh basil, leaves removed and torn (about 1 cup; reserve the stems if using dried beans)

Kosher salt

4 shallots, finely chopped

¼ cup red wine vinegar, or more to taste

6 medium tomatoes (about 2 pounds), cored and cut into 1-inch cubes

Freshly ground black pepper

½ cup extra-virgin olive oil, or more to taste

**4 to 6 servings**

If using dried beans, soak them overnight in water to cover, then drain. Or, to quick-soak the beans, rinse them well in cold water, place them in a large pot, and cover with 3 inches of cold water. Bring the water to a simmer, remove from the heat, and let sit for 1 hour; drain.

Cover the soaked beans with water by 5 inches in a large deep saucepan. Add the onion and basil stems and bring to a boil, then reduce the heat to low and simmer, uncovered, until the beans are very creamy but still whole, 1 to 1½ hours. Remove and discard the onion and basil stems, season with 1 teaspoon salt, and let cool in the cooking liquid. (*The beans can be cooked up to 3 days in advance.*)

Meanwhile, put the shallots in a large bowl, add the red wine vinegar, and marinate for 1 to 2 hours.

In a large bowl, combine the tomatoes with the marinated shallots. Season with salt and pepper. Drain the beans. Add the beans, basil leaves, and oil and gently mix into the tomatoes. Adjust the oil, vinegar, salt, and pepper if necessary and serve.

# The Restaurant Mama

Pretty much everyone at all the Union Square Hospitality Group restaurants has heard of Carolyn Wandell-Widdoes, even if they have never worked at the Union Square Cafe. In her twenty-three years at the Cafe, slender, ponytailed Carolyn, with her signature vintage cat's-eye glasses, has been a host, a bartender, and, now, a server. A restaurant regular, or even one of her coworkers, might assume that she has been in the hospitality business forever, and that is correct but incomplete. She has also been a licensed social worker; a caretaker for her mother, who had Alzheimer's disease; and a fledgling environmental activist.

Carolyn has been around long enough and cares about her work deeply enough to have achieved a special status: She is the restaurant's official mama, who shares any piece of what she knows with someone who may not even know enough to ask. One afternoon, right before family meal, when the restaurant was quiet, Carolyn huddled at the back end of the bar with Mike, a young staffer, for a quick lesson in wine service—the proper angle to present the bottle for the diner's approval, the change in position

to open it, and the best way to cut away the wrapper and get the corkscrew in true.

Presenting and opening a bottle of wine tableside is not as simple as it sounds. There is nothing solid like a counter on which to balance the bottle, nor can the servers tuck the bottle under their arm like a football, to steady it. They have no fancy technologically enhanced opener, just a classic waiter's corkscrew. When Mike tried to translate Carolyn's seamless maneuvers, he fumbled. She mimed the correct gestures, and he tried again.

After a few more minutes of concerted effort, he was capable enough to survive his shift, so Carolyn walked over to survey the tables in her section, appraising the smoothness of the tablecloth at one, checking the position of a napkin and flatware at another. On her way to the back of the restaurant for family meal, she noticed a bowl of flowers that needed to be two inches to the left, moved them, and then reassured the server whose table it was that she was just helping, not judging. That's what a good mama does: She leads by example and pitches in without criticism.

*The key here is to do less:* Stop cooking the lentils when they still have a little bite to them, and don't cook the squash at all, because you want it to have crunch. The thyme and shallots in the lentil cooking water add flavor, and the dried cherries contribute tart and sweet accents. All you need to do is introduce these seemingly unlikely ingredients to each other. They'll get along fine.

# Lentil Salad with Summer Squash & Dried Cherries

2 large shallots

2 cups French green lentils, rinsed and picked over

3 fresh thyme sprigs

5 medium green or golden zucchini, cut into ¼-inch cubes

1 cup dried cherries

Kosher salt and freshly ground black pepper

¼ cup sherry vinegar

3 tablespoons extra-virgin olive oil

6 to 8 servings

Cut 1 of the shallots in half, leaving the root end intact. Finely chop the remaining shallot and set aside.

Bring 6 cups water to a boil in a large saucepan. Add the lentils, thyme, and halved shallot. When the water returns to a boil, reduce the heat to medium-low and simmer, uncovered, until the lentils are just tender, 20 to 25 minutes. Drain the lentils, discarding the thyme sprigs and shallot, and let cool to room temperature.

In a large bowl, combine the lentils, zucchini, dried cherries, chopped shallot, and salt and pepper to taste. (*The salad can be prepared to this point up to 1 day ahead, and refrigerated, covered.*)

Add the sherry vinegar and oil, stir gently to combine, and serve.

*This dish makes virtue delicious:* In a single forkful, you get a cruciferous vegetable, a whole grain, and beans. The first time he made it, Gramercy Tavern sous chef Geoff Lazlo built the dish layer by layer, starting with farro, an ancient whole grain with a nutty flavor (it's increasingly easy to find alongside rice at the market). He appropriated some cauliflower florets from a coworker's cutting board and then added beans and three distinct kinds of heat: harissa paste, red pepper flakes, and jalapeño. He stirred, he tasted, he added, and then he laughed. "Look at that," he said. "I think I just made vegan chili."

# Farro & Beans

⅔ cup dried red or white beans, such as kidney, cannellini, Great Northern, or cranberry, or one 15-ounce can beans, drained and rinsed

Kosher salt

½ cup olive oil or Garlic Oil (page 95)

½ teaspoon red pepper flakes

½ teaspoon fennel seeds

½ teaspoon cumin seeds

1 large onion, finely chopped

3 garlic cloves, thinly sliced

1 jalapeño, halved, seeded, and finely chopped

¼ cup apple cider vinegar

¼ cup sherry vinegar

2 cups farro

1 teaspoon harissa paste

4 cups Vegetable Stock (page 38)

3 medium carrots, peeled, cut lengthwise in half, and sliced ¼ inch thick

2 cups bite-sized cauliflower florets

¼ cup chopped fresh Italian parsley

**6 to 8 servings**

If using dried beans, soak them overnight in water to cover, then drain. Or, to quick-soak the beans, rinse them well in cold water, place them in a large pot, and cover with 3 inches of cold water. Bring to a simmer, remove from the heat, and let sit for 1 hour; drain.

Cover the soaked beans with water by 5 inches in a large deep saucepan. Bring to a boil, then reduce the heat to low and simmer, uncovered, until the beans are creamy but still whole, 1 to 1½ hours. Season with 1 teaspoon salt, and let cool in the cooking liquid. (*The beans can be cooked up to 3 days in advance.*)

Heat the oil in a large Dutch oven over medium-low heat. Add the spices and toast, stirring frequently, until fragrant, about 5 minutes. Add the onion, garlic, and jalapeño, season with salt, and cook, stirring, until tender, about 10 minutes. Stir in the vinegars and simmer for 15 minutes.

Add the farro, harissa, and stock, bring to a simmer, and cook, covered, stirring occasionally, until the farro is tender, about 45 minutes.

Stir in the beans and vegetables and cook, covered, stirring frequently, until the vegetables are tender, 15 to 20 minutes. Adjust the salt, add the parsley, and serve.

# Teamwork

Anyone can have a bad day in the kitchen, and the giveaway is often the outsized gesture—a wild lunge for a pan that is bubbling too fast, a grab for a teetering cutting board, a downward swoop with a bit too much momentum. Arrhythmia can disrupt everything, but drawing attention to a coworker's problems only makes matters worse.

Geoff Lazlo, a Gramercy Tavern sous chef, was having quite the opposite of a bad day, shaping an array of baby carrots into colorful sculpted jewels, glazing them until they shined, all the while tending a big pot of farro and beans for family meal. He was ahead of the curve; he had time to consider just how to layer three different kinds of heat into his grain dish instead of settling for one-note predictability.

Most of the time, Geoff expedites while other people cook, but on this shift, he had stepped in for a cook who hadn't come in. He liked being back on the line, and he liked the combination of absolute precision (the carrots) and absolute improvisation (the farro and beans).

But on this particular night, after family meal, Geoff picked up some warning signs from a cook at a nearby station—small hints that the guy was not quite on top of things. A saucepan clattered when he aimed for the burner in haste. He was moving around too much, and his station wasn't as organized as it should be. Geoff watched as he worked to see whether the cook might right himself, making little encouraging comments, exuding what he hoped was a reassuring vibe.

Within the hour, everyone on the line would be working at a furious pace, reaching arm over arm to plate the meat or fish, sauce, vegetables or maybe a grain, and garnish, five cooks assembling a single dish in seconds. Then they'd turn back to a burner, an oven, or a cutting board and ready their part of the next order. There was no room for anyone to be a minute late.

Geoff stepped over to the struggling cook and murmured quietly, "C'mon, man. You've got it." Geoff doesn't like kitchens that run on melodrama. A stern but supportive word for a wobbling colleague, and he gets the results he is after.

*Seasonal produce comes to restaurant kitchens in waves,* redefining family meal; abundance makes the menu. This basic risotto showcases spring peas, though it can be made year-round with frozen ones. It also rewards the home cook who keeps an eye on the nutritional balance sheet. Unlike classic versions, this lighter one works without butter; traditionalists can add it at the end.

# Risotto with Peas

1 cup shelled fresh peas (about 1 pound unshelled) or thawed frozen peas

Kosher salt

6 cups Chicken Stock (page 39)

2 tablespoons olive oil

2 garlic cloves, finely chopped

1¾ cups Arborio rice

¾ cup dry white wine

2 tablespoons finely chopped fresh thyme

2 tablespoons finely chopped fresh Italian parsley

Freshly ground black pepper

½ cup grated Pecorino Romano

2 tablespoons unsalted butter (optional)

**4 to 6 servings**

If using fresh peas, bring 4 cups water to a boil in a medium saucepan. Prepare a bowl of ice water. Add 1 teaspoon salt to the boiling water, then add the peas and blanch for 3 minutes, or until tender. Immediately plunge the peas into the ice water to stop the cooking. Drain and set aside.

Bring the stock to a simmer in a large saucepan over medium heat, then reduce the heat and keep at a bare simmer.

Warm the oil in a large skillet or Dutch oven over medium heat. Add the garlic and cook, stirring, for 1 minute. Add the rice, stir to coat, and cook, stirring, for 1 minute. Add the wine and stir until it is absorbed by the rice. Add a ladleful of the stock and cook, stirring, until it has been absorbed by the rice. Continue adding stock a ladleful at a time and stirring until most of the stock has been absorbed and the rice is al dente, 20 to 25 minutes.

Stir in the peas, thyme, parsley, and salt and pepper to taste and cook, stirring, for 1 minute to warm the peas. Remove the pan from the heat, stir in the grated cheese and the butter, if using, and serve.

*It was 3:35, with less than half an hour before the usual 4:00 supper,* and Gramercy Tavern sous chef Kyle Knall was making the starch for a Middle Eastern–themed family meal. Plain couscous wasn't good enough, so Kyle scanned the kitchen, considering his options. Across the aisle, sous chef Geoff Lazlo was preparing four different kinds of carrots for a glazed carrot dish that calls for carrot juice—so that became part of Kyle's dish. He added star anise and cinnamon to the couscous, poured in carrot juice and stock, and let the couscous sit to absorb the liquid while he turned out a quick raw salad of onions, raisins, and herbs dressed with lemon juice and olive oil. The couscous went into the bowl with the salad, and an otherwise plain grain was transformed.

You can find carrot juice in the fresh-juice section of a gourmet market or health-food store.

# Couscous with Carrot Juice

1½ cups Vegetable Stock (page 38)

1½ cups carrot juice

1 star anise

1 cinnamon stick

2 large garlic cloves

1½ cups instant couscous

1 small red onion, thinly sliced

⅓ cup golden raisins

¼ cup finely chopped fresh cilantro

2 tablespoons finely chopped fresh mint

2 tablespoons fresh lemon juice

2 tablespoons extra-virgin olive oil

Kosher salt and freshly ground black pepper

**4 to 6 servings**

Combine the stock, carrot juice, star anise, cinnamon stick, and garlic in a medium saucepan and bring to a boil. Add the couscous, cover, and remove from the heat. Let sit until the liquid has been absorbed, about 10 minutes.

Combine the onion, raisins, herbs, lemon juice, olive oil, and salt and pepper to taste in a bowl large enough to hold the couscous.

Remove and discard the star anise, cinnamon stick, and garlic from the couscous and fluff with a fork. Toss the couscous with the onion and raisin mixture. (*The salad can be prepared up to 1 day ahead and refrigerated, covered.*)

Serve warm, at room temperature, or cold.

*Union Square Cafe cook Monica Reese* is known for her vegetables, her salads, her sense of humor, and her drawings—she was an artist before she became a cook. It's her mission to rescue the kitchen's extra vegetables from oblivion and give them a handsome new reason for being. That's how this novel grain salad full of slender Japanese eggplant, peanuts, and fresh herbs came to be.

# Herbed Japanese Eggplant & Bulgur Salad

3–4 Japanese eggplants (about 1 pound)

6 tablespoons plus 1 teaspoon olive oil

Kosher salt and freshly ground black pepper

1 cup raw unsalted peanuts

1 shallot, cut in half

1 cup medium-grain bulgur

½ cup rice wine vinegar

2 scallions, thinly sliced

3 tablespoons finely chopped fresh mint

⅓ cup finely chopped fresh cilantro

¼ cup finely chopped fresh basil (Thai basil if you can find it)

**4 to 6 servings**

Preheat the oven to 350 degrees. Line a baking sheet with parchment paper.

Cut the eggplants in half lengthwise and slice into ½-inch-thick half-moon shapes. In a large bowl, toss the eggplant with 3 tablespoons of the oil and salt and pepper to taste. Spread the eggplant on the baking sheet and roast for 25 minutes, or until just tender; set aside. Leave the oven on.

Toss the peanuts with the 1 teaspoon oil. Spread them in a baking dish in a single layer and toast in the oven for 7 to 10 minutes, until they smell toasty, watching carefully so that they do not burn. Set aside.

In a medium saucepan, bring 2 cups water to a boil. Stir in ½ teaspoon salt, then add the shallot and bulgur, reduce the heat to medium-low, and simmer until the bulgur has absorbed all the water, about 10 minutes. Remove the pan from the heat, cover, and let sit for 10 minutes. Remove and discard the shallot.

Put the bulgur in a serving bowl and fluff with a fork. Stir in the eggplant, peanuts, vinegar, scallions, herbs, and the remaining 3 tablespoons olive oil. Adjust the seasonings to taste and stir again. Serve warm or at room temperature.

*If you like risotto but dread standing over a pan* and stirring for half an hour, this dish is the solution: It provides all the creaminess without the constant vigilance.

Wheat berries, one of an increasing number of whole grains available in the market aisle, need to cook for an hour and a half, but they don't require watching and can be made ahead. The carrots need only the occasional glance, and you can put the dish together in minutes when you're ready to eat. There's an intriguing array of collaborative flavors and textures here—the nutty, earthy wheat berries, which have more bite than rice, play against sweet corn and pureed carrots, all unified by lemon, parsley, butter, and cheese.

# Corn, Carrot & Wheat Berry "Risotto"

### For the wheat berries

1 tablespoon vegetable oil

2 cups wheat berries

1 medium carrot, halved crosswise

½ large yellow onion, halved

1 celery stalk, halved

3 tablespoons fresh lemon juice

4 tablespoons (½ stick) unsalted butter

Kosher salt

### For the carrot puree

2 tablespoons unsalted butter

4 medium carrots (about 1 pound), peeled and thinly sliced

### To finish the dish

4 tablespoons (½ stick) unsalted butter

1 cup corn kernels (from 1–2 ears)

¾ cup grated Parmigiano-Reggiano

Kosher salt and freshly ground black pepper

¼ cup coarsely chopped fresh Italian parsley

6 to 8 servings

TO COOK THE WHEAT BERRIES: Heat the oil in a large saucepan over medium heat. Add the wheat berries and toast, stirring frequently, for 5 minutes. Add 6 cups water and the vegetables, bring to a simmer, and cook, uncovered, stirring occasionally, for 1½ hours, or until the wheat berries are tender and have absorbed most of the liquid.

Remove and discard the vegetables and drain the wheat berries, reserving the liquid. Stir in the lemon juice, butter, and salt to taste. Set aside. (*The wheat berries can be made up to 1 day ahead and refrigerated, covered; refrigerate the cooking water separately.*)

TO MAKE THE CARROT PUREE: Melt the butter in a medium skillet over low heat. Add the carrots and ½ cup water and cook, covered, until the carrots are tender, 12 to 15 minutes. Uncover and simmer until about ¼ cup liquid remains.

Transfer the carrots and liquid to a blender and puree until smooth. Set aside.

TO FINISH THE DISH: Heat 2 tablespoons of the butter in a large saucepan over medium heat until it begins to foam. Add the corn and cook, stirring, for 2 minutes. Add the wheat berries, stir to combine, and warm through.

Turn off the heat and stir in the carrot puree, Parmigiano, the remaining 2 tablespoons butter, and salt and pepper to taste. If the "risotto" seems dry, add some of the reserved wheat berry cooking water as necessary. Garnish with the parsley and serve.

*On some summer days,* Gramercy Tavern cook Margot Protzel can barely keep up with the fresh basil from the nearby Union Square Greenmarket, pouring batch after batch of smooth deep green pesto into quart containers arranged on the counter. Plenty of pesto-centric dishes appear on the family meal menu, including this celebration of asparagus and garlic scapes, the curly tops of the hardneck garlic plant.

Scapes, which have a milder flavor than garlic cloves, are trimmed in late spring and early summer to allow the garlic bulb to form and so have a short season, less than a month in some places. If you miss them, scallions are a good stand-in.

The pesto recipe makes more than you will need for this dish. Toss the leftover pesto with pasta, or spread on bread with a tomato slice; having extra is always a good thing.

# Barley & Spring Vegetables with Pesto

5 tablespoons olive oil

1½ cups pearl barley, rinsed and drained

1 medium leek, white part only, cut lengthwise in half, thinly sliced, and well washed to remove grit

Kosher salt

6 tablespoons dried currants or raisins

¼ cup sherry

1 bunch asparagus, tough ends snapped off, cut into ½-inch pieces

5 garlic scapes, flower tops removed, thinly sliced, or ½ cup thinly sliced scallion greens

½ cup Pesto (recipe follows)

½ cup coarsely chopped fresh Italian parsley

4 to 6 servings

Heat 3 tablespoons of the oil in a large skillet over medium-high heat. Add the barley and toast, stirring constantly to prevent burning, until it is deep golden brown and has a nutty aroma, 5 to 10 minutes. Reduce the heat to medium, add the leek and 1 teaspoon salt, and cook for 1 to 2 minutes, stirring, until the leek is just beginning to soften. Add 3 cups water, bring to a simmer, cover, and cook, checking frequently and adding more water if needed, until the barley is al dente, 30 to 45 minutes. Drain off any excess water and spread the barley on a baking sheet or in a shallow baking dish to cool.

Meanwhile, put the currants and sherry in a small saucepan and bring to a boil. Remove from the heat, cover, and let stand for 5 minutes, or until the currants have plumped. Drain, reserving the liquid.

Heat the remaining 2 tablespoons oil in a large skillet over high heat. Add the asparagus, garlic scapes, and a pinch of salt and cook, stirring, until the asparagus is tender, about 5 minutes. Remove from the heat.

In a large bowl, gently stir together the barley, pesto, asparagus and garlic scapes, and currants. If the salad needs a bit more liquid, add some of the reserved currant soaking liquid and mix well. (*The salad can be made up to 1 day ahead, covered, and refrigerated.*)

Serve warm or at room temperature, garnished with the parsley.

# Pesto

4 cups tightly packed fresh basil leaves

3 tablespoons pine nuts

1–2 garlic cloves, coarsely chopped

1 teaspoon kosher salt

¾ cup extra-virgin olive oil

½ cup grated Parmigiano-Reggiano

½ cup grated Pecorino Romano

**2 cups**

In a food processor, pulse together the basil, pine nuts, garlic, and salt. With the motor running, slowly drizzle in the oil. Scrape down the sides with a rubber spatula to make sure everything is incorporated, then add the cheeses and pulse briefly to combine. (*The pesto can be refrigerated in an airtight container for up to 1 week.*)

# Pasta & Noodles

*For this summer pasta salad* with vegetables, mint, and parsley, the zucchini and tomatoes are cooked briefly with onions and garlic, just long enough to bring out their flavor without sacrificing their crisp texture.

# Orzo Salad with Zucchini, Tomatoes & Fresh Herbs

Kosher salt

1 pound orzo

½ cup olive oil

1 small red onion

3 medium zucchini, quartered lengthwise and cut into ½-inch slices

3 small tomatoes, cored and cut into ½-inch pieces

1 garlic clove, finely chopped

Freshly ground black pepper

3 tablespoons fresh lemon juice

2 tablespoons finely chopped fresh mint

2 tablespoons finely chopped fresh Italian parsley

**4 to 6 servings**

Bring 4 quarts water to a boil in a large pot and add 2 tablespoons salt. Add the orzo, stir, and cook until just al dente, stirring frequently, 8 to 10 minutes. Drain and rinse briefly under cold water to keep the orzo from sticking together. Set aside in a large bowl.

Heat 2 tablespoons of the oil in a large skillet over medium heat. Add the onion and cook, stirring, until soft, about 5 minutes. Add the zucchini, tomatoes, and garlic, season with salt and pepper, and cook, stirring, for 3 to 5 minutes; the zucchini should still be crunchy. Remove from the heat and cool.

Toss the vegetables with the orzo and the remaining 6 tablespoons oil. (*The salad can be made to this point up to 1 day ahead, covered, and refrigerated; bring to room temperature before serving.*)

Add the lemon juice, mint, and parsley to the orzo salad and stir well. Adjust the seasonings to taste and serve.

*White miso might sound like* the kind of ingredient that sends you in search of a specialty store, but in fact it is the most common type of miso paste, and you're likely to find it in the international or Asian food section of the supermarket. It's a lighter, sweeter alternative to dark miso, which is generally used in soup, and it often appears in dressings like the one for this easy Japanese noodle salad.

You can make the dressing in the time it takes to cook the soba, and if you add some thinly sliced cooked chicken, beef, or shrimp, you'll have a one-dish meal.

# Soba Salad with Miso Dressing

Kosher salt

### For the dressing

5 tablespoons white miso paste

½ cup chopped peeled fresh ginger

¼ cup soy sauce

3 tablespoons fresh lime juice

1 large egg

1 cup vegetable oil

Freshly ground black pepper

1 pound soba noodles

4 medium carrots, peeled and coarsely grated (about 4 cups)

2 bunches scallions, thinly sliced on the bias (about 2½ cups)

2 bunches radishes, thinly sliced (about 4 cups)

**6 to 8 servings**

Bring 4 quarts water to a boil in a large pot and add 2 tablespoons salt.

MEANWHILE, MAKE THE DRESSING: Combine the miso paste, ginger, soy sauce, and lime juice in a blender and blend, at medium speed until smooth. Add the egg and blend until combined. With the motor running, slowly add the oil. Once the dressing is smooth, add pepper to taste; you won't need salt, because the miso and soy sauce are salty. (*The dressing can be made up to 1 day ahead and refrigerated, covered.*)

Add the soba noodles to the boiling water and cook, stirring often, until al dente. Drain the noodles and rinse well under cold running water. Drain well, transfer to a baking sheet, then spread out and let cool.

In a large bowl, combine the noodles with the carrots, scallions, and radishes. Toss with the miso dressing and serve at room temperature or cold. (*The soba salad can be made up to 2 hours in advance.*)

*Union Square Cafe chef Carmen Quagliata's wife* planted cherry tomatoes when their two sons were little so that the boys could eat them off the vine, but they couldn't keep up with the yield. Carmen oven-dried the rest and re-created a dish that his mother had once made for him. Like her, he uses capellini, because the juicy sauce clings well to the fine pasta.

Since you oven-dry the tomatoes in advance, the entire kitchen will smell like summer by the time you're ready to cook the pasta.

# Capellini with Garden Tomatoes

1 pint cherry tomatoes, such as Sweet 100s, or grape tomatoes, halved

1 tablespoon balsamic vinegar

¾ cup olive oil

Kosher salt

4 garlic cloves, finely chopped

½ teaspoon red pepper flakes

1 cup torn fresh basil leaves

1 large beefsteak tomato, cored, peeled, and chopped, juice and seeds reserved

8 ounces capellini

½ cup grated Pecorino Romano

**4 servings**

Preheat the oven to 200 degrees.

Place the cherry tomato halves close together on a baking sheet, cut side up. Mix the balsamic vinegar and ¼ cup of the oil together and spoon evenly over the tomatoes. Sprinkle with a healthy pinch of salt.

Bake the tomatoes for 2 to 3 hours, or until they look shriveled and slightly dry but are still moist when you bite into one. Cool on the baking sheet. (*The tomatoes can be made several hours in advance.*)

Bring 4 quarts water to a boil in a large pot and add 2 tablespoons salt.

Meanwhile, in a large skillet, heat the remaining ½ cup oil over medium heat until it shimmers. Add the garlic and cook until light golden, about 3 minutes. Add the red pepper flakes, basil, beefsteak tomato, with its juice and seeds, and ½ teaspoon salt and bring to a boil, then remove from the heat.

Add the capellini to the boiling water, stir, and cook until al dente.

Ladle ½ cup of the cooking water into the skillet, then drain the pasta, add to the sauce, and stir to combine. Add the oven-dried tomatoes, with all their oil and juices, and stir once or twice. Transfer to a wide shallow bowl, top with the Pecorino Romano, and serve immediately.

# The Coach

There's nothing like constraint to get the creative juices going. No matter where he stands, chef Carmen Quagliata, who took over the Union Square Cafe kitchen from Michael Romano in September 2007, is in the middle of things, which is just how he likes it. His office is a rabbit warren up a tight spiral staircase from the compact main kitchen, a jam-packed space that hems him in no matter which way he turns. His culinary imagination appreciates the tension of tight space and time—as though too much freedom were a bad thing—and he tries to wring as much as possible out of every hour of the day.

Carmen has trained his cooks to define tasks the way he does, in terms of how many quarter-hour units they require, and yet there isn't a clock-watcher among them. It has become second nature: Family meal planning starts at 2:30, and the food heads out to the rear dining room with absolute precision at 4:00.

Carmen steps in, frequently and on the run, wherever he sees a need. It's not unusual to find him trimming Brussels sprouts, stirring a pot on the line, or dressing a salad to conform to a diner's special request. Occasionally he even makes a dish for family meal, usually because a puzzle has presented itself: six ingredients, not enough of any one of them to stand on its own, with just thirty minutes to turn some combination of them into a dish.

He works fast, more comfortable with the sprint than the marathon, the brisk pace a counterbalance to the other side of his personality, the moments when he might get emotional about his sons' baseball games or his wife's garden. His eyebrows angle up in the middle, as though he always has a question on his mind, which, in a way, he does: Everybody ready for whatever's coming next?

*Union Square Cafe cook Joe Anthony* likes what he calls "clean" food with lots of vegetables, but he's aware that he can't send staffers out hungry at the start of an eight-hour shift. So he frequently turns a new vegetable combo, like this Sicilian-influenced mix of fennel and spinach cooked with raisins, orange zest, and red pepper flakes, into a pasta sauce.

Be sure the washed spinach is completely dry, because any water that clings to it will dilute the sauce.

# Penne with Fennel, Spinach & Golden Raisins

1 medium white onion, thinly sliced

1 medium fennel bulb, trimmed, halved, cored, and thinly sliced, preferably on a mandoline

1 cup golden raisins

Finely grated zest of 1 orange

Kosher salt

½ teaspoon red pepper flakes

1 cup dry red wine

2½ cups Maialino Marinara (page 114)

12 ounces baby spinach (about 5 cups)

1 pound penne

1 cup finely grated Pecorino Romano, plus more for serving

1 cup finely grated Parmigiano-Reggiano, plus more for serving

**6 to 8 servings**

In a large skillet, combine the onion, fennel, raisins, orange zest, 1 teaspoon salt, and the red pepper. Add the wine, bring to a simmer over medium-low heat, cover, and cook until the vegetables are tender, 20 to 30 minutes.

Meanwhile, bring 4 quarts water to a boil in a large pot and add 2 tablespoons salt.

Add the marinara and spinach to the vegetables and simmer over medium heat, stirring frequently, until the spinach wilts and the liquid thickens slightly into a sauce, about 10 minutes.

Meanwhile, add the penne to the boiling water, stir, and cook until al dente. Drain.

Add the pasta to the sauce, stirring well to combine. Stir in both cheeses and serve immediately, with more cheese on the side.

*Cacio e pepe, a classic Roman pasta* with cheese and lots of black pepper, is a standard item on Maialino's menu, but for family meal, the traditional tonnarelli, a long pasta with squared-off edges, gives way to shorter penne, which is less likely to flick a drop of sauce onto a staffer's clothes. There's a simple secret to the velvety sauce: The more finely ground the Pecorino Romano, the smoother the sauce—which is why at Maialino it's pulverized to a powder in a food processor. You can also use the finest side of a box grater to get the right consistency, but don't use a Microplane grater, since the cheese shreds will be so fine that they will clump.

The pasta cooking water and butter form what sous chef Jean-Paul Bourgeois likes to call "a liaison of goodness," a foundation for the blended cheese. For the bite, Maialino uses Tellicherry pepper, a full-flavored black pepper from India, but the peppercorns in your cabinet will work as well.

# Penne Cacio e Pepe

2 tablespoons kosher salt

1 pound penne

2 tablespoons olive oil

1 tablespoon medium-coarse ground black pepper, or more to taste

4 tablespoons (½ stick) cold unsalted butter, cut into small pieces

1¼ cups finely grated Pecorino Romano

**4 to 6 servings**

Bring 4 quarts water to a boil in a large pot and add the salt. Add the pasta, stir, and cook until al dente.

Meanwhile, heat the oil in a large skillet over medium-low heat. Add the pepper and warm for 1 to 2 minutes to release its flavor. Ladle 1¼ cups of the pasta cooking water into the skillet and remove the pan from the heat.

When the pasta is al dente, drain it and add to the skillet. Return the pan to medium-high heat, add the butter, and cook, stirring constantly, for about 1 minute. Remove from the heat and gradually sprinkle 1 cup of the cheese over the pasta, stirring briskly and shaking the pan until the cheese is fully incorporated and forms a creamy sauce. Taste and add more pepper if you like.

Transfer to a platter, top with the remaining ¼ cup grated cheese, and serve immediately.

*For Saturday night's midnight family meal at The Modern,* chef de cuisine Sandro Romano turns out a huge batch of spaghetti carbonara. You can make carbonara with bacon, but it's even better with pancetta, pork belly cured with salt and spices. Best of all is guanciale, cured pork cheeks, which has a fuller flavor and is authentic to this Roman dish. The pasta cooking water added to the sauce gently warms the beaten eggs so they won't scramble when the hot pasta hits the bowl, and the heat of the pasta finishes cooking the sauce.

# Spaghetti Carbonara

Kosher salt

2 tablespoons olive oil

6 ounces thinly sliced guanciale or pancetta (see headnote), cut into small strips

½ cup plus 2 tablespoons finely grated Pecorino Romano

Freshly ground black pepper

1 large egg

1 large egg yolk

12 ounces spaghetti

**4 to 6 servings**

Bring 4 quarts water to a boil in a large pot and add 2 tablespoons salt.

Meanwhile, heat the oil in a large skillet over medium-low heat. Add the guanciale and cook until browned but not quite crisp, about 10 minutes. Drain the contents of the pan through a strainer set over a metal bowl large enough to hold the cooked pasta, then set the guanciale aside.

Slowly whisk the ½ cup grated cheese into the guanciale fat to form a creamy sauce. Season abundantly with pepper. When the mixture is cool, beat the egg and egg yolk together and whisk in the beaten eggs.

Add the pasta to the boiling water, stir, and cook until just al dente. Ladle out about ¼ cup of the cooking water and whisk 2 tablespoons of the water into the egg mixture. Stir in the guanciale.

Drain the pasta and add it to the bowl. Place the bowl over low heat and toss the pasta gently but thoroughly with a spatula or kitchen tongs, removing it from the heat as soon as the pasta is coated and the sauce is no longer runny, about 1 minute. If the sauce is too thick or becomes grainy, immediately add some of the remaining reserved cooking water, a tablespoonful at a time, to restore it to the proper consistency.

Top the pasta with the remaining 2 tablespoons Pecorino Romano and serve immediately.

*A family meal cook doesn't have to play by the rules,* geographical or cultural. "I bet it would be good if I added this" is the operative notion behind some of the restaurants' most satisfying dishes—in this case, a surprising blend of mushrooms, curry powder, smooth coconut milk, and tart citrus, all brightened up with fresh ginger, cilantro, and jalapeño.

# Coconut Curry Pasta

Kosher salt

2 tablespoons vegetable oil

1 large garlic clove, thinly sliced

1 tablespoon finely grated peeled fresh ginger

½ medium jalapeño, seeded and finely chopped

10 ounces cremini mushrooms, trimmed and thickly sliced (about 4 cups)

Freshly ground black pepper

1 tablespoon curry powder

1 14-ounce can unsweetened coconut milk

1 pound penne or other short pasta

⅓ cup finely chopped fresh cilantro

2 tablespoons fresh lime juice

**4 to 6 servings**

Bring 4 quarts water to a boil in a large pot and add 2 tablespoons salt.

Meanwhile, heat the oil in a large skillet over medium-low heat. Add the garlic, ginger, and jalapeño and cook, stirring occasionally, until the jalapeño is softened, about 5 minutes. Add the mushrooms and a pinch each of salt and pepper and cook, stirring, for 5 minutes, until the mushrooms begin to soften. Add the curry powder and cook for 1 minute. Add the coconut milk, stirring well, bring to a gentle simmer, and cook until the liquid has reduced to the consistency of a sauce, about 5 minutes. Turn off the heat.

Add the pasta to the boiling water, stir, and cook until al dente. Drain.

Add the pasta to the pan with the sauce and mix well. Turn the heat to medium-low and cook until heated through. Add the cilantro and lime juice and stir to combine. Adjust the seasonings and serve immediately.

*These rice noodles are a little salty, a little sweet, and a little hot.* The thinly sliced cabbage cooks up quickly, but if you want more crunch, toss in a cup of grated carrots or lightly steamed broccoli florets.

White soy sauce, which you can find in Asian markets, is more subtle and slightly sweeter than the dark, but you can use all dark soy sauce. Rice noodles come in a range of sizes and widths, so follow the package directions for cooking times.

# Rice Noodles with Cabbage & Leeks

⅓ cup Garlic Oil (recipe follows)

1 medium head Savoy or Napa cabbage, halved, cored, and cut into ⅛-inch-wide slices

2 medium leeks, white and light green parts only, finely chopped and well washed to remove grit (about 2 cups)

1 tablespoon finely grated peeled fresh ginger

1 small jalapeño, halved, seeded, and minced

1 cup rice wine vinegar

¾ cup white soy sauce (see headnote)

⅓ cup sugar

3 tablespoons kosher salt

1 pound wide dried rice noodles

2 tablespoons toasted sesame oil

2 tablespoons dark soy sauce or mushroom-flavored soy sauce

1 tablespoon Sriracha hot sauce

5 scallions, thinly sliced

**6 to 8 servings**

In a large skillet or Dutch oven, heat the garlic oil over medium heat. Add the cabbage, leeks, ginger, and jalapeño and cook, stirring, until soft, 8 to 10 minutes. Add the vinegar, white soy sauce, and sugar, bring to a simmer, and cook 10 to 12 minutes, until reduced by half.

Meanwhile, bring 6 quarts water to a boil in a large pot and add the salt. Stir the rice noodles into the boiling water and cook according to the package directions. Drain.

Scrape the vegetable mixture into a large bowl. Add the rice noodles and toss well. Drizzle in the sesame oil, dark soy sauce, and Sriracha. Top with the sliced scallions, and serve.

# Garlic Oil

2 cups olive oil

½ cup sliced garlic

**2 cups**

This is a staple in the Gramercy Tavern kitchen, a quick way to add garlic flavor at just the level of intensity that seems right to you. Brush some of the oil onto slices of country bread and grill it, then top with sliced summer tomatoes and fresh basil or a white bean puree for bruschetta. A teaspoon will improve a soup, sauce, or salad, or just about anything else. It also flavors Farro and Beans (page 70).

Heat the oil in a small saucepan over medium heat. Reduce the heat to low, add the garlic, and simmer, stirring, for 5 minutes, or until the garlic has started to brown slightly. Remove from the heat and let cool.

Strain the oil. (*The oil can be stored in a tightly sealed container in the refrigerator for up to 1 week.*)

*Ricotta serves as the mild-mannered diplomat* between bitter greens and hot or spicy sausage in this Eleven Madison Park family meal pasta. Goat's-milk ricotta is leaner than cow's-milk, but if you can't find it, use cow's-milk ricotta—as the cooks there do.

# Orecchiette with Broccoli Rabe, Sausage & Ricotta

2 bunches broccoli rabe (about 2 pounds)

Kosher salt

¼ cup olive oil

1 pound Italian sausage, hot, sweet, or a combination, casings removed, cut into bite-sized pieces

4 garlic cloves, finely chopped

Freshly ground black pepper

1 pound orecchiette

1 cup ricotta (see headnote)

¼ cup grated Pecorino Romano

6 to 8 servings

Remove and discard any tough outer or damaged leaves from the broccoli rabe. Tear the remaining leaves and florets off the main stems and into large pieces and wash well in cold water. Prepare a bowl of ice water.

Place the leaves and florets in a large saucepan and cover with cold water by 2 inches. Bring to a simmer over high heat. Add ½ teaspoon salt to the water, and remove from the heat. Reserve ¾ cup of the cooking water, drain the broccoli rabe, and immediately plunge it into the ice water to stop the cooking. When it is cool, drain well and pat dry.

Bring 4 quarts water to a boil in a large pot and add 2 tablespoons salt.

Meanwhile, heat 1 tablespoon of the oil in a large skillet or Dutch oven over medium-high heat. Add the sausage and cook, stirring, until the meat is lightly browned, 4 to 6 minutes. Add the garlic and cook for 1 minute. Add the broccoli rabe, the reserved cooking water, and the remaining 3 tablespoons oil, and stir thoroughly. Season with salt and pepper to taste; keep warm.

Stir the orecchiette into the boiling water and cook until al dente. Drain.

Add the pasta to the skillet. Stir in the ricotta and heat to warm through. Remove from the heat, sprinkle with the Pecorino Romano, and serve immediately.

*Maialino cooks have adapted Bolognese sauce* for family meal, creating a tasty main-dish pasta with whatever ingredients are on hand, which in this case includes their marinara sauce and lamb, not beef. Improvisation yields impressive results. This hearty pasta, with a respectful nod to Bologna, is one of the reasons staffers at Maialino line up early, plates in hand, before family meal even emerges from the kitchen.

You'll need to make the marinara sauce in advance.

# Lamb Bolognese

¼ cup olive oil

1 pound ground lamb

Kosher salt

Pinch of red pepper flakes

4 fresh thyme sprigs

2 bay leaves

2 cups dry red wine

4 cups Maialino Marinara (page 114)

1 3-inch piece Parmigiano-Reggiano or Grana Padano rind (optional)

4 tablespoons (½ stick) unsalted butter

¼ cup heavy cream

½ cup grated Parmigiano-Reggiano, plus more for sprinkling

Freshly ground black pepper

1 pound fresh fettuccine (store-bought or homemade, page 108)

**4 to 6 servings**

Heat the oil in a 12-inch skillet over medium-high heat. Add the ground lamb and brown slowly, scraping the bottom of the pan and reducing the heat as necessary to keep the lamb from browning too fast, until the moisture evaporates and the meat is well browned, 15 to 20 minutes. Add a pinch of salt and the red pepper flakes and cook for 1 minute more. Drain off the fat.

Turn the heat to high, add the thyme, bay leaves, and wine, and stir well. Bring to a boil and reduce until only a small amount of liquid is left in the pan, 5 to 10 minutes.

Add the marinara and the cheese rind, if using, and simmer for 20 minutes, or until the sauce thickens.

Meanwhile, bring 4 quarts water to a boil in a large pot and add 2 tablespoons salt.

When the sauce has thickened, remove and discard the thyme sprigs, bay leaves, and cheese rind, if you used it. Stir in the butter, cream, and grated cheese, bring to a simmer, and remove from the heat. Season to taste with salt and pepper. (*The sauce can be made up to 3 days ahead, covered, and refrigerated; rewarm over medium-low heat.*)

Add the fettuccine to the boiling water, stir to separate the strands, and cook for 2 to 3 minutes, until al dente. Drain.

Add the pasta to the sauce and stir to coat well. Sprinkle with cheese and serve immediately.

*For the final Tabla Thanksgiving family dinner,* shortly before the restaurant closed, the mandate was simple: Make a dish you love. For sous chef Zia Sheikh, now a sous chef at North End Grill, it was an amplified macaroni and cheese, with mustard, thyme, shallots, garlic, and Grana Padano livening up the sauce and a crusty cheese-and-bread-crumb topping.

# "The Dish You Love Best" Macaroni & Cheese

### For the sauce

3 tablespoons unsalted butter

1 cup thinly sliced shallots (3–4 medium)

3 large garlic cloves, thinly sliced

Freshly ground black pepper

2 fresh thyme sprigs

2 tablespoons all-purpose flour

3 cups Chicken or Vegetable Stock (page 39 or 38)

3 cups heavy cream

3 cups coarsely grated sharp cheddar (about 1 pound)

1¼ cups grated Grana Padano (about 7 ounces)

2 teaspoons Dijon mustard

Kosher salt

Butter for the pan

2 tablespoons kosher salt

1 pound penne, fusilli, or other short pasta

¾ cup panko bread crumbs or fine dried bread crumbs

⅓ cup grated Grana Padano

**10 to 12 servings**

TO MAKE THE SAUCE: Melt the butter in a large saucepan over medium-low heat. Add the shallots, garlic, 1 teaspoon pepper, and the thyme and cook, stirring, until the shallots are translucent, 5 to 7 minutes.

Slowly add the flour, stirring constantly, and cook for 5 minutes, so that the flour loses its raw taste. Add the stock, stirring constantly, then increase the heat to medium and bring to a boil. Reduce the heat to medium-low and simmer for 10 to 15 minutes, stirring occasionally, so the flavors come together.

Add the cream, bring to a simmer, and cook until the sauce is thick enough to coat the back of a wooden spoon, 7 to 10 minutes longer. Strain the sauce into a bowl.

Clean the saucepan, add the sauce, and return it to low heat. Add the cheeses and mustard, stirring constantly. Once the cheese is completely melted, season to taste with salt and pepper and remove from the heat. (*The sauce can be made up to 1 day ahead, covered, and refrigerated. Bring to room temperature and reheat slowly before using.*)

TO ASSEMBLE AND BAKE: Preheat the oven to 400 degrees. Butter a 9-x-13-inch baking dish.

Bring 4 quarts water to a boil in a large pot and add the salt. Add the pasta to the boiling water, stir, and cook until just al dente. Drain well.

Combine the pasta with the sauce and pour into the baking dish.

In a small bowl, combine the panko and Grana Padano. Sprinkle over the pasta. Bake until the top is golden brown and bubbling, 20 to 25 minutes. Serve.

*Baked ziti answers any busy cook's* constant quest for more flavor in less time, and it's the kind of dish that the chefs of Blue Smoke make for exactly the same reason for their work family. The allure is simple: It delivers all the satisfaction of lasagna with none of the architectural effort. The pasta, tomato sauce, meats, and cheeses are mixed together, spread in a pan under a layer of grated mozzarella, and baked. Prepare the tomato sauce in advance, and the process becomes even faster.

# Baked Ziti

2 tablespoons olive oil

½ medium onion, finely chopped (½ cup)

Kosher salt

3 garlic cloves, finely chopped

¼ cup chopped fresh basil

¾ pound sweet Italian fennel sausage, casings removed

12 ounces ground beef chuck

½ cup dry red wine

2½ cups Maialino Marinara (page 114)

Freshly ground black pepper

Butter for the pan

1 pound ziti

1 large egg, beaten

½ cup ricotta

2 cups grated mozzarella

**6 to 8 servings**

Heat 1 tablespoon of the oil in a 12-inch skillet over medium heat. Add the onion with ½ teaspoon salt and cook, stirring, until translucent, about 8 minutes. Add the garlic and cook for 2 minutes, or until softened. Stir in the basil. Transfer the onion and garlic to a bowl and set aside; wipe out the skillet.

Heat the remaining 1 tablespoon oil in the skillet over medium-high heat. Add the sausage and brown well, stirring occasionally and breaking it up with a spoon, about 15 minutes. Using a slotted spoon, transfer the sausage to a plate and set aside, leaving the fat in the pan.

Add the ground beef to the pan and cook, stirring occasionally, for 15 to 20 minutes, until any liquid the meat gives off has evaporated and the meat is well browned. Transfer to the plate with the sausage.

Add the onion-garlic mixture to the skillet. Pour the wine into the skillet, stir to deglaze the pan, and boil to reduce the wine by half, 3 to 4 minutes. Add the marinara, and simmer for 8 minutes over medium-low heat until slightly thickened.

*recipe continues*

Add the cooked meats to the sauce and simmer for 5 minutes more. Season with salt and pepper to taste. Remove from the heat and allow to cool.

Meanwhile, preheat the oven to 375 degrees. Butter a 9-x-13-inch baking dish.

Bring 4 quarts water to a boil in a large pot and add 2 tablespoons salt.

Add the ziti to the boiling water, stir, and cook until just al dente. Drain the pasta and spread it on a baking sheet while you finish the sauce.

Mix the beaten egg with the ricotta and stir into the meat sauce.

In a large bowl, combine the pasta and meat sauce and stir well. Spread the mixture in the baking dish and top with the mozzarella. Bake for 12 minutes, or until the pasta is hot and the mozzarella has melted. Serve.

# In a Father's Footsteps

Other kids might have a swing set in the backyard or a collection of video games, but when Andrea Czachor, Maialino's general manager, was a little girl, she invited her friends to her dad's restaurant after school. Located in Rutland, Vermont, it served up New England specialties—homemade popovers and breads, clam chowder, steaks, and, for the girls, Shirley Temples.

For Andrea, it was an exciting place to be, the only place she could imagine herself when she grew up. Her mother, an elementary school teacher and librarian, preached a more structured life, with regular hours, in an environment that was more welcoming to women than restaurants often were. Andrea was not swayed.

Everything her mother said about the crazy hours was true, but there was still plenty of time to be a family, one way or another. During the school year, her father carved out a window of time between lunch and dinner so that he could pick up the kids at school or attend their sporting events. On holidays, her mother stepped in as maître d' at the restaurant, and Andrea and her brother hung out there—so they were together just like other families. And Sundays were sacrosanct, family day, no electronics allowed, usually involving a long drive in the car that culminated with a meal at a restaurant her father wanted to try out.

When it was time to go to college, Andrea picked a school that was only hours away and came home on weekends to work at the restaurant. She was going to be her dad's maître d'—still the only career that made sense to her.

But when her father died during her junior year, that nice, tidy future evaporated in an instant. That summer her mother sold the restaurant, and Andrea moved in with two girlfriends in New York City. She got her first job in 2005, working in food service at the U.S. Open tennis tournament, three weeks of grueling eighteen-hour days without a day off. Four years and two front-of-the-house jobs later, she got a job at Maialino as the dining room manager, and after two years, she was promoted to general manager. Part of her position involves guiding younger staffers onto the path she had to find for herself, and it isn't unusual, after the lunch rush, to see her at a back table with an employee who wants to talk about what the right next move might be.

Andrea thinks her dad would be proud to see what she's done, and her fiancé, a sommelier, understands her odd-hours schedule. She always knew she'd end up in the restaurant business. Now, she says, she's a lifer in the company, in what feels to her like a familiar small town.

*This lasagna is worth every minute of effort* devoted to getting it just right. Homemade meatballs, made from a mix of beef, pork, and veal, then cooked and sliced, provide more flavor and texture than mere ground beef. For best results, ask the butcher at your market for very finely ground meat. A from-scratch but simple tomato sauce, a blend of cheeses, and fresh pasta all contribute to a harmonious dish.

# Mama Romano's Lasagna

### For the meatballs

6 slices white sandwich bread

¾ cup milk

8 ounces finely ground beef

8 ounces finely ground pork

8 ounces finely ground veal

2 tablespoons chopped fresh Italian parsley

3 tablespoons grated Parmigiano-Reggiano

3 tablespoons grated Pecorino Romano

2 large eggs, beaten

2 teaspoons kosher salt, or more to taste

⅛ teaspoon freshly ground black pepper, or more to taste

¼ cup olive oil

### For the sauce

½ cup olive oil

1 cup coarsely chopped onion

2 garlic cloves, thinly sliced

2 28-ounce cans plum tomatoes, passed through a food mill or pureed with their juice in a food processor

1 teaspoon kosher salt

⅛ teaspoon freshly ground black pepper

3 fresh basil sprigs, tied together with kitchen twine

TO MAKE THE MEATBALLS: In a large bowl, soak the bread slices in the milk for 2 minutes.

Squeeze the bread and mash it until it becomes a smooth paste. Add all the remaining ingredients and mix thoroughly with a rubber spatula or your hands. Form a little of the meat into a thin 1-inch patty and cook it in a teaspoon or so of olive oil in a small skillet over medium heat until cooked through, about 2 minutes. Taste and adjust the seasonings in the meat mixture if necessary.

With moistened hands, form the meat mixture into 10 equal-sized meatballs; they will be very moist and soft. Lay the meatballs on a baking sheet and refrigerate until needed. (*The meatballs can be refrigerated for up to 3 hours.*)

Heat the oil in a Dutch oven or large saucepan over medium heat. Add only as many meatballs as will fit comfortably in the pot without crowding and cook, turning once, until browned on both sides, 8 to 10 minutes total. As the meatballs are seared, remove them from the pot and set them aside on a plate. When all of the meatballs are browned, pour out and discard the remaining oil.

TO MAKE THE SAUCE: Add the oil to the pot and heat over medium heat. Add the onion and cook, stirring, until it begins to soften, 3 to 4 minutes. Add the garlic and cook, stirring, until the onion and garlic are lightly browned, 4 to 5 minutes. Using a skimmer or slotted spoon, remove and discard the onion and garlic, leaving as much of the olive oil as possible in the pot.

Add the tomatoes, salt, and pepper to the pot. Bring to a boil, then add the basil, lower the heat, and simmer for 15 minutes.

*recipe continues*

Add the meatballs to the pot, along with any juices that have accumulated on the plate. Continue simmering the sauce for about 45 minutes, stirring occasionally, until thickened. Remove from the heat and set aside to cool. Remove and discard the basil.

Carefully transfer the meatballs from the sauce to a platter or baking sheet, scraping the sauce that adheres to them back into the pot. Slice the meatballs into ¼-inch-thick slices and refrigerate, covered.

### For the cheese mixture

3 ounces Parmigiano-Reggiano, grated (1 cup)

10 ounces mozzarella, grated (2½ cups)

1¾ pounds (3½ cups) whole-milk ricotta

3 large eggs, beaten

1 teaspoon kosher salt

### For the pasta

2 tablespoons kosher salt

8 5-x-10-inch sheets fresh pasta, homemade (page 108) or store-bought

Olive oil

¼ cup grated Parmigiano-Reggiano

**8 to 10 servings**

TO MAKE THE CHEESE MIXTURE: Combine all the ingredients in a large bowl and mix thoroughly with a rubber spatula or your hands. Refrigerate, covered.

TO COOK THE PASTA: Bring 4 cups water to a boil in a large pot and add the salt. Lightly oil a baking sheet. Fill a large bowl with ice water.

Cook the pasta sheets one by one just until al dente. Carefully transfer each sheet with a slotted spoon to the ice water to cool, then immediately transfer the pasta sheet to the baking sheet and lightly oil the top of it.

TO ASSEMBLE AND BAKE THE LASAGNA: Preheat the oven to 350 degrees. Lightly oil a 9-x-13-inch baking pan.

Spread a thin layer of sauce over the bottom of the baking pan. Fit 2 of the pasta sheets into the pan and, using a rubber spatula, spread half the cheese mixture in an even layer over it. Top with a second layer of 2 sheets of pasta. Spread a good amount of sauce over the pasta, then arrange the sliced meatballs, slightly overlapping, on top. Spread more sauce over the meatballs and top with the third layer of 2 sheets of pasta. Spread the remaining cheese mixture over the pasta and then top with the final 2 sheets of pasta. Spread the remaining sauce over the pasta.

Cover the pan with parchment paper and then with aluminum foil, making sure the parchment is completely covered by the foil. Poke a few holes in the foil and parchment with the point of a paring knife. Bake the lasagna for 1 hour.

Remove the foil and parchment and sprinkle the Parmigiano over the top of the lasagna. Continue baking, uncovered, for 20 to 30 minutes longer, until the top of the lasagna browns lightly and looks set. Allow the lasagna to rest for at least 30 minutes before serving. (*The lasagna can be cooled and refrigerated, tightly covered, for up to 1 day. Reheat, covered with parchment and foil, in a 325-degree oven until it is hot in the center.*)

*There are two ways to make fresh pasta* and two ways to roll it out—by hand and by machine. Making it by hand will give you a better sense of how to produce pasta that has the right texture, with a bit of a bite to it, but if you're pressed for time, a food processor is a perfectly acceptable substitute. To roll out the dough, a hand-cranked or electric pasta machine yields the best results.

# Fresh Pasta Dough

2 cups all-purpose flour, plus more for rolling

½ teaspoon kosher salt

3 large eggs

About 1 tablespoon olive oil

**1 pound**

TO MAKE THE DOUGH BY HAND: Combine the flour and salt on a work surface, shape into a mound, and make a well in the center large enough to hold the eggs. Crack the eggs into the well and beat lightly with a fork, then begin using it to pull flour from the base of the well and incorporate it into the eggs. When the mixture is thick, use your hands to push all the remaining flour into the center and knead until a dough forms. When the dough is fairly stiff, move it away from any remaining flour and small bits of dough. Clean your hands, then scrape the remaining flour and bits of dough from the work surface with a pastry scraper and transfer to a fine-mesh strainer. Shake the flour from the strainer onto one side of the work surface and discard the bits of dough.

Place the dough on the floured surface and knead, incorporating as much of the flour as necessary, until it holds together well and is no longer sticky; the dough should not be hard or dry.

Transfer the dough to a clean surface and knead with clean hands until smooth and elastic, about 5 minutes. Form the dough into a ball. Drizzle with the oil, turn to coat with the oil, wrap tightly in plastic wrap, and let rest for at least 30 minutes and up to 8 hours.

TO MAKE THE DOUGH BY MACHINE: Combine the flour and salt in a food processor and pulse a few times to aerate. With the machine running, add the eggs through the feed tube and process until the dough starts to form a ball. If the dough is too dry, add 1 to 2 teaspoons water and continue to process.

Turn the dough out onto an unfloured work surface and knead until smooth and elastic. Form it into a ball. Oil and wrap the dough as above and let it rest for at least 30 minutes.

TO ROLL OUT THE PASTA: Sprinkle some flour on a baking sheet and set aside. Set up a hand-cranked or an electric pasta machine and lightly flour the work surface in front of it.

Cut the pasta dough into quarters. Wrap 3 of the quarters in plastic wrap and set aside. Pass the remaining quarter through the widest setting on the pasta machine. Decrease the setting a notch, pass the dough through again, and then repeat, decreasing the setting again.

On the floured work surface, fold the dough into thirds, bringing the two ends over the center as though folding a letter. Flatten it with your fingertips and run it through the widest setting a second time. Repeat this process 5 or 6 times, dragging the dough through the flour if it becomes sticky, until it is silky and elastic. Then continue rolling the dough, decreasing the setting each time, until you get to the next-to-the-last setting. Roll the dough through this setting 3 times; you will have a long sheet of pasta that is silky, elastic, and about as wide as the rollers.

Cut the sheet into thirds (each will be about 10 inches long) using a sharp knife or a pasta cutter. Then cut into the shape your recipe calls for using an attachment for the pasta machine or a long sharp knife. For fettuccine, wind the strands around your fingers to make nests and toss gently with the flour on the baking sheet. For lasagna sheets, cut rectangles 5 inches by 10 inches. Repeat with the remaining dough.

(*The pasta can be refrigerated, tightly covered, for up to 1 day or carefully wrapped and frozen for up to 3 weeks.*)

*Savory pork, crispy potatoes, greens, garlic,* and a little red pepper heat all build step-by-step in a single skillet before they are mixed with pasta and cheese and just the right amount of made-in-advance marinara sauce. Everything benefits from the combination, resulting in a dish that serves up a variety of textures as well as flavors. This can be a second-night supper, designed to use up what's left of a pork (or lamb) roast served the night before, but it's so good, you may want to make a bigger roast next time to guarantee that you'll have enough leftovers.

# Skillet Pasta with Roast Pork, Crunchy Potatoes & Greens

Kosher salt

1 pound Yukon Gold potatoes (about 2 medium)

8 ounces fusilli or other short pasta

6 tablespoons olive oil

1½ cups ½-inch cubes leftover roast pork or lamb

4 garlic cloves, thinly sliced

1 teaspoon red pepper flakes

3 loosely packed cups baby spinach or coarsely chopped escarole

1½ cups Maialino Marinara (page 114)

½ cup grated Pecorino Romano, plus more for sprinkling

**4 to 6 servings**

Bring 3 quarts water to a boil in a large pot and add 1 tablespoon salt.

Meanwhile, put the potatoes in a medium saucepan, add cold water to cover, and bring to a boil. Add 1½ teaspoons salt, reduce the heat to low, and simmer for 4 minutes. (The potatoes will not be cooked.) Drain and cool.

Slice the potatoes in half lengthwise and then into ¼-inch-thick half-moons. Set aside, covered, until you're ready to finish the dish. (*The potatoes can be refrigerated, covered, up to 2 days ahead.*)

Add the pasta to the boiling water, stir, and cook until al dente. Drain, toss with 1 tablespoon of the oil, and set aside.

Heat ¼ cup of the oil in a 12-inch skillet over medium-high heat. Add the potatoes and cook, turning once and shaking the pan often or loosening the potatoes with a spatula, until evenly golden brown, about 5 minutes per side. Move the potatoes to one side of the pan and add the meat in a single layer. Press it down with a spatula, season with salt, and cook, without stirring, until brown and crisp on the first side, 3 to 5 minutes.

Move the meat to the side of the pan with the potatoes and add the remaining 1 tablespoon oil and the garlic to the empty space. Cook the garlic over medium-low heat, stirring, until lightly browned, 2 to 3 minutes. Stir everything together and add the red pepper flakes. Add the spinach or escarole and cook, stirring, until wilted (spinach will start to wilt immediately; escarole will take 4 to 5 minutes).

Meanwhile, warm the marinara in a small saucepan over low heat, stirring occasionally.

Stir the pasta and grated cheese into the meat and greens.

Ladle the marinara onto a platter or ladle onto individual plates and pile the pasta on top. Sprinkle with a little more cheese and serve immediately.

# The Family Man

Terry Coughlin, a managing partner at Maialino, can tell the story of his life restaurant by restaurant. Yes, he grew up in California, got a degree in theater education, and planned to teach, but his real life began when he headed east and "bluffed my way into Gramercy Tavern," thanks to a friend who got him an interview for a waiter's position. He was hired for a job he didn't think he could do and went to work "waiting for someone to tap me on the shoulder and say, 'Sorry, we made a mistake.'"

That didn't happen, so he kept at it, grateful for the chance to catch up with what opportunity had handed him. He met his future wife at Gramercy Tavern, where she was the maître d', and announced their engagement at a family meal. After eight years, having been promoted to captain and looking for a new challenge, Terry stood up at family meal again to tell everyone of another transition: He was leaving Gramercy Tavern to take a management position at Tabla. He shared the news of his wife's first pregnancy at that restaurant and, two years later, of a second child on the way.

Months later, his coworkers noticed that he did not seem his usual easygoing self and started asking whether everything was all right. At a family meal, Terry told them that his second daughter would be born with Down syndrome.

"We share what's good, and now what's difficult," he told the staff, "and this is an opportunity to tell you what I'm going through. We're going to use this as an opportunity to make a difference. It's a great gift." As people lined up to offer a hug or a handshake or a comment about someone they knew in a similar situation, it hit him that what might sound like a greeting card sentiment to an outsider was in fact the plain truth: This was his family.

When Maialino opened, Terry moved there as its general manager, the head of the household, along with chef Nick Anderer, and took on one extra responsibility. He worked with a local group that finds jobs for adults with special needs and customized a job for a man who lived nearby. By the time Terry was promoted to managing partner, the restaurant family had grown by one more.

*Make this homemade tomato sauce,* freeze half for later, and then walk right by the prepared-sauce display at the market, thinking how much better and more economical your own is. Steeping the fresh basil in the sauce as it cools, rather than cooking it in the sauce the whole time, contributes just the right amount of a fresher flavor.

At Maialino, the sauce is passed through a food mill rather than a food processor, which would make it too smooth. If you don't have a food mill, chop the onion and carrot very fine before you cook them and omit the food-mill step.

# Maialino Marinara

⅔ cup olive oil

⅔ cup chopped white onion

¼ cup chopped peeled carrot

4 garlic cloves, smashed and peeled

¾ teaspoon kosher salt

½ teaspoon freshly ground black pepper

1½ teaspoons sugar

2 28-ounce cans plum tomatoes, preferably San Marzano, crushed with your hands, with their liquid

3–4 large fresh basil sprigs

**8 cups**

Heat the oil in a large saucepan over medium-low heat. Add the onion, carrot, and garlic and cook, stirring, until the onion is translucent and the carrot is soft, 10 to 15 minutes.

Add the salt, pepper, and sugar, stir in the tomatoes and ½ cup water, and bring just to a simmer. Reduce the heat to low and simmer, uncovered, for 45 minutes. Remove from the heat.

Remove and discard the garlic and pass the sauce through a food mill into a bowl (see headnote). Add the basil sprigs and let the sauce cool to room temperature.

Remove and discard the basil and transfer the sauce to an airtight container. (*The sauce can be refrigerated, tightly covered, for up to 1 week or frozen for up to 3 months.*)

# Seafood

*This salad was born out of Gramercy Tavern sous chef* Geoff Lazlo's affection for delicatessen food and his hunch that egg salad and smoked fish would work well combined in a single dish. He took a geographical detour and added sesame oil to the mayonnaise dressing for a cold dish that's part Jewish comfort food, part Asian, and altogether delicious. At family meal, it's offered two ways: as a cold salad and as a sandwich filling.

# Smoked Fish & Chopped Egg Salad

### For the sesame mayonnaise

½ cup mayonnaise

2 teaspoons toasted sesame oil

2 teaspoons black sesame seeds

6 large eggs, at room temperature

5 ounces skinless smoked whitefish fillets (cod, hake, or pollock)

2 celery stalks, cut into ¼-inch pieces (about 1 cup)

1 small cucumber, quartered lengthwise and cut into ¼-inch dice (about 1 cup)

1 medium shallot, finely chopped

1 tablespoon finely chopped fresh dill

1 tablespoon finely chopped fresh Italian parsley

2 tablespoons capers, rinsed and drained

1 tablespoon fresh lemon juice

Kosher salt and freshly ground black pepper

**4 servings**

TO MAKE THE SESAME MAYONNAISE: Whisk the mayonnaise with the sesame oil and sesame seeds in a small bowl. Cover and refrigerate.

Preheat the oven to 350 degrees.

Place the eggs in a large saucepan, cover with cold water by at least 1 inch, and bring to a boil. Immediately remove the pan from the heat, cover, and let stand for 12 minutes.

Drain the eggs, return to the pan, cover with cold water, and let stand until completely chilled.

Peel the eggs under cold running water and finely chop.

Place the smoked fish in a baking dish and warm in the oven for 5 to 10 minutes so that it will flake apart easily.

Flake the fish into a medium bowl. Add the eggs, celery, cucumber, and shallot and mix well. Stir in the sesame mayonnaise, herbs, capers, and lemon juice. Season with salt and pepper to taste. Cover and refrigerate until cold before serving. (*The salad can be made up to 1 day ahead.*)

*Man—and woman—cannot live* by fried chicken and pulled pork alone. Sometimes the Blue Smoke staff craves fish, and the fillets that usually land on the menu find a new purpose in a popular family meal main course. The restaurant's assertive flavors slip into something a bit more subtle here: baked white fish in a buttery sauce seasoned with lemon and fresh herbs. Serve it with sides that are just as easygoing—a green salad and rice or boiled potatoes to soak up the sauce.

# Baked Fish with Lemon & Herb Butter

Butter for the pan

### For the herb butter

8 tablespoons (1 stick) unsalted butter, softened

¾ cup finely chopped scallions (about 4 scallions)

¼ cup finely chopped fresh Italian parsley

3 tablespoons finely chopped fresh oregano

3 tablespoons finely grated lemon zest

2 teaspoons kosher salt

¼ teaspoon freshly ground black pepper

1½–2 pounds skinless rock cod, flounder, red snapper, or other white-fleshed fish fillets (about 6 ounces each)

1 lemon, halved

4 to 6 servings

Preheat the oven to 400 degrees. Butter a 9-x-13-inch baking dish.

TO MAKE THE HERB BUTTER: Combine the butter, scallions, parsley, oregano, zest, salt, and pepper in a medium bowl and mix until smooth. (*Shaped into a log and wrapped well in plastic wrap, the butter will keep for up to 2 days in the refrigerator, or up to 1 month in the freezer; bring to room temperature before proceeding.*)

Arrange the fish fillets in a single layer in the baking dish. If you have thin fillets, tuck the tail ends under to create an even thickness. Using a rubber spatula, spread the herb butter evenly over the fish.

Bake for 15 minutes, or until the fish flakes easily with a fork. Squeeze the lemon over the fish and serve.

*This dish is a study in contrasts*—mild, sweet halibut served with a salad of crisp sugar snap peas, cherry tomatoes, and a mix of fresh herbs in a lemony vinaigrette. It relies on the bright flavors of ripe produce and requires very little time at the stove, just the right combination for summertime meals.

You can substitute cod, scrod, or hake for the halibut—whtatever is freshest.

# Grilled Halibut with Cherry Tomatoes, Sugar Snap Peas & Lemon

### For the salad

Kosher salt

8 ounces (about 2 cups) sugar snap peas, trimmed

3 lemons

2 tablespoons finely chopped shallots

¼ cup extra-virgin olive oil

Freshly ground black pepper

3 tablespoons chopped mixed fresh herbs, such as Italian parsley, tarragon, and chives

1 pint cherry tomatoes, halved

### For the fish

4 5-ounce Pacific halibut fillets (see headnote)

Kosher salt and freshly ground white pepper

2 tablespoons olive oil

4 servings

TO MAKE THE SALAD: Bring 8 cups water to a rapid boil in a large saucepan and add 2 tablespoons salt. Prepare a bowl of ice water and set a colander in it.

Drop the snap peas into the boiling water and blanch for 1 to 2 minutes, until crisp-tender. Drain the peas and place them in the colander in the ice water to stop the cooking.

When the snap peas are cool, drain and place them on a towel to dry, then cut them in half on the bias.

Zest 1 of the lemons using a Microplane grater. Juice all 3 lemons. Whisk together the zest, juice, shallots, and olive oil in a medium bowl. Season with salt and black pepper. Stir in the herbs, cherry tomatoes, and peas. Adjust the seasonings to taste. Set aside.

TO MAKE THE FISH: Prepare a hot fire in a grill or preheat a ridged grill pan over high heat.

Season the halibut with salt and white pepper. Rub it all over with the olive oil.

Place the fillets on the grill or in the grill pan and cook, turning once, until opaque throughout, 3 to 5 minutes on each side, depending on the thickness of the fillets.

Place the fish on a serving platter, top with the salad, and serve.

*Fish doesn't arrive in the restaurant kitchens* in neat portion sizes, and once the butcher has done his orderly work, the leftover pieces are a family meal waiting to be made. A cook at Union Square Cafe turned swordfish trimmings into this dish, but salmon works just as well. A vivid vinaigrette, a quick sear, and dinner is served, accompanied by lavash bread and lemon wedges.

You can cook the fish on a hot grill or in a ridged grill pan.

# Charred Swordfish with Mint Vinaigrette

2 pounds swordfish steaks or salmon fillets, skin removed, cut into 2-inch chunks

½ cup plus 1 tablespoon olive oil

Kosher salt and freshly ground black pepper

2 anchovy fillets

2 garlic cloves, smashed and peeled

½ teaspoon fennel seeds

¼ teaspoon red pepper flakes

2 teaspoons finely chopped shallot

1 tablespoon finely grated lemon zest

5 tablespoons fresh lemon juice

¼ teaspoon sugar

¼ cup lightly packed coarsely chopped fresh mint

4–6 lemon wedges

Lavash bread (optional)

**4 to 6 servings**

Toss the fish with the 1 tablespoon oil and season with salt and pepper.

Put the anchovy fillets, garlic, and fennel seeds on a cutting board and finely chop them together.

Heat the remaining ½ cup oil in a small skillet over medium heat until it just starts to shimmer. Remove from the heat, stir in the anchovy mixture and red pepper, and stir constantly until the oil cools.

Combine the shallot, lemon zest, juice, sugar, and ½ teaspoon salt in a large bowl. Scrape in the anchovy mixture and stir to combine.

Prepare a medium-hot fire in a grill or preheat a ridged grill pan over medium-high heat.

Cook the fish in batches, if necessary, turning to sear on all four sides, for 2 to 3 minutes per side. Toss the pieces of fish in the vinaigrette and let sit for 4 minutes.

Stir the mint into the vinaigrette and let it sit for 1 minute more. Using a slotted spoon, transfer the fish to a serving platter or individual plates, garnish with lemon wedges, and serve with the lavash, if using.

*Family meal gives sous chefs and line cooks* the chance to shine outside the boundaries of the menu. Union Square Cafe executive sous chef Chad Shaner turned coleslaw into the perfect companion for a fried fish sandwich, creating one that is full of unexpected flavors, sweet, sour, and spicy. The fried fish has some secrets up its sleeve as well. It goes into the coating mix straight from a quick soak in seltzer, which yields a crisp crust with a light, almost airy feel. Graham crackers add sweetness and help the fish to brown more quickly.

# Summer Fish Sandwiches

### For the coleslaw

1 cup shredded green cabbage

2 tablespoons finely chopped red onion

2 large radishes, grated

1 tablespoon chopped capers

1 tablespoon chopped sour pickles

1 teaspoon chopped sweet pickles

3 tablespoons mayonnaise

1 tablespoon sour cream

1 teaspoon fresh lemon juice

1 teaspoon white wine vinegar

½ teaspoon Dijon mustard

½ teaspoon prepared horseradish

Pinch of salt

5–8 twists freshly ground black pepper

### For the fish

3 cups vegetable oil

2 cups seltzer

1 pound skinless halibut, cod, grouper, or red snapper fillets, cut into 1½-inch chunks

1½ cups all-purpose flour

½ cup graham cracker crumbs

Old Bay Seasoning

Kosher salt and freshly ground black pepper

TO MAKE THE COLESLAW: Mix all the ingredients together in a medium bowl. Refrigerate.

TO MAKE THE FISH: In a large saucepan, heat the vegetable oil over high heat until it reaches 350 degrees on a deep-fat thermometer. (A bread cube dropped into the oil will turn golden brown in 45 seconds.)

Meanwhile, put the seltzer in a medium bowl. Add the fish and let soak for 10 minutes. Mix the flour and cracker crumbs in a small bowl.

Without drying the fish, dredge it in the flour mixture and place on a plate until all the fish is coated. Fry in batches until golden brown, 2 to 3 minutes, turning once. Remove with a slotted spoon and drain on paper towels. Season with a sprinkle of Old Bay and salt and pepper to taste.

4 large tomato slices

4 hamburger buns or brioche rolls, split and toasted

4 servings

TO ASSEMBLE THE SANDWICHES: Place a tomato slice on each of the bottom halves of the toasted buns. Cover with the fish, top with the coleslaw, and serve.

*A home cook might see a peach on the counter* and some black beans in the pantry without making a connection between them. A cook at Maialino saw the same two ingredients and envisioned a salsa. Sweet peaches and mild beans, tied together with citrus and heat, turn a familiar fish taco into a new dish.

Like many inspirations, this one is fleeting: Once you add the peaches to the salsa, the acid in the citrus will start to break down the fruit, and the peaches will soften. If you don't think you will finish all the salsa at one meal, combine everything but the peaches and divide the salsa into two batches. Add half the peaches to the first batch 1 to 3 hours before serving to let the flavors blend, but don't add the remaining peaches to the rest of the salsa until you're ready to serve; the peachless batch will keep for a couple of days, covered, in the refrigerator.

# Cornmeal-Crusted Fish Tacos with Black Bean & Peach Salsa

### For the salsa

4 ripe peaches (skin on), halved, pitted, and cut into ¼-inch dice

1 15-ounce can black beans, drained and rinsed

1 small red onion, finely chopped (about ½ cup)

¼ cup finely chopped fresh cilantro

¼ cup finely chopped fresh oregano

½ jalapeño, seeded and finely chopped

3 tablespoons fresh lime juice

3 tablespoons fresh orange juice

2 teaspoons kosher salt

¼ teaspoon freshly ground black pepper

### For the sour cream

½ cup sour cream

1 tablespoon fresh lime juice

Kosher salt and freshly ground black pepper

TO MAKE THE SALSA: Combine all the ingredients in a bowl and refrigerate for 1 to 3 hours.

TO MAKE THE SOUR CREAM: Put the sour cream in a small bowl and whisk in the lime juice. Season with salt and pepper to taste and refrigerate until ready to use.

## For the tacos

½ cup cornmeal

3 tablespoons cornstarch

1½ cups buttermilk

4 corn tortillas, preferably white corn

3 cups vegetable oil

1½ pounds skinless red snapper, cod, grouper, or halibut fillets, cut into 1-x-2-inch chunks

Kosher salt and freshly ground black pepper

2 cups shredded romaine lettuce

1 cup coarsely chopped fresh cilantro

4 servings

TO MAKE THE TACOS: Preheat the oven to 300 degrees.

Combine the cornmeal and cornstarch in a medium bowl. Slowly add the buttermilk, stirring with a fork.

Toast the tortillas briefly on a grill pan or in a large skillet over high heat, about 30 seconds per side. Immediately wrap them in foil and let them steam in the oven while you cook the fish.

Heat the vegetable oil in a large saucepan over high heat until it reaches 350 degrees on a deep-fat thermometer.

Season the fish with salt and pepper. Working in batches, dip the pieces of fish into the cornmeal batter and shake off the excess. Fry the fish a few pieces at a time until golden brown, turning once, about 3 minutes per side. Drain on paper towels, transfer to a baking sheet, and keep warm in the oven while you fry the rest.

Serve the fish in the warm tortillas, garnished with the romaine, salsa, sour cream, and cilantro, or put all the ingredients in separate bowls and allow diners to assemble their own tacos.

*For this cultural collaboration* between Mexican fish tacos and Louisiana blackened fish, Union Square Cafe executive sous chef Chad Shaner coats firm white fish fillets with a dry rub full of heat, blackens them quickly, and serves the fish wrapped in warm tortillas with chipotle sour cream, cheese, and thin slices of scallions and radishes.

# Blackened Fish Tacos

### For the toppings
6 scallions, slivered

5 radishes, thinly sliced

8 ounces cheddar, grated (about 2 cups)

1½ cups sour cream

2 canned chipotle chiles in adobo, finely chopped

### For the tacos
2 tablespoons chili powder

2 tablespoons garlic powder

2 tablespoons paprika

1 tablespoon ground cumin

1 teaspoon red pepper flakes

2 skinless red snapper, cod, or other firm white fish fillets (about 1 pound total)

1 teaspoon kosher salt

1 teaspoon freshly ground black pepper

12 white corn tortillas

3 tablespoons canola oil

*4 servings*

TO MAKE THE TOPPINGS: Lightly oil a ridged grill pan or large skillet and heat over high heat. Add the scallions and cook for 1 minute on each side, or until charred. Put the scallions, radishes, and cheese in separate bowls.

Blend the sour cream and chipotles in a small bowl. Set aside.

TO MAKE THE TACOS: Preheat the oven to 350 degrees.

Combine the chili powder, garlic powder, paprika, cumin, and red pepper flakes in a shallow dish. Season the fish fillets on both sides with the salt and pepper, then press them into the spice mixture, turning to coat.

Toast the tortillas briefly in a large skillet over high heat, about 30 seconds per side. Immediately wrap them in foil and let them steam in the oven while you cook the fish.

Heat the oil in the same skillet over medium-high heat until it starts to shimmer. Add the fillets and cook until well browned, 4 to 5 minutes on each side. Drain on paper towels and cut crosswise into 1-inch-wide strips or simply break the fish apart into chunks.

Serve the fish in the warm tortillas, garnished with the scallions, radishes, cheese, and chipotle sour cream, or put all the ingredients in separate bowls and allow diners to assemble their own tacos.

*Restaurant cooks know the two secrets to crisp zucchini*—cook it fast and don't salt it, which would release water and turn the vegetable soft. Here the zucchini cooks just enough in the heat of a dressing that contains stir-fried ginger, garlic, peppers, and scallions.

That's where the dish was going to end, until the lightbulb in the cook's head went on. If the zucchini was good on its own, wouldn't it be even better with poached shrimp, vermicelli, and a refreshing bit of pineapple and fresh basil?

# Thai Shrimp with Summer Squash & Vermicelli

### For the shrimp

1 2-inch piece fresh ginger, thinly sliced

1 lemon, cut in half

3 tablespoons kosher salt

3 garlic cloves

24 medium shell-on shrimp (about 1 pound)

### For the zucchini

2 large zucchini (about 1½ pounds), halved lengthwise and then cut into ½-inch half-moons

3 tablespoons vegetable oil

2 tablespoons minced garlic

2 tablespoons minced peeled fresh ginger

1 small Thai bird pepper or jalapeño, seeded and finely chopped

½ cup thinly sliced scallions

2 medium red bell peppers, cored, seeded, and very thinly sliced

1 cup mirin (sweet rice wine)

½ cup soy sauce

3 tablespoons fish sauce

1 teaspoon toasted sesame oil

TO POACH THE SHRIMP: Combine 6 quarts water, the ginger, lemon halves, salt, and garlic cloves in a large pot. Bring to a boil over high heat and boil for 5 minutes.

Add the shrimp. As soon as the water boils again, remove the pot from the heat, remove the shrimp with a slotted spoon, and refrigerate until cool enough to handle.

Shell and devein the shrimp. (*The shrimp can be cooked up to 2 days ahead and refrigerated, covered.*)

TO MAKE THE ZUCCHINI: Put the zucchini in a large shallow bowl.

Heat the oil in a wok or a large skillet over high heat until it shimmers. Add the minced garlic, ginger, and chile pepper and cook, stirring constantly, for 15 seconds. Add the scallions and stir-fry for 15 seconds. Add the bell peppers and stir-fry for 10 seconds. Add the mirin, soy sauce, fish sauce, and seseame oil, bring to a boil, and immediately pour over the zucchini slices; stir well. Refrigerate while you cook the vermicelli.

8 ounces rice vermicelli

1 cup diced (½-inch) fresh pineapple

15 fresh basil leaves, torn

**4 to 6 servings**

TO COOK THE VERMICELLI: Bring 8 cups unsalted water to a boil.

Spread out the noodles in a large flat dish in a shallow layer and pour the boiling water over them. After 2 minutes, gently separate the noodles with a large fork. Let them sit until softened, 5 to 8 minutes. Drain and cool to room temperature.

Toss the noodles with the zucchini and shrimp on a platter, top with the pineapple and basil, and serve.

*Transfer the shrimp from their garlic-intense marinade* into a skillet, cook for a couple minutes on a side, and that's that. If you like the idea of shrimp on a skewer, put 6 each on individual bamboo skewers short enough to fit in the skillet and cook by the same method, turning once.

You can also use this marinade for thick fish steaks, like swordfish, halibut, or salmon (let sit for 2 hours), or for chicken, pork, or beef (which should marinate overnight).

# Jerk Shrimp

### For the marinade

½ cup coarsely chopped scallions (about 2)

¼ cup coarsely chopped peeled fresh ginger

¼ cup chopped fresh Italian parsley

8 garlic cloves

1 jalapeño, coarsely chopped (with seeds)

¾ teaspoon kosher salt, or more to taste

1½ teaspoons freshly ground black pepper

½ teaspoon ground cinnamon

¼ teaspoon ground cloves

¼ teaspoon ground allspice

2 tablespoons vegetable oil

2 tablespoons soy sauce

¼ teaspoon sugar

24 medium shrimp (about 1 pound), shelled and deveined

Vegetable oil

4 servings

TO MAKE THE MARINADE: Combine all the ingredients and 2 tablespoons water in a blender and process to a paste; add a bit more water if necessary.

Pour the marinade into a bowl, stir in the shrimp, and refrigerate, covered, for 1 hour.

Remove the shrimp from the refrigerator and let stand for 15 minutes.

Heat a large nonstick skillet over medium heat and add just enough oil to coat the bottom of the pan. Remove the shrimp from the bowl, shake off the excess marinade, and put them in the pan in a single layer (cook in batches if necessary). Cook the shrimp, turning once, until browned on both sides, about 2½ minutes per side. Serve.

*A head of Bibb lettuce* becomes the basis of a creamy herb sauce that takes no time at all, and cubed bread is pressed into service for homemade croutons. Together they set the stage for the mussels, whose cooking liquid blends with the vegetal sauce to complete the dish.

# Mussels with Lettuce Sauce

2 cups ½-inch cubes brioche, focaccia, or white country bread

3 tablespoons unsalted butter

½ cup finely chopped shallots (about 2 large)

2 pounds mussels, scrubbed and debearded

1 cup dry white wine

1 cup heavy cream

1 teaspoon kosher salt, or more to taste

¼ teaspoon freshly ground black pepper

1 head Bibb lettuce, cored and coarsely chopped (about 4 cups)

2 tablespoons finely chopped fresh Italian parsley

1 tablespoon finely chopped fresh tarragon

**4 servings**

Preheat the oven to 400 degrees.

Spread the bread cubes on a baking sheet and toast until golden brown, 7 to 10 minutes. Set aside.

Melt the butter in a large skillet or Dutch oven over medium heat. Add the shallots and cook, stirring, for 2 minutes, or until translucent but not browned. Add the mussels and wine, cover, and steam for 5 to 6 minutes, until the mussels have opened. If any do not open, continue to cook for a few minutes longer, then discard the ones that do not open. Remove the pan from the heat, transfer the mussels and their juices to a serving bowl, and cover to keep warm.

Add the cream, salt, and pepper to the pan, bring to a boil over medium-high heat, and boil for 8 to 10 minutes to reduce the liquid by half.

Add the lettuce and herbs to the cream sauce, bring back to a boil, and remove from the heat.

Spoon the lettuce sauce over the mussels, top with the croutons, and serve.

*This beautiful, colorful seafood stew* is a dinner party waiting to happen. A young cook put it together as one of his inaugural family meal efforts at Maialino, and a seasoned colleague looked on approvingly. "You play the way you practice," he said. A serious cook does his or her best regardless of whether the diner is a customer or a coworker.

This is one of those dishes where having all the ingredients lined up in advance, measured and cut, is key.

# Cioppino

1 pound medium shrimp, shelled and deveined, shells reserved

¼ cup olive oil

6 garlic cloves, smashed and peeled

2 tablespoons fennel seeds

Pinch of red pepper flakes

2 small onions, quartered and thinly sliced (about 3 cups)

1 large fennel bulb, trimmed, halved, cored, and thinly sliced (about 2 cups)

1 large red bell pepper, cored, quartered lengthwise, seeded, and thinly sliced crosswise (about 2 cups)

1 small jalapeño, halved, seeded, and finely chopped (about 2 tablespoons)

1 bunch scallions, coarsely chopped (about 1 cup)

2 bay leaves

Kosher salt and freshly ground black pepper

1 tablespoon tomato paste

½ cup dry white wine

1 28-ounce can plum tomatoes, drained and crushed with your hands

18 Manila or littleneck clams, scrubbed

Bring 8 cups water to a boil in a large saucepan and add the shrimp shells. Reduce the heat to low and simmer for 20 minutes, covered. Remove from the heat, strain the stock, and set aside.

Meanwhile, heat the oil in a large Dutch oven over low heat. Add the garlic and cook, stirring occasionally, until golden brown, 10 to 12 minutes.

Add the fennel seeds and red pepper flakes and cook, stirring, for 1 minute. Raise the heat to medium, add the onions, fennel, bell pepper, jalapeño, scallions, bay leaves, and salt and pepper to taste, and cook, stirring occasionally, until the vegetables are softened, about 10 minutes.

Add the tomato paste and white wine, stirring to dissolve the tomato paste, and cook for 3 minutes. Add the stock and tomatoes, bring to a simmer, and cook, stirring occasionally, for 30 minutes, or until the liquid is reduced by one third.

18 mussels, scrubbed and debearded

1½ pounds assorted skinless white-fleshed fish fillets (such as sea bass, red snapper, cod, and/or swordfish), cut into 2-inch pieces

1 bunch fresh Italian parsley, leaves coarsely chopped (about 1½ cups)

*6 to 8 servings*

Increase the heat to medium, add the clams, and cover the pot. When the clams start to open, after about 3 minutes, add the mussels, shrimp, and fish chunks, stirring gently. Cover and cook the seafood until the mussels open, the shrimp are pink, and the fish chunks are opaque, 4 to 6 minutes. If any shellfish have not opened, cover and cook for a few more minutes, then discard any unopened shellfish.

Remove and discard the bay leaves. Taste for salt and serve in bowls, garnished with the parsley.

*Paella for family meal* starts with a smoky marinade, chicken, and rice. Then Sammy Kim, a cook at The Modern, takes it in whatever direction the refrigerator allows: The paella might be piled high with shellfish, as it is here, or end up being just the best chicken and rice dish you've tasted in recent memory. Add or subtract ingredients to make it your own. The only imperative is short-grain rice so that you get the proper texture and the prized crust, which the Spanish call *socarrat*, on the bottom of the pan.

# Paella

### For the marinade

2 fresh oregano sprigs

1 fresh thyme sprig

1 bay leaf

2 teaspoons smoked paprika

2 teaspoons kosher salt

½ teaspoon crushed black peppercorns

2 garlic cloves, smashed and peeled

2 teaspoons red wine vinegar

2 teaspoons finely chopped shallot

Grated zest of 1 lemon

½ cup olive oil

6 bone-in chicken thighs, with skin

TO MAKE THE MARINADE: Mix all the ingredients together in a small bowl.

TO MARINATE THE CHICKEN: Put the chicken thighs in a baking dish and rub all over with the marinade. Cover and refrigerate for 2 to 12 hours.

TO MAKE THE PAELLA: In a large paella pan or a 13- to 14-inch skillet, heat 2 tablespoons of the oil over medium heat. Add the bell pepper strips and cook, stirring, until crisp-tender, 3 to 5 minutes. Season with salt and pepper and remove from the pan, leaving the oil in the pan; set aside.

Remove the chicken pieces from the marinade and pat dry with paper towels. Raise the heat to medium-high and add the remaining 2 tablespoons oil to the pan. When it is hot, add the chicken, skin side down, and brown on both sides, about 5 minutes per side. Remove the chicken from the pan and set aside. Strain the oil in the pan through a fine-mesh strainer into a bowl.

Return 2 tablespoons of the oil to the pan (discard the rest), add the chorizo, and cook over medium heat, turning once, until it has browned and released some of its fat (this will help flavor the rice), about 4 minutes. Using a slotted spoon, transfer the chorizo to paper towels to drain.

## For the paella

¼ cup extra-virgin olive oil

1 red bell pepper, cored, seeded, and cut into thin strips

Kosher salt and freshly ground black pepper

2 links fresh Mexican chorizo sausage, casings removed, cut into ½-inch-thick slices

1 medium onion, chopped

4 garlic cloves, finely chopped

2 cups short-grain Spanish rice or Arborio rice

1 cup canned plum tomatoes, drained and crushed with your hands

4½ cups Chicken Stock (page 39)

½ teaspoon saffron threads

12 Manila or littleneck clams, scrubbed

12 mussels, scrubbed and debearded

12 jumbo shrimp, shelled and deveined

1 cup frozen peas, thawed

2 tablespoons coarsely chopped fresh Italian parsley

6–8 lemon wedges

**6 to 8 servings**

Add the onion and garlic to the pan and cook over medium-low heat, stirring and scraping up any browned bits with a wooden spoon, until softened, 2 to 3 minutes. Add the rice and stir to coat. Add the tomatoes and cook, stirring, for 2 minutes. Season with 1 tablespoon salt.

Meanwhile, bring the stock to a simmer in a medium saucepan. Add the saffron, turn off the heat, and let steep for 2 to 3 minutes.

Pour the stock into the paella pan and bring to a boil. Shake the pan gently or stir once to spread the rice evenly in the pan—after this, do not disturb the rice again. Bring the stock to a simmer and cook over low heat, uncovered, for 10 minutes.

Return the chicken pieces, skin side up, and the chorizo slices to the pan, tucking them into the rice. Cook for 8 minutes. Tuck the clams and mussels into the rice and cook for 8 minutes. Add the shrimp and cook for another 8 to 10 minutes, until the clams and mussels have opened, the shrimp are cooked through, and all of the liquid has been absorbed. The rice should look fluffy and moist and have pulled away from the sides of the pan. Remove and discard any unopened clams and mussels. If you are using a paella pan, turn the heat up to high for 1 minute, or until you smell the toasted rice at the bottom. Remove from the heat.

Place the reserved red bell peppers and the peas on top of the paella, cover with a damp kitchen towel, and let stand for 5 minutes to finish the cooking and heat the peppers and peas.

Garnish with the chopped parsley and lemon wedges and serve.

# Chicken & Turkey

*Rice sticks are a magic trick in a bag:* Crumble them into hot oil and they poof instantly into crispy, twisty little morsels of browned, puffed rice—ready in seconds to serve as a crunchy topping for bite-sized pieces of quick-cooked chicken, broccoli, and almonds.

# Chicken & Broccoli with Crispy Noodles

1 tablespoon dry sherry

1 tablespoon cornstarch

1 tablespoon grated peeled fresh ginger

2 pounds boneless, skinless chicken breasts, cut into 1-inch chunks

1 cup vegetable oil

4 ounces thin rice sticks or rice noodles

1½ pounds broccoli (1–2 heads), cut into small florets, stalks reserved for another use

½ cup skinless almonds or raw cashews

¾ cup kecap manis or ¾ cup soy sauce mixed with ¼ cup packed dark brown sugar

¾ cup Chicken Stock (page 39), plus more if needed

**4 to 6 servings**

In a large bowl, whisk together the sherry and cornstarch. Add the ginger, then add the chicken pieces and stir to coat. Set aside.

Heat the oil in a wok or a 12-inch skillet over high heat until it reaches 350 degrees on a deep-fat thermometer. The rice sticks cook almost instantly, so have a slotted spoon and paper towels ready before you start. Take a handful of rice sticks, break into 2- to 3-inch pieces, and drop into the hot oil. They should puff immediately and become opaque—remove them as soon as they do to prevent burning and drain on the paper towels. Repeat, bringing the oil back to 350 degrees before you add more rice sticks, until all of them are cooked.

Pour off all but 2 tablespoons of the oil and return the pan to the heat. When the oil is shimmering, add the chicken, broccoli, and almonds and cook, stirring frequently, until the chicken is lightly browned all over, about 3 minutes.

Add the kecap manis and chicken stock and bring to a boil, stirring. Reduce the heat to medium-low, cover, and simmer until the chicken is cooked through and the broccoli is tender, 3 to 4 minutes; add a little more stock if the mixture becomes too dry.

Divide the chicken and broccoli among the plates, top with the crispy noodles, and serve.

*Blue Smoke chef Kenny Callaghan* puts summer on a plate for his wife and young sons with a pounded chicken breast nestled inside what could be the perfect breading crust—crunchier than usual thanks to panko bread crumbs, tastier than usual because of grated cheese. On top of it is a salad of sweet corn, tomatoes, and peppery arugula.

# Chicken Cutlets with Corn & Tomato Salad

### For the salad

¾ cup plus 2 tablespoons olive oil

4 ears corn, husked and kernels cut from the cob

Kosher salt and freshly ground black pepper

¼ cup red wine vinegar

### For the chicken

4 6- to 7-ounce boneless, skinless chicken breast halves

3 cups panko bread crumbs

1¼ cups grated Pecorino Romano

2 cups all-purpose flour

4 large eggs

Kosher salt and freshly ground white pepper

⅓ cup vegetable oil, plus more if needed

### For finishing the salad

1 small red onion, halved and thinly sliced

1 pound (about 2 pints) cherry tomatoes, halved, or quartered if large

8 cups loosely packed baby arugula

4 servings

TO MAKE THE SALAD: Heat the 2 tablespoons olive oil in a large skillet over high heat. Add the corn and cook, stirring frequently, for 2 minutes, or until the corn is just tender. Season with salt and black pepper and set aside.

Whisk together the vinegar and the remaining ¾ cup olive oil in a large bowl. Add salt and pepper to taste and whisk again. Set aside.

TO MAKE THE CHICKEN: Butterfly each chicken breast by slicing it in half horizontally, stopping about ½ inch from the opposite side. Fold the butterflied breast open like a book. Place each breast between two pieces of plastic wrap and pound until ¼ inch thick.

Combine the panko and Pecorino in a shallow bowl. Put the flour in another shallow bowl. Whisk the eggs together in a third bowl. Generously season both sides of each chicken cutlet with salt and white pepper and dredge in the flour to coat evenly, shaking off the excess. Dip the floured cutlets in the eggs, allowing the excess to drip off, then place in the panko mixture and turn to coat thoroughly. Put each piece of chicken on a plate while you finish coating the other cutlets (do not stack them).

Heat the oil in a large skillet over medium heat until it shimmers. Add 2 chicken cutlets and cook until golden brown on one side, 1 to 2 minutes. Flip and cook on the other side until golden, 1 to 2 minutes longer. Transfer to a plate, cover loosely with foil, and repeat with the remaining chicken cutlets, changing the oil if it looks dark and burned.

TO FINISH THE DISH: Combine the corn, onion, tomatoes, and arugula with the reserved dressing, tossing to coat. Adjust the seasonings to taste. Place a cutlet on each plate. Arrange some of the salad on each cutlet, drizzle with the dressing remaining in the bowl, and serve.

*Erase every oversauced, too-cheesy memory* you have of chicken Parmigiano. This lighter version emphasizes flavor, and when cook Lena Ciardullo prepares it for family meal at Maialino, she always sets aside an extra batch for the late-night staff, who take their meal at around eleven. No matter how many pans she puts out in the afternoon, they disappear instantly.

Don't be surprised when the first layer of tomato sauce just covers the bottom of the baking pan. Don't be surprised that the baked cutlets come out of the oven looking a little paler than fried ones would. Don't worry that they're wading, not drowning, in cheese. And don't be surprised when people reach for second helpings, murmuring to themselves that they've never tasted chicken Parm quite like this.

This recipe is a tutorial in how to do the small things better: The garlic is started in cold olive oil, not hot, the better to bring out its flavor; and the basil steeps in the warm cooked sauce rather than being cooked along with it. And the dish is assembled using warm sauce, not room temperature—that way, it takes less time to heat up in the oven, which means the chicken won't dry out.

# Less-Is-More Chicken Parmigiano

### For the tomato sauce

3 garlic cloves, smashed and peeled

3 tablespoons olive oil

Pinch of red pepper flakes

½ cup dry red wine

1 28-ounce can plum tomatoes, crushed with your hands, with their liquid

3 large fresh basil sprigs, tied together with kitchen twine

1 4-inch Grana Padano rind (optional)

Kosher salt and freshly ground black pepper

### For the chicken

3 8-ounce boneless, skinless chicken breast halves

Kosher salt and freshly ground black pepper

TO MAKE THE TOMATO SAUCE: Put the garlic in the olive oil in a medium saucepan, turn the heat to low, and toast the garlic slowly, stirring occasionally, until it is golden brown, 5 to 10 minutes.

Add the red pepper flakes, wait a few seconds, and then add the wine. Raise the heat to high and boil to reduce the liquid by half, about 5 minutes. Add the tomatoes and their liquid, then reduce the heat to medium-low, add the bundle of basil leaves and the cheese rind, if using, and simmer, uncovered, for 35 minutes.

Add salt and pepper to taste and remove from the heat. Remove and discard the garlic, basil, and cheese rind, if you used it. (*The sauce can be cooled, covered, and refrigerated for up to 1 week.*)

TO MAKE THE CHICKEN: Preheat the oven to 475 degrees, with a rack in the lower third.

Slice each chicken breast in half horizontally to make 2 thin cutlets. Season them with salt and pepper.

1 cup all-purpose flour

4 large eggs

3 cups panko bread crumbs

Olive oil spray

2 cups grated mozzarella (about 8 ounces)

½ cup grated Grana Padano

4 to 6 servings

Put the flour in a shallow bowl. Beat the eggs in another shallow bowl. Put the bread crumbs in a third bowl. Dip the pieces of chicken in the flour and shake off the excess, then dip them in the eggs, allowing the excess to drip off, and place in the crumbs, turning to coat. Set them in one layer on a rack on a baking sheet. Spray each piece thoroughly on both sides with olive oil spray.

Bake for 15 to 20 minutes, until the chicken is lightly browned. Remove from the oven and reduce the oven temperature to 425 degrees.

Meanwhile, rewarm the sauce.

Spread half the sauce over the bottom of a 10-x-14-inch baking pan. Arrange the chicken cutlets in the pan in a single layer and top with the remaining sauce. Sprinkle with the mozzarella and Grana Padano.

Bake for 10 minutes, or until the cheese has melted and the sauce is bubbling. Serve hot.

*Food carts all over New York City* feature chicken or lamb seasoned with a Middle Eastern spice mix, seared on a griddle, and then stuffed into warm pitas or served over rice. Because the carts often stay open for business well past midnight, it was probably inevitable that a cook, inspired by his late-night snack, would create a similar version for family meal.

The key is to use a heavy cast-iron skillet over high heat—and to give the pieces of chicken some breathing room, because if they're crowded, they'll steam instead of browning.

Just like its street-corner predecessor, this chicken is short on looks but long on flavor. Some of the pieces of chicken will char, some will brown. Then mix them with lime juice, salt, and sugar and let them sit briefly, and the spices will combine with the juices to form a delicious seasoning. Serve like the original, in warm pitas or over rice.

# Pushcart Chicken

### For the spice paste

2 tablespoons ground cumin

2 tablespoons ground coriander

1½ teaspoons garlic powder

1½ teaspoons onion powder

½ teaspoon paprika

½ teaspoon ground cinnamon

¼ teaspoon freshly grated nutmeg

½ teaspoon ground allspice

¼ teaspoon smoked paprika

¼ teaspoon cayenne pepper

1 tablespoon tomato paste

2 tablespoons olive oil

2½ pounds boneless, skinless chicken thighs, cut lengthwise into thirds

⅓ cup fresh lime juice

1 tablespoon kosher salt

1 teaspoon sugar

2 tablespoons olive oil

4 to 6 servings

TO MAKE THE SPICE PASTE: In a large bowl, combine all the spices, the tomato paste, and olive oil, mixing well with a rubber spatula.

Add the chicken pieces to the spice paste and stir well to coat. Refrigerate, covered with plastic wrap, for at least 1 hour, or up to 4 hours.

About 30 minutes before you are ready to cook, remove the chicken from the refrigerator.

Mix the lime juice with the salt and sugar in a large bowl, stirring to dissolve the salt and sugar.

TO COOK THE CHICKEN: In a 12-inch cast-iron skillet, heat the oil over medium-high heat. Working in batches, cook the chicken, loosening and turning the pieces as they brown, 3 to 4 minutes per side. Transfer the cooked chicken to the lime juice mixure and toss to coat. Once all the chicken is cooked, let sit for 5 minutes, stirring occasionally, so that the lime juice mingles with the spice coating to make a sauce.

Remove the chicken from the lime juice mixture and serve.

*On Saturday mornings,* when prep cook Iris Batista prepares the Dominican dishes of her childhood for appreciative Gramercy Tavern staffers, one of her coworkers will inevitably tell her that she should have her own restaurant. She surveys the huge deserted Gramercy Tavern kitchen and shakes her head. "This *is* my kitchen," she says. "This is my restaurant."

Her signature dish is this chicken, which works whether you have an hour or a day to let it marinate. Then roast it in the oven, still coated in the vegetable and herb puree, which turns into a tangy, thick paste. This is great straight out of the oven or cold the next day, when the celery mysteriously asserts itself a little bit more.

# Dominican Chicken

### For the marinade

3 celery stalks, coarsely chopped

6 garlic cloves

⅓ cup packed fresh cilantro leaves

Juice of 2 small lemons (¼ cup)

2 teaspoons fresh thyme leaves

½ cup coarsely chopped green bell pepper

½ cup coarsely chopped red bell pepper

1 teaspoon kosher salt

½ teaspoon capers, rinsed and drained

2 tablespoons olive oil

1 4-pound chicken, cut into 10 pieces (legs, thighs, wings, and breasts split and halved again; back reserved for stock if desired)

4 to 6 servings

TO MAKE THE MARINADE: Combine all the ingredients in a blender or food processor and puree. Transfer to a large bowl.

Add the chicken to the marinade, and turn to coat. Refrigerate, covered with plastic wrap for at least 1 hour, or as long as overnight.

About 1 hour before cooking, remove the chicken from the refrigerator.

Preheat the oven to 375 degrees. Place a rack on a large baking sheet.

Arrange the chicken pieces skin side up on the rack, leaving them well coated with the marinade. Roast for 40 to 45 minutes, until the skin is golden brown and the internal temperature of a thigh reaches 165 degrees on an instant-read thermometer. Serve immediately or cool and refrigerate to serve cold.

# The Reunion

"Whew. Flashback."

Blue Smoke pastry chef Jennifer Giblin, laden with bags of baking ingredients, surveyed the Tabla kitchen, where she had worked twelve years earlier. Tonight was the Tabla alumni dinner—held on December 7, which happened to be the restaurant's twelfth anniversary, the final big event before the restaurant would close in three weeks.

Jennifer took up her old station alongside other alums: a chef from a new restaurant near Union Square, who arrived bearing boxes of gourmet pizzas for the staff; another graduate who now had a place of his own an hour out of the city; one from a seafood restaurant; and one who had flown in from Los Angeles to make a single course. The manager at Maialino, who used to work at Tabla, arrived after work to work some more. A one time cook showed up without a plan or an assignment, simply because staying away was not an option.

Everyone had a cell phone or a camera at the ready to record the event, and chef Floyd Cardoz couldn't say hello to an employee before being waylaid by someone else who wanted to have a picture taken with him.

Everything mattered a little more than usual.

Even the staffer who taped the white tablecloth onto the service counter, pulling it as taut as a trampoline, appreciated the magnitude of the event. Once he finished, another staffer set out dozens of champagne flutes and began to pour two inches of champagne into each one. The dinner guests, who were part of the Tabla extended family, would arrive at 6:00 for hors d'oeuvres and a tasting menu, and the next morning a group of longtime purveyors would attend a farewell breakfast.

When the glasses had been filled, Floyd introduced each of the visiting chefs in order of their Tabla seniority. He acknowledged his chef de cuisine, Ty Kotz, "who's been with me the longest, who you all know and love," and his general manager, Kevin Richer.

He raised his glass. "Before we disappear," he said, "I want to offer everyone a glass of champagne from Kevin and myself and to thank everybody for this, for such an important part of my life." He clinked his glass against each one of the others.

"Pretty cool day," muttered Ty, trying to focus on the assembled group instead of the reason they were together. "Once in a lifetime."

*A tomatillo looks like a small green tomato* dressed up in a gauzy cape and tastes like equal parts tomato and citrus, sweet and puckery. Charring it, as North End Grill chef Floyd Cardoz does for his version of this traditional Mexican dish, brings out a more subtle set of flavors. The pumpkin seeds, spices, garlic, and onion are toasted as well, forming the basis of a thick sauce that's tart and comforting all at once.

# Chicken Pipián

3 allspice berries or ⅛ teaspoon ground allspice

3 bay leaves

2 tablespoons vegetable oil

¾ cup hulled raw green pumpkin seeds (pepitas)

3 garlic cloves

1 medium onion, coarsely chopped

12 ounces tomatillos (about 5), husks removed, rinsed

2 serrano chiles or 1 jalapeño, seeds removed, coarsely chopped

1½ cups coarsely chopped romaine lettuce

1½ cups loosely packed chopped fresh cilantro, plus more for garnish

Kosher salt

¼ teaspoon freshly ground black pepper

3 pounds boneless, skinless chicken, preferably dark meat, cut into 1-x-2-inch pieces

1½ cups Chicken Stock (page 39) or water

6–8 warm tortillas

Lime wedges for serving

*6 to 8 servings*

Toast the allspice berries (if using ground allspice, reserve it for later) and bay leaves in a small dry skillet over medium heat, stirring occasionally, until fragrant, about 3 minutes. Remove from the heat and grind to a fine powder in a spice grinder or coffee mill; set aside.

Warm the oil in a medium cast-iron skillet over medium-low heat. Add the pumpkin seeds, stir, and toast, continuing to stir, until the seeds are fragrant and the oil begins to darken slightly, 3 to 5 minutes. Remove the pumpkin seeds from the pan and set aside.

Pour off the oil and wipe the pan dry. Add the garlic and onion and toast over medium-high heat, stirring once or twice, until the garlic is charred on one side, 4 to 5 minutes. Transfer to a plate and set aside.

Add the tomatillos to the pan and cook over medium heat, turning occasionally, until charred on all sides, about 3 minutes per side.

Transfer the tomatillos to a blender or food processor, add the pumpkin seeds, garlic and onion, chiles, lettuce, cilantro, 1 tablespoon salt, and the pepper and blend to a smooth puree.

In a large Dutch oven, combine the puree and the ground spices (if using preground allspice, add it now) and cook over medium heat, stirring, until the puree starts to boil. Add the chicken and stock and bring to a boil again. Reduce the heat to medium-low and simmer until the chicken is tender and the sauce has thickened, 50 to 60 minutes. Remove from the heat and let cool slightly. Remove the chicken, shred, and return it to the sauce to reheat. Season to taste with salt. (*The dish can be made up to 1 day ahead, covered, and refrigerated.*)

To serve, wrap the chicken and sauce in warm tortillas, garnished with cilantro, with lime wedges on the side, or serve everything in separate bowls and allow diners to assemble their own.

*This lively version of roast chicken* is sparked by a marinade that includes fresh ginger and hot and sweet peppers. It came to life when Robert Lilly, one of Tabla's cooks, grabbed a blender, surveyed his options, loaded in ten compatible ingredients, and hit Puree.

Cutting each split chicken breast in half ensures that all the pieces will cook in the same amount of time. Leave the pureed marinade on the chicken when you put it in the oven—it will turn into a flavorful insulation that keeps the chicken moist and tender.

# Tabla Chicken with Ginger & Peppers

### For the marinade

1 cup soy sauce

1 small red bell pepper, cored, seeded, and coarsely chopped

1 small red onion, coarsely chopped

1 small jalapeño, halved, seeded, and coarsely chopped

3 garlic cloves

1 1-inch piece fresh ginger, peeled

¼ cup vegetable oil

2 tablespoons toasted sesame oil

1 tablespoon light brown sugar

1 tablespoon freshly ground black pepper

1 4-pound chicken, cut into 10 pieces (legs, thighs, wings, and breasts split and halved again; back reserved for stock if desired)

**4 to 6 servings**

TO MAKE THE MARINADE: Combine all the ingredients in a blender or food processor and process until smooth. Transfer to a large shallow bowl or baking dish.

Add the chicken to the marinade and turn to coat. Refrigerate, covered with plastic wrap, for at least 1 hour, or as long as overnight.

About 30 minutes before you plan to cook it, remove the chicken from the refrigerator.

Preheat the oven to 375 degrees.

Do not wipe off the marinade. Arrange the chicken pieces on a rack on a baking sheet. Roast for 40 to 45 minutes, or until the internal temperature of a thigh reaches 165 degrees on an instant-read thermometer. Remove from the oven and let sit for 5 minutes before serving.

*Yes, these boneless, skinless chicken breasts* require two quarts of buttermilk for their twice-dipped preparation. According to chef Daniel Humm, the chicken juices dilute the liquid during the first long soak, so a second buttermilk bath is needed. And the second dredge in the seasoned flour ensures a more consistent coating.

# Eleven Madison Park Fried Chicken

8 boneless, skinless chicken breast halves (about 4 pounds), cut crosswise in half

1 medium white onion, thinly sliced

5 garlic cloves, thinly sliced

8 cups buttermilk

4 cups all-purpose flour

Kosher salt

1½ teaspoons freshly ground black pepper

½ teaspoon cayenne pepper

½ teaspoon paprika

½ teaspoon chopped fresh thyme

½ teaspoon chopped fresh rosemary

Vegetable oil for deep-frying

**6 to 8 servings**

Combine the chicken, onion, and garlic in a large bowl. Cover with 4 cups of the buttermilk. Cover and refrigerate for at least 4 hours, or as long as overnight.

Combine the flour, 1½ teaspoons salt, the black pepper, cayenne, paprika, and herbs in a large bowl, mixing well. Pour the remaining 4 cups buttermilk into another bowl. Remove the chicken pieces from the marinade (some of the onion and garlic will remain stuck to the chicken) and dredge in the seasoned flour, shaking off the excess. Then dip the chicken pieces, one at a time, into the bowl of fresh buttermilk and return to the seasoned flour for a second dredging. Place the dredged chicken pieces on a plate in a single layer.

Heat 2 inches of vegetable oil in a deep 12-inch cast-iron skillet or Dutch oven over medium-high heat until it reaches 365 degrees on a deep-fat thermometer. Using tongs, carefully add the chicken pieces to the oil, in batches, and fry for 4 minutes, or until cooked through. Remove from the oil and drain on paper towels; bring the oil back to 365 degrees before each batch.

Season the chicken with salt and serve immediately.

*What distinguishes this fried chicken* is the crunch from two ingredients that don't usually appear together in a recipe—Japanese panko bread crumbs, which are coarser and crunchier than standard ones, and graham cracker crumbs, which lend a slightly sweet, nutty flavor to the crust. Add a little bit of heat and garlic for balance, and you have one of Union Square Cafe's most beloved family meal dishes, as interpreted by line cook Ian "Moose" Muse from his mother's original recipe.

# Union Square Cafe Fried Chicken

1 3- to 3½-pound chicken, cut into 10 pieces (legs, thighs, wings, and breasts split and halved again; back reserved for stock if desired)

2 cups buttermilk

1 cup all-purpose flour

1 cup panko bread crumbs

1 cup graham cracker crumbs

2 tablespoons paprika

2 tablespoons kosher salt

1 tablespoon garlic powder

¾ teaspoon cayenne pepper

Vegetable oil for deep-frying

**4 to 6 servings**

Put the chicken pieces in a large bowl, add the buttermilk, and let soak for 30 minutes at room temperature, turning occasionally.

Combine the flour, crumbs, paprika, salt, garlic powder, and cayenne in a medium bowl, mixing well. Drain the chicken pieces and dredge in the seasoned flour, shaking off the excess.

In a large deep cast-iron skillet, heat about 2 inches of oil over medium-high heat until it reaches 325 degrees on a deep-fat thermometer. Using tongs, carefully add the chicken pieces in batches, without crowding. Cook wings for 6 minutes and the rest of the chicken pieces for 8 minutes. Turn with the tongs and cook on the second side for another 6 minutes for wings, 8 minutes for the rest, or until the interior temperature of a thigh reaches 165 degrees on an instant-read thermometer. Remove the chicken from the oil and drain on paper towels; bring the oil back to 325 degrees before you fry each batch.

Serve immediately.

*Employees at Union Square Tokyo* have developed their own family meal repertoire. Their version of fried chicken has the requisite crunch thanks to potato starch, which is found in the baking or kosher food section of most supermarkets. Boneless chunks of marinated chicken are lightly coated in egg white and potato starch, then twice-fried briefly until crisp. The first frying cooks the chicken through, and the second frying, at a higher temperature, turns it to golden brown perfection.

# Union Square Tokyo Twice-Fried Chicken

### For the marinade

8 garlic cloves, grated (about 3 tablespoons)

4 teaspoons grated peeled fresh ginger

½ cup soy sauce

¼ cup sake

2 tablespoons sugar

2 teaspoons salt

1 teaspoon freshly ground black pepper

3 pounds boneless, skinless chicken, preferably dark meat, cut into 1½-inch pieces

3 large egg whites, lightly beaten

¾ cup potato starch

Vegetable oil for deep-frying

6 to 8 servings

TO MAKE THE MARINADE: Combine all the ingredients in a bowl large enough to hold the chicken. Add the chicken to the marinade and stir to coat. Cover and refrigerate for at least 30 minutes, or up to 2 hours.

About 30 minutes before you want to cook it, remove the chicken from the refrigerator.

Drain the chicken and discard the marinade; return the chicken to the bowl. Add the egg whites and stir and turn to coat all the pieces. Add the potato starch and mix well.

Heat 2 inches of oil over medium heat in a wok or heavy pot until it reaches 325 degrees on a deep-fat thermometer. Fry the chicken in batches, without crowding the pan, until cooked through, about 4 minutes. Remove the chicken with a slotted spoon and drain on paper towels. Heat the oil to 375 degrees. Using the slotted spoon, return the chicken to the oil in batches and fry until crisp, 1 to 2 minutes. Drain on clean paper towels and serve immediately.

# Mom's Legacy

"Moose" Muse floats: He works other cooks' shifts on their days off. But for family meal, he doesn't budge; his coworkers won't let him. His mother's fried chicken and her macaroni and cheese are on the short list of Union Square Cafe family meal favorites, which is why he makes them frequently, usually together.

Moose's real name is Ian, but no one has called him that in years. There used to be another Ian at the restaurant, and so Muse became Moose, and it stuck. The dishes are emphatically his: To everyone at the Cafe, they are known as "Moose'sfriedchicken" and "Moose'smac'n'cheese." No one else would dare attempt them.

For two hours, Moose zoomed from the basement prep kitchen to the upstairs kitchen to the deep-fry station, back to the stovetop, where the pasta was cooking, and to the walk-in refrigerator for the cheese for his casserole. Word spread, and the rest of the afternoon was like an extended game of musical chairs. Everyone wanted to be in the right position to secure a spot in the front of the family meal line at four o'clock.

The more opportunistic eaters forgot etiquette altogether. One cook walked past a pan of mac 'n' cheese just out of the oven, scooped out a corner chunk, headed back to his station, and inhaled an appetizer-sized portion to give him the stamina to wait for the real thing. Another cook passing by liberated a wing from a heaping pan of fried chicken. Moose pretended to be dismayed, but he is a better cook than an actor.

"That ought to be enough," he said with pride, as the chicken headed out to the dining room. "And it'll all be gone in a minute." He was in no hurry to join everyone. The last part of the process for him was to take a moment to relish the way this food made him feel.

"It gives people a memory," he said. "You eat something, and it takes you back to a good day you remember, or your family. When I was growing up, my mom made this food all the time for us, but when she got older, she stopped—so I started, and now it reminds me of her."

*A whole turkey can frustrate even a dedicated cook,* sparking annual holiday debates about how to get the white meat and the dark meat done at the same time. This brined turkey breast solves all sorts of problems. It's easier to cook because it's all white meat, and the brine adds flavor and seals in moisture. Let the turkey soak in the brine for at least a day, let it air-dry, and the tasty, tender results will retire the question of what process works best. Chris Bradley developed the brine at Gramercy Tavern, where he worked before moving over to run the kitchen at Untitled at the Whitney.

# Maple-Brined Turkey Breast

### For the brine

8 cups Chicken Stock (page 39) or water

2 cups kosher salt

1½ cups pure maple syrup

2 tablespoons black peppercorns

1 tablespoon juniper berries

1½ teaspoons whole cloves

4 bay leaves

8 fresh thyme sprigs

6 quarts ice water


1 6- to 8-pound bone-in turkey breast

3 cups coarsely chopped peeled carrots (about 3 large)

3 cups coarsely chopped onions (about 2 medium)

3 cups coarsely chopped celery (about 6 stalks)

8 tablespoons (1 stick) unsalted butter, cut into thin slices

½ cup pure maple syrup

**8 to 10 servings**

TO MAKE THE BRINE: Bring the stock, salt, maple syrup, spices, and herbs to a simmer in a large pot, stirring to dissolve the salt. Remove from the heat and cool completely.

Add the ice water to the brine. Place the turkey breast in a container large enough to hold it and the brine (a cooler works nicely), cover with the chilled brine, and refrigerate for at least 8 hours, or as long as overnight.

Remove the turkey from the brine, rinse, and pat dry. Put it on a platter or in a large baking dish and return it to the refrigerator, uncovered, to air-dry for at least 2 hours, or up to 24 hours.

TO COOK THE TURKEY: Preheat the oven to 400 degrees.

Place all the vegetables in a roasting pan. Loosen the turkey skin by gently prying it away from the breast meat with your fingers, without detaching it completely, then insert the pats of butter under the skin over the surface of the breast, being careful not to tear the skin. Place the turkey skin side up on top of the vegetables and roast for 40 to 50 minutes, or until the internal temperature reaches 165 degrees on an instant-read thermometer. Brush the turkey with the maple syrup during the last 15 minutes of cooking.

Let the turkey breast rest for 10 minutes before you slice it, and serve with the vegetables as an accompaniment if you like.

*At Maialino, a cook and a pastry cook* faced with a lot of leftover turkey conspired to come up with a new and improved potpie, one that benefited from adjustments to the basic proportions—a lighter sauce, more vegetables, and a New England biscuit topping instead of a double pastry crust. Roll or pat out the biscuit dough, cut into rounds, and place on top of the filling.

The result is more like a stew with a crust, so it's best to serve this in shallow bowls, with soupspoons as well as forks to scoop up the flavorful liquid.

# Turkey & Vegetable Potpie with Biscuit Crust

### For the filling

8 tablespoons (1 stick) unsalted butter

½ cup all-purpose flour

4 cups Chicken Stock (page 39) or water

1 cup half-and-half or cream (depending on how rich you want the sauce to be)

1 cup diced (½-inch) peeled carrots

1 cup diced (½-inch) celery

1 cup diced (½-inch) red or yellow onion

1 bay leaf

2 fresh thyme sprigs

1 fresh sage sprig

3 cups diced (½-inch) vegetables of your choice: mushrooms, bell pepper, green beans, potatoes, fresh corn, and fresh or frozen peas

Kosher salt and freshly ground black pepper

6 cups diced (1-inch) cooked turkey, white or dark meat (see page 162 or your own recipe)

Nancy Olson's Biscuit dough (page 260)

2 tablespoons unsalted butter, melted

**10 to 12 servings**

TO MAKE THE FILLING: Melt the butter in a large saucepan over low heat. Slowly stir in the flour with a wooden spoon and cook over medium-low heat, stirring often, until the roux is light golden, about 10 minutes.

Gradually whisk in the stock, increase the heat to medium-high, and bring the liquid to a simmer, continuing to whisk. Stir in the half-and-half, increase the heat to high, and bring the sauce to a boil, then reduce the heat to low. Add the carrots, celery, onion, bay leaf, thyme, and sage. If using bell pepper, green beans, and/or potatoes, add them now. Stir well and simmer over medium-low heat until the vegetables are tender, 10 to 12 minutes. Remove and discard the herb sprigs and bay leaf and season with salt and pepper. (*The sauce can be refrigerated, covered, for up to 2 days; rewarm it gently when you're ready to make the potpie.*)

Preheat the oven to 350 degrees.

Add the turkey and the remaining vegetables to the sauce and simmer for 5 to 10 minutes, or until the vegetables are just tender. Pour the mixture into a 9-x-13-inch baking dish.

On a floured surface, roll or pat the biscuit dough out ½ inch thick. Using a 2- to 3-inch biscuit cutter or drinking glass, cut rounds out of the dough and cover the top of the potpie. Brush the tops of the biscuits with the melted butter.

Bake for 30 to 40 minutes, or until the biscuit crust is golden brown and the sauce is bubbling. Serve hot.

*Magic Dust, a spice blend* created by Blue Smoke partner and Illinois barbecue legend Mike Mills, is the go-to solution for a family meal cook who wants to turn a traditional recipe into a take-notice dish. This Union Square Cafe turkey meat loaf is a smoky, spicy version, spiked with Mike's signature blend and barbecue sauce.

# Turkey Meat Loaf with Magic Dust

2 pounds ground turkey

1¼ cups panko bread crumbs

½ cup finely chopped onion

¼ cup finely chopped peeled carrot

2 tablespoons thinly sliced fresh basil

1 tablespoon chopped fresh oregano

1 tablespoon chopped fresh thyme

1 tablespoon chopped fresh Italian parsley

2 teaspoons Magic Dust (recipe follows)

1 tablespoon kosher salt

½ teaspoon freshly ground black pepper

2 large eggs, beaten

¼ cup your favorite barbecue sauce or Maialino Marinara (page 114), pureed

**4 to 6 servings**

Preheat the oven to 350 degrees. Line a baking sheet with parchment paper.

In a large bowl, combine the ground turkey, bread crumbs, onion, carrot, herbs, Magic Dust, salt, and pepper. Add the eggs and mix thoroughly.

Shape the mixture into a 4-x-10-inch log on the baking sheet. Bake for 30 minutes.

Remove the pan from the oven and brush the meat loaf with the barbecue sauce to cover. Return to the oven and bake for another 20 minutes, or until the internal temperature reaches 160 degrees on an instant-read thermometer.

Loosely tent the meat loaf with aluminum foil and let rest for 10 minutes, then slice and serve.

# Magic Dust

1 teaspoon celery seeds, crushed with the side of a chef's knife

½ cup paprika

¼ cup kosher salt

¼ cup sugar

2 tablespoons dry mustard (such as Colman's)

¼ cup chili powder

¼ cup ground cumin

2 tablespoons freshly ground black pepper

¼ cup granulated garlic

2 tablespoons granulated onion

1 tablespoon cayenne pepper

**About 2½ cups**

Everything that goes into Magic Dust is sitting right on the supermarket shelf, so what's the magic part? Two generations of barbecue royalty—southern Illinois' Mike Mills and his daughter Amy—say that in this case, smaller is better. Taking your spices for a spin in a grinder makes all the difference. "One thing that's special about our Magic Dust," says Mike, "is that all of the ingredients are finely ground and there are no larger particles in the rub that would give a burst of a particular flavor. All of the flavors are there in every bite."

Combine all the ingredients in a spice grinder or food processor and process until finely ground. Store in a tightly closed container for up to 1 month.

# Beef, Pork & Lamb

*A patty melt is essentially a merger* between a cheeseburger and a grilled cheese sandwich. At Union Square Events, the company's catering division, even such a supposedly simple sandwich undergoes a period of research and development, during which the staff evaluates various interpretations of the dish, before it ever heads out to events in Central Park or to Mets games. Versions showed up at family meal until the cooks found the rendition they liked best—this one. It's good topped with ketchup, mustard, or coleslaw.

# Patty Melt

1½ pounds ground beef chuck

1 medium onion, halved, ½ grated, ½ thinly sliced

¼ teaspoon garlic powder

1 teaspoon kosher salt

1 teaspoon freshly ground black pepper

2 tablespoons vegetable oil

4 tablespoons (½ stick) unsalted butter, melted

8 slices rustic bread

8 slices American, Monterey Jack, or mild cheddar cheese

**4 sandwiches**

Combine the beef, grated onion, garlic powder, salt, and pepper in a medium bowl and mix well. Form into 4 patties about ½ inch thick.

Heat 1 tablespoon of the oil in a large heavy skillet over medium-high heat. Add 2 of the patties and cook for about 3 minutes on each side for medium-rare, or longer if you want them more well done. Drain on paper towels. Wipe out the pan, heat the remaining 1 tablespoon oil, and cook the second batch of patties. Discard the fat in the skillet and wipe it out again.

Brush the butter on one side of each slice of bread. Turn 2 slices of bread butter side down. Top each with a slice of cheese, some of the sliced onion, and a hamburger patty. Add another slice of cheese to each and top with a second slice of bread, butter side up.

Add the sandwiches to the pan and cook for 2 minutes over medium-high heat until the bottom slices of bread are golden brown, about 2 minutes. Turn the sandwiches and cook for 2 minutes on the second side, or until golden. Keep the sandwiches warm in a low oven while you assemble and cook the remaining 2 sandwiches. Serve hot.

# A Taste of Home

Jean-Paul Bourgeois's first family meal did not go well at all. Three months after Maialino opened in the fall of 2009, Jean-Paul started on the plancha station, cooking anything that benefited from contact with scorching heat on the big flat-top griddle. He was twenty-four years old, a hefty, grinning, eager guy from Thibodaux, Louisiana (population 10,000), who thought his dad was the best cook he knew and dreamed of someday acquainting New Yorkers with his childhood cuisine at his own place. He'd arrived in New York City with a freshly minted BA in culinary arts and a passion for Cajun food.

In the meantime, he planned to use family meal to show what he could do. Maialino is a Roman trattoria, but Jean-Paul looked at the kitchen's raw materials and saw a chance to rearrange them into dishes from back home. Since oxtail stew was on the menu, there were always lots of small bony pieces left over. Jean-Paul had grown up eating them, and he knew they were too tasty to discard, so he braised them, added some mushrooms and potatoes, and served them up with the braising liquid over rice. Then he stood back and waited to be anointed an instant family meal hero.

It backfired. The small chunks of oxtail weren't cutlery food, they were pick-it-up-with-your-fingers food. Staffers eat under time constraints and depend on fairly effortless meals. Why hadn't Jean-Paul pulled the meat off the bone for them?

Determined to obliterate the memory of the unfortunate stew, Jean-Paul came back with plenty of less messy dishes: pulled pork or brisket with red-eye gravy and sides of mashed potatoes and collard greens and whatever else he had time to make—all of it cutlery-friendly. Jambalaya made the menu, and a brined turkey became a biscuit-topped potpie.

Before long, Jean-Paul had become "the family meal man," in constant competition with himself for the next memorable meal. Staffers had to be warned to "coffee up" after particularly sumptuous spreads, lest the fragrant homemade corn bread, pulled pork sandwiches, and slaw made them want to curl up for a nice afternoon nap.

When Jean-Paul got promoted to sous chef just over a year later, he was also promoted out of family meal, which is the cooks' responsibility at Maialino. Sometimes, though, he can't help stepping back in.

*On a summer day, with the outdoor grill going,* this is a perfect watch-the-sunset meal: thin slices of steak served with grilled onions, tomatoes, and baby spinach in a mustard dressing spiked with Tabasco. If it's raining, use a grill pan to make the dish indoors, and it will summon up memories of better weather.

# Steak & Spinach Salad with Mustard Vinaigrette

### For the vinaigrette

1 cup vegetable oil

4 teaspoons white wine vinegar

1 tablespoon whole-grain mustard

A dash of Tabasco sauce, or more to taste

Kosher salt and freshly ground black pepper to taste

2 pounds flat-iron, flank, or skirt steak, excess fat trimmed

Kosher salt and freshly ground black pepper

2 medium red onions, sliced into ½-inch-thick rings

Vegetable oil

10 ounces baby spinach (about 4 cups)

2 cups Sun Gold or other cherry tomatoes, halved

**4 to 6 servings**

TO MAKE THE VINAIGRETTE: Combine all the ingredients in a container with a tight-fitting lid or a small bowl and shake well or whisk to emulsify. Set aside.

Prepare a hot fire in a grill or preheat a ridged grill pan over high heat.

Season the steak on both sides with salt and pepper. Grill the steak or cook in the grill pan for about 4 minutes per side for medium-rare. Transfer to a cutting board and let rest for 10 minutes.

Meanwhile, brush the onions with vegetable oil and season on both sides with salt and pepper. Grill until charred and slightly softened, turning once, about 4 minutes. Transfer to a cutting board and, when cool enough to handle, cut into 2-inch pieces.

Thinly slice the steak against the grain.

Toss the spinach with the tomatoes, grilled onions, and vinaigrette in a large bowl. Adjust the salt and pepper to taste and serve the salad with the steak.

*For family meal cooks, marinades are essential*—they're the best way to make the same cut of meat or piece of chicken taste completely different than it did the week before. Flank steak and its relatives, hanger and skirt steak, are flavorful cuts that can stand up to a distinctive marinade like this one, which is full of citrus and hot, salty Asian flavors. The steak is served on top of chopped romaine, which wilts slightly under the heat.

# Thai Beef

### For the marinade

¼ cup olive oil

¼ cup fish sauce

¼ cup soy sauce

¼ cup light sesame oil (not toasted)

2 tablespoons Sriracha hot sauce

Greens from 1 bunch scallions, coarsely chopped

1 2-inch piece fresh ginger, peeled and thinly sliced

1 stalk lemongrass, root and dry top cut off, outer leaves removed, thinly sliced

Grated zest of 2 oranges

Grated zest of 2 lemons

1 teaspoon ground ginger

1 teaspoon ground coriander

1½ pounds flank, hanger, or skirt steak, excess fat trimmed

1 head romaine lettuce, cored and coarsely chopped

**4 to 6 servings**

TO MAKE THE MARINADE: Combine all the ingredients in a large bowl. Spoon out 3 tablespoons and reserve for the romaine.

Add the steak to the marinade, turning to coat, and marinate, covered and refrigerated, for at least 2 hours, or up to 24 hours.

About 30 minutes before you want to start cooking, remove the steak from the refrigerator.

Preheat a large ridged grill pan or a 12-inch skillet over high heat. Remove the steak from the marinade and wipe off the excess marinade. Cook for 4 to 5 minutes on each side for medium-rare flank or skirt steak, depending on the thickness, or 8 to 10 minutes for medium-rare hanger steak. Transfer the meat to a cutting board and let it rest for 5 minutes.

Toss the romaine with the reserved 3 tablespoons marinade and put it on a platter. Thinly slice the steak against the grain and serve over the romaine.

*Once in a while, a favorite family meal dish* makes the jump to the menu. If it's beloved by a bunch of restaurant professionals, why not share it with the customers? Victor Estrella, a porter at Union Square Cafe, has been serving up this traditional Dominican beef stew at family meal since he came to the Cafe in the early 1990s, and over time it's become part of restaurant lore, an informal entry on the list of standard employee benefits. Now it's part of the weekend brunch menu so that patrons can enjoy it as well.

Serve over rice.

# Dominican Beef

3 pounds hanger or skirt steak, excess fat trimmed

3 tablespoons olive oil

1 small red onion, sliced

1 small red bell pepper, cored, seeded, and cut into ½-inch-wide slices

4 garlic cloves, thinly sliced

1 tablespoon tomato paste

2 teaspoons kosher salt

½ teaspoon freshly ground black pepper

4 cups Chicken Stock (page 39)

½ cup coarsely chopped fresh cilantro

2 scallions, cut into ¼- to ½-inch pieces

3 tablespoons red wine vinegar

**6 to 8 servings**

Slice the hanger steak into thin strips about 3 inches long and ⅛ inch thick, or slice the skirt steak against the grain into strips about 3 inches long and 1 inch wide.

Heat the oil in a 12-inch skillet or Dutch oven over medium heat. Add the onion, bell pepper, and garlic and cook for 3 to 5 minutes, or until softened. Add the tomato paste, beef, salt, and pepper and cook for 2 to 3 minutes, stirring frequently.

Add the chicken stock and bring to a boil, then lower the heat and simmer gently, uncovered, until the beef is very tender but not falling apart, about 2 hours; if the dish gets too dry, add up to ½ cup water at a time, but no more—you don't want it to be soupy. (*The beef can be cooked to this point up to 1 day ahead, cooled, covered, and refrigerated; you may need to add water when reheating.*)

Add the cilantro and scallions and cook for 10 minutes. Add the vinegar and cook for 5 minutes longer, then serve.

*Arepas are corn fritters native to Colombia and Venezuela* that can be served on their own or split and filled with cheese, meat, or even seafood salad. They showed up at an impromptu family meal at the Bar Room in the Museum of Modern Art one day because there was a window of time and the right ingredients at hand and because executive sous chef Michael Cooperman encouraged one of the cooks to make up a batch as a treat for the kitchen staff.

The three components of this version—arepas, steak, and black bean salsa—can stand on their own, so you can mix and match as time and ambition allow, or substitute mozzarella for the steak for a quicker vegetarian version.

If you want a chunkier salsa, mash the beans with a potato masher or fork instead of using a blender and then stir in the spices, lime juice, and olive oil.

# Stuffed Arepas with Black Bean Salsa

### For the salsa

1 15-ounce can black beans, drained and rinsed

1 garlic clove, smashed and peeled

6 fresh cilantro sprigs

½ teaspoon ground cumin

½ teaspoon ground coriander

2 tablespoons fresh lime juice

2 tablespoons olive oil

1 plum tomato, cored, seeded, and finely chopped

½ cup finely chopped red onion

1 small jalapeño, seeded and finely chopped

Kosher salt and freshly ground black pepper

1–2 tablespoons Sriracha hot sauce (optional)

TO MAKE THE SALSA: In a blender or food processor, combine the black beans, garlic, cilantro, cumin, coriander, lime juice, and olive oil and process until smooth. Transfer to a small bowl and stir in the tomato, onion, and jalapeño. Season with salt and pepper, then add the hot sauce to taste, if using. (*The salsa can be made up to 1 day ahead, covered, and refrigerated.*)

TO MAKE THE AREPA DOUGH: Bring the milk and butter to a boil in a small saucepan, stirring to melt the butter. Remove from the heat and cool to room temperature.

Combine the cornmeal, ⅔ cup flour, sugar, and salt in a medium bowl. Add the milk mixture and mix with an electric mixer or stir with a wooden spoon until well incorporated. Add the grated cheese and mix well. If the dough feels sticky, add a little more flour. Cover with plastic wrap and refrigerate for at least 1 hour, or up to 1 day.

### For the arepas

¾ cup whole milk

6 tablespoons (¾ stick) unsalted butter

1⅓ cups cornmeal

⅔ cup all-purpose flour, plus up to 2 tablespoons more if needed

¼ cup sugar

½ teaspoon kosher salt

1 cup grated mozzarella (about 4 ounces)


Vegetable oil for deep-frying

### For the filling

12 ounces mozzarella, thinly sliced or grated, or Grilled Flank Steak with Garlic (recipe follows), at room temperature

**6 servings as a main course or 8 to 10 servings as an appetizer; 12 arepas**

**TO SHAPE AND FRY THE AREPAS:** On a lightly floured work surface, roll the dough out about ½ inch thick. With a cookie cutter or a drinking glass, cut out 3-inch circles.

In a 12-inch skillet, heat about 1½ inches oil over medium-high heat until it reaches 350 degrees on a deep-fat thermometer. Fry the arepas, in batches, until golden brown, 2 to 3 minutes per side, turning carefully with tongs or a slotted spoon. Remove from the oil and drain well on paper towels.

**TO STUFF THE AREPAS:** *If filling the arepas with cheese*, preheat the oven to 300 degrees. Split the arepas open, tuck some of the mozzarella inside, and wrap each one in foil. Arrange on a baking sheet and warm in the oven for about 5 minutes to allow the cheese to melt.

*If filling the arepas with steak*, split them open and fill with slices of the steak.

Top the stuffed arepas with the salsa and serve.


# Grilled Flank Steak with Garlic

### For the marinade

1 cup olive oil

3 garlic cloves, thinly sliced

4 fresh rosemary sprigs

1 teaspoon Aleppo pepper (see headnote, page 32) or red pepper flakes

2 bay leaves


2 pounds flank steak

Kosher salt

**6 servings**

**TO MAKE THE MARINADE:** Combine all the ingredients in a large baking dish and mix well.

Add the steak to the marinade, turning to coat, and marinate in the refrigerator for at least 2 hours, or up to 24 hours.

About 45 minutes before cooking, remove the steak from the marinade and bring to room temperature. Season the steak with salt.

Preheat a ridged grill pan or a large skillet over high heat. Add the meat and cook for 4 to 5 minutes on each side, depending on the thickness, for medium-rare. Transfer to a cutting board and let rest for 10 minutes.

Slice the steak on an angle against the grain, as thin as possible.

*Thinly sliced Korean barbecue* is piled into lettuce wraps and served with fresh and pickled vegetables. Making the marinade and slicing the beef take just 15 minutes the night before, and the beef can marinate for 1 to 24 hours, whatever works best with your schedule. You might want to invest a little more time and make a double batch, because the marinated beef freezes beautifully, which means that you can have an almost instant home-cooked meal when you want to serve the dish again.

Either way, it's a fast and flavorful alternative to more familiar preparations, one that cooks in less time than it takes to set the table.

# Seared Short Rib Wraps

### *For the marinade*

2 tablespoons Korean chili powder or red pepper flakes

½ cup packed dark brown sugar, or more to taste

½ cup plus 2 tablespoons soy sauce, or more to taste

5 garlic cloves

1 tablespoon chopped peeled fresh ginger

½ onion, coarsely chopped

1 bunch scallions, sliced

2½ pounds boneless beef short ribs

### *For the wraps*

12–18 Bibb lettuce leaves

About ½ cup Chinese black bean paste (optional)

Cooked white rice

Thinly sliced peeled carrots

Thinly sliced peeled daikon radish

Store-bought kimchi or sliced sour pickles

**4 to 6 servings**

TO MAKE THE MARINADE: Combine all the ingredients except the scallions in a blender and process until smooth. Transfer to a large bowl and stir in the scallions. Adjust the sugar and/or soy sauce to taste if necessary.

Slice the short ribs across the grain into thin strips, about ⅓ inch thick. Stir the beef into the marinade and mix well. (*The beef can be refrigerated, tightly covered, for at least 2 hours, or up to 24 hours, or frozen for up to 1 month.*)

Bring the meat to room temperature before cooking. In a large nonstick skillet, sear the meat, in batches, over high heat, 1 to 2 minutes on each side until browned and medium-rare.

TO ASSEMBLE THE WRAPS: Spread each lettuce leaf with a small amount of bean paste, if using. Fill with some rice, vegetables, kimchi, and beef, fold into a package, arrange on a platter, and serve.

*This braise incorporates* soy sauce and rice wine, daikon radish, and shiitake mushrooms in a traditional Korean short rib dish known as *galbijjim*. It's a nice change from familiar tomato-based preparations.

There won't be a great deal of liquid left when you turn up the heat on the ribs to evaporate the excess and glaze the ribs, which takes only a few minutes. Watch the pot closely to make sure they don't get too dry.

# Korean Short Ribs

2 pounds 2-inch-thick bone-in beef short ribs

6 tablespoons soy sauce

1 tablespoon rice wine

¾ cup finely chopped onion

8 garlic cloves, finely chopped

1 tablespoon dark brown sugar

1 medium carrot, peeled, halved lengthwise, and cut into 1-inch pieces

1 5-inch-long piece daikon radish, peeled, halved lengthwise, and cut into 1-inch pieces

10 shiitake mushrooms, stems discarded

1 tablespoon light corn syrup

1 tablespoon toasted sesame oil

½ teaspoon freshly ground black pepper

**4 servings**

Fill a heavy medium pot with water, bring to a boil, and add the short ribs. Simmer for 5 minutes, skimming off any foam that rises to the surface. Remove the ribs and rinse them well with cold water. Set aside.

Skim the fat off the water you boiled the ribs in, then transfer 2 cups of the water to a small bowl; discard the rest. Clean out the pot and put the short ribs back into it. Add the soy sauce, rice wine, onion, garlic, and brown sugar to the reserved 2 cups cooking water, stir well, and add to the meat. Cover the pot and bring to a boil, then simmer over medium-low heat for 45 minutes.

Add the carrot, daikon, and shiitake mushrooms to the pot, reduce the heat to low, cover, and simmer for about 1 hour, stirring occasionally with a wooden spoon and basting the meat with the liquid in the bottom of the pot. To see if the ribs are done, check the meat with a chopstick or a paring knife: If it pierces the meat smoothly, the ribs are cooked.

Add the corn syrup, sesame oil, and pepper, stir well, and bring to a boil over high heat. Boil to reduce the liquid for about 5 minutes, until syrupy, turning the ribs to glaze them.

Transfer the meat to a platter and serve.

*Once a month, several of the restaurants* cook extra servings of family meal for the families and staff at a nearby hospital's hospice center. The cooks at Tabla viewed those days as a particular challenge, because the food had to be flavorful enough to satisfy both their coworkers and the hospice families and staff, who craved something other than institutional cuisine but were also looking for comfort food. This curry is substantial enough to be satisfying, tasty enough to be intriguing, and special enough to convey the feelings that went into making it.

It's the kind of curry a home cook can master easily without an advanced degree in Indian cuisine.

# Easy Beef Curry

2 pounds boneless beef chuck, cut into 1-inch cubes

3 tablespoons olive oil

1 medium onion, thinly sliced

2 garlic cloves, finely chopped

1 tablespoon ground cumin

1 tablespoon turmeric

1 tablespoon ground coriander

1 teaspoon ground allspice

¼ teaspoon ground cloves

¼ teaspoon ground cinnamon

1 28-ounce can plum tomatoes, crushed with your hands, with their juices

½ cup Beef Stock (page 39) or water

Kosher salt

6 fresh cilantro sprigs, finely chopped

Cooked basmati rice for serving

**4 to 6 servings**

Pat the beef dry with paper towels. Heat 2 tablespoons of the oil in a large skillet or Dutch oven over medium-high heat. Add half the beef and brown for 5 to 7 minutes, turning the pieces so that they brown on all sides. Using tongs or a slotted spoon, transfer the meat to a plate. Heat the remaining 1 tablespoon oil, brown the second batch of beef, and transfer to the plate.

Reduce the heat to medium, add the onion and garlic, and cook, stirring frequently, until softened, about 5 minutes. Add the spices and cook for 1 minute, stirring.

Return the beef to the pot, add the tomatoes with their juices, and bring to a simmer. Reduce the heat to medium-low and simmer, covered, for 1 hour, or until the beef is tender.

Add the stock, cover, and simmer for another 2 hours, until the beef is falling apart.

Season the curry to taste with salt. Garnish with the cilantro and serve over the rice.

*A braise is the best friend an inexpensive cut of meat can have.* After searing the meat to caramelize its exterior, slow-cook it in liquid until it's tender enough to cut with a fork. That liquid always includes an element of acidity, and in the South, cola is a popular choice. Jean-Paul Bourgeois, one of the Maialino sous chefs, grew up on cola braises in a little town south of New Orleans. He takes mischievous pleasure in introducing his northern coworkers to a recipe that makes for a lot of raised eyebrows—until people taste the results.

Once the short ribs are in the oven, you can abandon them. Come back 2 hours later, reduce the cooking liquid to a tasty sauce, and you have a hearty main dish, with leftovers for sandwiches. A favorite Maialino combination involves the shredded meat, horseradish mayonnaise, and spicy arugula piled on slices of rustic bread.

# Cola-Braised Short Ribs

5 pounds bone-in beef short ribs, 7–8 inches long

Kosher salt and freshly ground black pepper

2 tablespoons olive oil

4 small onions, halved and cut into 1-inch chunks (about 4 cups)

3 carrots, peeled and cut into 1½-inch pieces (about 2 cups)

2 celery stalks, cut into 1½-inch pieces (about 2 cups)

6 garlic cloves, smashed and peeled

1 bay leaf

10 fresh thyme sprigs

2 tablespoons tomato paste

4 cups cola (not diet)

8 cups Beef Stock (page 39)

**4 to 6 servings, with leftovers**

Season the ribs with salt and pepper. Heat the oil in a 14-x-16-inch roasting pan set over two burners on medium-high heat. Add the ribs, in batches, and brown on all sides, about 20 minutes, then remove them from the pan.

Drain off all but 3 tablespoons of the fat from the pan. Reduce the heat to medium-low and add the vegetables, garlic, bay leaf, and thyme. Cook, stirring occasionally, until the vegetables soften, about 15 minutes.

Preheat the oven to 350 degrees.

Stir in the tomato paste and cook for 5 minutes, occasionally scraping the bottom of the pan, until the color darkens. Add the cola, turn the heat up to high, and boil for 15 minutes, or until the liquid is reduced by half, stirring a few times to make sure it doesn't stick or burn.

Add the stock, bring to a boil, and add the ribs. Reduce the heat to medium-low so that the liquid is barely simmering, cover the pan tightly with foil, transfer to the oven, and braise for 2 to 2½ hours, or until the meat is fork-tender.

Skim the fat from the broth. (*The ribs and vegetables can be cooked up to 1 day ahead, covered, and refrigerated; remove the hardened fat before proceeding.*)

Use a slotted spoon to transfer the ribs to a platter, along with the vegetables, and cover to keep the meat from drying out while you reduce the sauce. Remove and discard the bay leaf and thyme sprigs. Boil the liquid over high heat until it is reduced by half, 15 to 20 minutes.

Reduce the heat to medium-low, return the meat and vegetables to the pan, and cook for 5 minutes, or 30 minutes if the ribs have been refrigerated, spooning the sauce over the ribs to glaze them. Serve.

# The Full-Tilt Kitchen

In terms of sheer volume, Blue Smoke exists in its own universe in the Union Square Hospitality Group. In an average summertime week, it serves over a ton of brisket, 1,750 pounds of pork butt, 2,950 pounds of beef ribs, 3,220 pounds of baby back ribs, 5,600 pounds of Kansas City spareribs, and almost 6,600 pounds of chicken. People stand eight deep at the long bar that stretches from the front door to the dining room, and hosts learn how to run the human gauntlet to a back table without misplacing their parties of four along the way.

Let's say everyone at your table of four orders two courses each and some dishes for the table to share. Here's what happens next: Inside the kitchen, a computer printer in a squat gray box spits out two copies of what you told the waiter. The expediter hands one copy to the cooks and keeps the other. Their shared goal is to deliver each round of dishes to you and your companions simultaneously and at the right pace, timing the courses appropriately depending on how fast you eat, with shared dishes sandwiched in between the others. It's not easy to be seamless. Some Blue Smoke cooks have a recurring nightmare in which the printer spews orders nonstop, faster and faster, and there is no way to keep up.

Printout in hand, the expediter calls out each order to the kitchen, sometimes talking so fast that he sounds like an auctioneer. Usually the cook who's responsible for making a particular dish sings it out in response, loudly, to show that the order came through above the general din, but every restaurant has its own style. The cooks might all call out, "*Oui*, chef!"

in unison every time the expediter announces an order, or one at a time, but everything gets a confirmation. The expediter notes the time the order was placed, clips each new printout to the tail end of a row of orders—dozens at once during peak hours—and then, depending on the pace, cajoles, encourages, or sounds a note of urgency.

In the course of a minute or two, "Let's have that salad" becomes "I need that salad right now" and then "You're killing me here with that salad." A Blue Smoke expediter has been known to step behind the line to help out on a busy night rather than let any station fall even a minute behind.

In a perfect world, a party's plates all appear together in the pass-through window that separates the cooks from the expediter, who grabs one plate at a time and double-checks to make sure it matches the order. He hands them to a food runner standing at his side, arm outstretched, with a folded side towel in place for insulation. The runners ferry the food out to the tables and come right back for the next order.

A dining room traffic jam or a customer with a question can leave the expediter with nobody there to take the next plate. At that point, all he can do is yell for help. Since Blue Smoke gets almost half its business from walk-ins, the kitchen is often operating at full tilt and there's no time even to enunciate properly. "P'gup," is what "pick up" sounds like, barked rather than spoken. "P'gup, p'gup, p'gup', p'*gup!*" A predictable rhythm is rarely established: The only certainty is speed.

*Maialino sous chef Jean-Paul Bourgeois* often likes to serve the food he grew up on for family meal, like this rubbed brisket braised in a traditional Southern gravy flavored with coffee and a smoked ham hock.

If you set aside some of the gravy, you can give your morning eggs a jolt: Fill individual ceramic ramekins with ½ cup gravy, make a well in the middle, and break an egg into it. Bake in a preheated 350-degree oven for 5 minutes, and serve with sliced rustic bread.

You may need to special-order second-cut brisket, which has the deckle, the succulent top layer, still attached, since it is usually trimmed away before it reaches the meat case. The deckle bastes the meat as it cooks, keeping it extra moist.

This is even better made a day ahead.

# Brisket with Red-Eye Gravy

### For the rub

2 tablespoons onion powder

2 tablespoons garlic powder

2 tablespoons paprika

1 tablespoon coffee grounds

1 tablespoon dark brown sugar

2 tablespoons kosher salt

1 teaspoon freshly ground black pepper

1 6- to 7-pound brisket with deckle (see headnote)

¼ cup vegetable oil

1 medium onion, finely chopped

½ cup finely chopped celery

½ cup finely chopped red bell pepper

2 tablespoons finely chopped garlic

1 tablespoon tomato paste

½ cup strong coffee

1 28-ounce can plum tomatoes, crushed with your hands, with their liquid

2 cups Beef or Vegetable Stock (page 39 or 38), plus more if needed

TO MAKE THE RUB: Combine the onion powder, garlic powder, paprika, coffee grounds, brown sugar, salt, and pepper in a small bowl, mixing well.

Rub the spice mixture into the brisket on all sides.

Heat the oil in a Dutch oven over medium-high heat until it shimmers. Brown the meat on all sides, 5 to 10 minutes per side (it will blacken, but the braising liquid will balance out the flavors). Remove the meat to a platter and cover with foil while you make the braising liquid.

Pour all but 2 tablespoons of the fat out of the pot and reduce the heat to medium-low. Add the onion, celery, bell pepper, and garlic and cook, stirring occasionally, for 15 minutes, or until soft. Add the tomato paste and cook until it turns deep red, about 5 minutes.

Deglaze the pot with the coffee, stirring to loosen the browned bits. Add the tomatoes with their liquid, the stock, and ham hock, bring to a simmer, and cook over low heat, uncovered, for 5 minutes, stirring occasionally. Add the salt, pepper, sugar, and vinegar.

Return the brisket and any accumulated juices to the pot. The braising liquid should come halfway up the side of the brisket; add more stock or water if the level is too low. Cover, bring just to a simmer, and cook over low heat for 4 to 4½ hours, until the brisket is very tender; a paring knife inserted into the meat should meet no resistance. (Alternatively, you can braise the brisket in a preheated 350-degree oven.)

1 smoked ham hock

2 tablespoons kosher salt,
or more to taste

¼ teaspoon freshly ground black
pepper, or more to taste

½ teaspoon sugar, or more to taste

2 tablespoons red wine vinegar,
or more to taste

**8 to 10 servings**

Let the brisket cool in the braising liquid for at least 1 hour, then skim the fat from the surface of the liquid. (*The brisket can be cooked a day in advance, cooled, covered, and refrigerated. To rewarm, preheat the oven to 350 degrees. Put the pot on top of the stove, remove the congealed fat from the surface, and bring the liquid to a low simmer, then cover the pot and warm the brisket in the oven for 30 to 40 minutes.*)

Taste the gravy and adjust the seasonings if necessary. Remove the ham hock and reserve for another use or pull apart the meat into the gravy. Remove the brisket to a cutting board and slice it against the grain. Serve with the red-eye gravy.

*Union Square Cafe cook Glen Vasquez* sees a tray of pork chops as a blank canvas and the restaurant pantry as his art supply store. Teriyaki sauce is only the first step in a marinade that's spicy, gingery, a little hot, a little sweet. An hour's turn, and the chops are ready for the grill.

# Teriyaki Pork Chops

### For the marinade

1½ cups teriyaki sauce

⅓ cup sherry vinegar

1 jalapeño, coarsely chopped (with seeds)

1 1-inch piece fresh ginger, peeled and coarsely chopped

1 scallion, coarsely chopped

2 pieces star anise

1 garlic clove, smashed and peeled

3 tablespoons honey

2 tablespoons Sriracha hot sauce

6 8-ounce center-cut rib pork chops

**6 servings**

TO MAKE THE MARINADE: Combine all the ingredients in a bowl or baking dish large enough to hold the pork chops in a single layer.

Add the chops to the marinade, turning to coat well, and marinate for 1 hour at room temperature.

Prepare a medium-hot fire in a grill or preheat a ridged grill pan over medium heat.

Remove the pork from the marinade and pat dry with paper towels. Grill the pork, turning once, until just cooked through, 12 to 15 minutes; the internal temperature should reach 150 degrees on an instant-read thermometer.

Let the pork rest for 5 minutes before serving.

# Picnic Time

As members of the kitchen crew stepped up to bat at the softball game at the annual Gramercy Tavern Memorial Day weekend picnic in Brooklyn's Prospect Park, they tried to look confident.

They were not. With grim smiles, they sized up the front-of-the-house team even as they pretended not to care, slapping each other on the back, clapping their hands, tying and retying their shoelaces. It was the forced cheerfulness of players who had lost too many times before. Who was that huge guy in the professional-looking pinstriped baseball pants, towering over the waiters and the bartenders and the back waiters and the beverage staff? Nobody quite recognized him, and while he might be a new hire, the kitchen team muttered about ringers and looked for preemptive excuses.

"Sure," said one cook, eyeing his rivals. "They have time to go to the gym."

Aside from the man in the pinstripes, players on both sides looked like every other weekend athlete in the park: T-shirts a little too big, baggy shorts, awkward socks, an indoor pallor. A female cook with the capable air of someone who'd played her share of slow-pitch, wearing sports attire that fit, was not enough to stave off the feeling of impending doom.

Dozens of fans had showed up to cheer the players on. What distinguished this game from those at adjacent baseball diamonds was the quality of the spectator snacks. Back at the park's Picnic House, which Gramercy Tavern had taken over for the day, two long buffet tables sagged under the weight of containers of green salads, potato salad and coleslaw, grilled vegetables, sausages, sandwiches, and an array of desserts and homemade ice creams that drew people's kids like a magnet. A father and son team manned a huge grill full of burgers and hot dogs. People balanced laden plates as they grabbed cold drinks, beer, or wine. Three front-of-the-house staffers had traipsed across the field with a bottle and a corkscrew and three glasses, and when they sat down behind the third-base line, the conversation was not about the shortstop's chops but about the vintner.

It didn't take long to see that sports history was going to repeat itself, as the waiters started to rack up runs and the kitchen staff resorted to loud comments about having more important things on their minds than learning to field a fly ball. Other staffers, who were already too full or too hot to walk over to the field, set up an enclave within aroma's reach of the grill, spread out their blankets under the shade trees, and waited for the game to end, signaling that it was time for another round of food.

*All year, Union Square Events,* the company's catering division, creates beautiful parties for other people. Then, as the winter holiday season starts to wind down, the staff takes an afternoon off to celebrate with its own holiday buffet, a Mexican feast assembled by prep cook Betsy Retamar.

The centerpiece of the meal, a dish spoken of in reverent anticipation for weeks, is what's become known as "holiday pork," a brined and slow-cooked roast with a citrus-and-apple-cider tang. You can slice it or shred it or cut it into chunks and crisp it in a skillet for instant carnitas. Ask for Boston butt or pork shoulder at your market; they are the same cut.

# Holiday Roast Pork

### For the brine

1 cup packed dark brown sugar

⅔ cup kosher salt

3 tablespoons freshly ground black pepper

2 cups coarsely chopped onions

2 heads garlic, cut horizontally in half

12 fresh thyme sprigs

6 fresh oregano sprigs

4 fresh rosemary sprigs

5 bay leaves

1⅓ cups coarsely chopped apples (not peeled)

1⅓ cups apple cider

2 oranges, halved

2 limes, halved

2 lemons, halved

1 6- to 8-pound bone-in pork shoulder (see headnote)

**12 to 15 servings**

TO MAKE THE BRINE: Combine the brown sugar, salt, pepper, onions, garlic, thyme, oregano, rosemary, bay leaves, apples, and apple cider in a container or pot large enough to hold the pork and brining liquid. Squeeze in some juice from the citrus halves and then add them to the container.

Add the pork and enough water to cover. Refrigerate for at least 2 hours, or as long as overnight.

About 1 hour before you want to start roasting the pork, remove it from the refrigerator.

Preheat the oven to 350 degrees.

Remove the pork from the brine and pat dry. Transfer to a Dutch oven and roast, covered, for 4 hours.

Uncover and continue cooking until the pork is browned and meltingly tender, 20 to 30 minutes more. The pork is done when it can be shredded easily with a fork.

Carve and serve.

*At Eleven Madison Park, German Victorio* invented a roast pork dinner out of the trimmings remaining when he had finished transforming various cuts of pork into individual portions. The dish proved so popular that the staffers paid its creator the ultimate compliment and named it after him.

German has an array of cuts at his disposal and might use a combination of pork belly, loin tips, rub ends, and cheeks, which you should try if you have access to them. But variety is not what matters; and all you need is a balance between lean pieces and some with more fat for added flavor, which you can achieve with a combination of pork shoulder and loin.

For roasting, line the baking sheet with parchment paper to keep the juices from scorching and the meat from drying out.

# German's Pork

2 pounds each boneless pork shoulder and loin, cut into 1½-inch chunks

1 large head garlic, cloves separated, smashed, and peeled

8–10 fresh thyme sprigs

½ cup fresh lemon juice

2 tablespoons kosher salt

1½ teaspoons coarsely ground black pepper

1 teaspoon red pepper flakes

2 lemons, cut into wedges

**6 to 8 servings**

In a large bowl, toss the pork with the garlic and thyme sprigs. Pour the lemon juice over the meat, sprinkle with the salt, black pepper, and red pepper flakes, and stir to coat evenly. Cover the bowl and marinate in the refrigerator for at least 2 hours, or up to 24 hours.

Preheat the oven to 225 degrees. Line a 12-x-18-inch baking sheet with parchment paper.

Spread the pork on the baking sheet in a single layer. Roast for 1 hour, stirring once or twice.

Remove the pan from the oven and increase the temperature to 350 degrees. Stir the pork to coat it with the juices, then return it to the oven. Roast for 1 hour more, or until the meat is tender and browned.

Transfer the meat to a serving dish, garnish with the lemon wedges, and serve.

*Floyd Cardoz, the chef of North End Grill,* inherited this recipe from his mother, who got it from her mother, who got it from Floyd's great-grandmother. This is family food from Goa, which lies along the western coast of India. Now the dish has entered its fifth generation on the Cardoz table, as Floyd continues to make it for his children. He grinds whole spices to get the most intense flavors possible, but we've provided ground-spice equivalents to make things easier.

# Goan-Spiced Braised Pork

### For the spice rub

2 tablespoons kosher salt

1 teaspoon freshly ground black pepper

2 tablespoons ground cumin

½ teaspoon turmeric

¼ teaspoon ground cinnamon

¼ teaspoon ground cloves

1 large onion, halved and thinly sliced

2 garlic cloves, smashed and peeled

1 tablespoon minced peeled fresh ginger

2 tablespoons apple cider vinegar

1 pound boneless pork shoulder

**4 servings**

TO MAKE THE SPICE RUB: Combine all the ingredients in a large bowl, mixing well.

Add the pork to the bowl, rub the spices into the pork, cover, and refrigerate for at least 6 hours, or up to 8 hours.

Preheat the oven to 350 degrees.

Bring the meat to room temperature. Transfer the meat and any juices to a large Dutch oven and bring to a simmer over medium heat. Cover, place the pot in the oven, and roast for 1 hour, or until the internal temperature reaches 160 degrees on an instant-read thermometer. Remove from the oven and let the meat rest for at least 15 minutes.

Skim off the fat from the meat juices. Slice the pork and serve with the juices spooned over it.

*Untitled at the Whitney chef Chris Bradley* grew up in the town of Statesville, North Carolina. He says he has sausage and gravy in his DNA, but he loves Gramercy Tavern pastry chef Nancy Olson's fresh biscuits so much that he credits her with this dish, which was part of the family meal rotation when he worked there. Olson, in turn, says its success is all about the sausage and gravy. Either way, their legacy is this pleasant surprise: What sounds like a heavy dish isn't, thanks in part to the addition of buttermilk or crème fraîche, which imparts a little tanginess to the gravy.

If you don't own a meat grinder attachment, ask the butcher at your market to grind the pork for you.

# Unexpectedly Light Pork Sausage & Gravy with Biscuits

### For the sausage

1¼ pounds boneless pork shoulder, excess fat trimmed, cut into 1-inch cubes

2 tablespoons minced fresh sage

1 tablespoon grated peeled fresh ginger

1 large garlic clove, finely chopped

1 tablespoon kosher salt, or more to taste

½ teaspoon freshly ground black pepper, or more to taste

½ teaspoon ground allspice

½ teaspoon freshly grated nutmeg

¼ teaspoon cayenne pepper

### For the gravy

2 tablespoons unsalted butter

¼ cup all-purpose flour, plus more if necessary

4 cups whole milk, or more if necessary

½ cup buttermilk or crème fraîche

Kosher salt and freshly ground black pepper

Nancy Olson's Biscuits (page 260)

4 to 6 servings

TO MAKE THE SAUSAGE: Put the pork in a bowl, add all the remaining ingredients, and stir to coat the pork. Refrigerate until the pork is cold.

Using a food processor or a stand mixer fitted with a grinder attachment, grind the mixture through the small die. Cook a small patty of the pork mixture in a little oil in a skillet over medium heat; taste and adjust the seasonings if necessary. Set aside.

TO MAKE THE GRAVY: Melt the butter in a large heavy saucepan over medium heat. Add the sausage and brown it thoroughly, stirring occasionally to break it up, 6 to 8 minutes.

Reduce the heat to low, sprinkle the flour over the sausage, and stir to incorporate. Add additional flour if needed, stirring until all the fat has been absorbed. Cook, stirring, for 2 minutes. Slowly add the milk and buttermilk, stirring constantly until smooth. Bring to a simmer and cook for 20 minutes, stirring frequently to prevent scorching, until the flour is cooked. If desired, adjust the consistency with more milk. Season with salt and pepper. (*The sausage and gravy can be made up to a day ahead, cooked, covered, and refrigerated; add a little water when reheating if necessary.*)

Spoon the sausage and gravy over the biscuits and serve.

# Master of His Universe

Chris Bradley, the chef of Untitled since it opened at the Whitney Museum in the spring of 2011, stood between the cafe's small, airy dining room and its equally small, narrow kitchen, surveying his proportionately lean staff, maybe a dozen people working a breakfast or lunch shift at any given time.

"This is as close to normal working hours as I've ever gotten," said Chris, whose friends used to refer to him as the "ghost roomie" because he was so rarely home at night. After four years as a sous chef in Gramercy Tavern's bustling kitchen, he was initially homesick. "The first few weeks were like the first few weeks of summer camp," Chris recalled. "I really missed the people there, but now I'm acclimated."

He rattled off the multiple roles he plays, using Gramercy Tavern counterparts as shorthand: "I'm Mo [Batista, who buys all the produce], I'm Nancy [Olson, the pastry chef], I'm Michael [Anthony, the chef], and I like it. It's such an education. I was overworked for the first six months, and then I learned to delegate, even if I still have my finger in everything." He shows up for work having grabbed something useful at the farmers' market on his way in; he dashes out if a pastry cook is in the middle of a recipe and down a quart of cream. And he corrals his mini staff for the afternoon family meal, even on the days when the staff fills just three booths.

There is no room for an outsized chef's ego in such a compact operation. "We all spend so much time together that attitude just has to go away," he said. "We're so close."

There is no room for an extensive or elaborate menu either; the kitchen can't handle it, and the customers, who are either fueling up for a day of museum-gazing or taking a break between viewings, don't have the time or the inclination. Chris had to come up with his best versions of familiar food, whether breakfast egg dishes or variations on grilled cheese, meals that might sound simple but aren't.

Family meal works the same way: Smaller in scope than what Chris contributed to for years at Gramercy Tavern, it is still a showcase for staff favorites, like the pulled pork and beans in a vinegar-based sauce from his North Carolina childhood.

As the Whitney prepares to move to a new space downtown, Chris is getting ready to run two restaurants there. "I've got a lot of input," he said. "They feel like my restaurants, with the insurance policy of the Union Square Hospitality Group—I'm talking about color, china patterns, design, the number of tables, the number of seats; I'm in on all the meetings." A larger universe, a different blueprint, but a family meal twice a day, no matter what.

*These Moroccan-spiced meatballs* show up at family meal at Gramercy Tavern, where they're served with a simple yogurt sauce that provides a creamy counterpoint and a cooling cucumber salad (page 47). They are seasoned with *ras el hanout*, a spice blend found in Middle Eastern markets. According to Doron Levy, an Israeli cook, *ras el hanout* is the Arabic term for "head of the spice store," and each merchant blends his own customized product. You can do the same, starting with equal parts ground anise, fennel, allspice, cardamom, cloves, black pepper, cinnamon, coriander, cumin, ginger, and nutmeg.

You bake the meatballs on a rack set on a baking sheet, rather than browning them on the stovetop, for another dish that cooks while you do something else.

# Lamb Meatballs with Yogurt Sauce

### For the meatballs

1 tablespoon pine nuts

1 pound ground lamb shoulder

1 tablespoon *ras el hanout* (see headnote), or more to taste

1 tablespoon kosher salt, or more to taste

2 garlic cloves, finely chopped

### For the sauce

2 cups Greek yogurt or labneh

Kosher salt and freshly ground white pepper

½ cup olive oil

¼ cup finely chopped fresh Italian parsley

**4 servings**

TO MAKE THE MEATBALLS: Preheat the oven to 425 degrees. Set a rack on a baking sheet.

Toast the pine nuts in a small skillet over medium heat for 3 to 4 minutes, stirring so that they don't burn. Transfer to a plate to cool, then chop them.

Put the lamb in a large bowl. Flatten it out, sprinkle the pine nuts, *ras el hanout*, salt, and garlic over it, and mix well by hand. To test for seasonings, flatten a tablespoon of the mixture into a patty, sear it in a small nonstick skillet over medium-high heat, and taste it. Add more salt and/or *ras el hanout* if necessary to the rest of the lamb mixture.

Moisten your hands and form the lamb mixture into 8 meatballs, about 2 inches in diameter, moistening your hands again if the mixture starts to stick. Arrange on the rack on the baking sheet and bake for 15 minutes, or until golden brown. Remove the meatballs from the oven and let stand for 5 minutes to finish cooking.

MEANWHILE, MAKE THE SAUCE: Put the yogurt in a bowl and season with salt and white pepper to taste. Stir in the oil. Slowly add up to ½ cup water, until the sauce is the consistency you like. Stir in the parsley.

Put the meatballs on a platter, spoon the sauce over them, and serve.

*This is a perfect rainy weekend recipe,* one that will fill the house with great smells and make it difficult to wait for supper. The chili is made with ground lamb as well as ground beef, and Union Square Cafe cook Glen Vasquez adds red wine vinegar to brighten the flavors, stirring in a little more at the end. There's a threshold, as there is with salt, so stir in the vinegar a bit at a time, and keep tasting until you get the balance you like.

As for heat, you can make the chili as mild or spicy as you like by adding red pepper flakes, Tabasco, or any other vinegar-based hot sauce.

While it's hard to be patient when something smells this good, chili only gets better if made a day ahead.

# Black Bean Chili

1½ cups dried black beans or two 15-ounce cans black beans, drained and rinsed

1 bay leaf (if using dried beans)

Kosher salt

7 tablespoons vegetable oil

2 pounds ground lamb

1 pound ground beef chuck

3 tablespoons ground cumin

2 tablespoons smoked paprika

1 tablespoon garlic powder

1 tablespoon onion powder

1 tablespoon ground coriander

½ teaspoon ground cinnamon

¼ teaspoon ground cloves

2 medium onions, finely chopped (3 cups)

1 red bell pepper, cored, seeded, and finely chopped (1 cup)

1 green bell pepper, cored, seeded, and finely chopped (1 cup)

2 medium jalapeños, halved, seeded, and finely chopped (or with seeds if you like spicy chili)

1 tablespoon tomato paste

If using dried beans, soak them overnight in water to cover, then drain. Or, to quick-soak the beans, rinse them well in cold water, place them in a large pot, and cover with 3 inches of cold water. Bring the water to a simmer, remove from the heat, and let sit for 1 hour; drain.

Place the soaked beans in a large saucepan with the bay leaf and enough unsalted water to cover them by 3 inches. Bring to a boil, then reduce the heat to low and simmer until the beans are tender but not falling apart, 1 to 2 hours. Remove from the heat, add salt to taste, and cool in the cooking liquid.

Meanwhile, heat 3 tablespoons of the oil in a Dutch oven over medium heat. Add the lamb and beef and slowly brown it, breaking it up with a wooden spoon, 10 to 15 minutes. Drain the meat in a colander and wipe any remaining fat from the pot.

Add the remaining ¼ cup oil to the pot, then add the spices and cook over medium heat, stirring, for 2 minutes. Add the onions, bell peppers, and jalapeños and cook, stirring occasionally, until tender, about 10 minutes. Add the tomato paste, stir well, and cook for 4 minutes, until the tomato paste has darkened.

# A Perfect Fit

Union Square Cafe was built before the era of showcase kitchens, cobbled out of an existing vegetarian restaurant that opened in 1936. It requires vertical imagination: There is barely enough room for two people to pass each other in the basement hallway, so one cook has to hoist a hotel pan full of marinating chicken above his head while the other tucks a bucket of spuds under his arm. A cook coming out of the walk-in refrigerator must cautiously open the door just a crack before stepping out, to make sure he won't bump into someone.

Glen Vasquez always stands on the left-hand side of the prep counter in the basement kitchen. No matter who else is on his shift, Glen holds down the same spot, which allows him to angle into the aisle and give his wide shoulders a few extra inches of valuable space at a counter that is exactly three cutting boards long. The other two slots might be occupied by cooks with seniority, like him, or by newcomers just months out of culinary school, like the twenty-year-old chopping and watching Glen out of the corner of his eye, asking questions with a mixture of deference and ambition.

Glen settled in at Union Square Cafe after stints at Tabla and Blue Smoke and one at a restaurant outside the company. He's seen kids like the one standing next to him, fresh out of school, their heads full of dreams. He has no desire to do anything but what he does,

no interest in moving up even one rung to sous chef.

In a few hours, he'd head upstairs to the grill station on the hot line. But first he had to prep potatoes for the gratin that is a standard item on the menu and make as much of family meal as possible in advance. As grill cook, Glen is responsible for the main dish, while other kitchen staffers contribute the salad, vegetables, and a starch.

On a quick tour of the pantry shelves and the walk-in refrigerator, he discovered enough pork chops to feed everyone and pulled out the makings of a marinade: teriyaki sauce and Sriracha hot sauce, sherry vinegar, garlic, scallions, fresh ginger, star anise, and honey. With a jalapeño added for more heat, the dish made sense in his head. He stacked everything high on a sheet pan—a big steel hotel pan of marinating chops, pans of potato gratin, prep containers, some sauces, and his knives—and lugged it all upstairs, zigging this way and that as he encountered hallway traffic.

From the moment he hit the main floor landing, it was nonstop, from family meal straight through dinner service, until after midnight. When he got home, Glen's three-year-old daughter, who has taught herself to wake up when he walks in the door, made her usual request: pancakes. So he made her a little batch, and she ate two bites before falling back to sleep.

1 15-ounce can plum tomatoes, crushed with your hands, with their liquid

2 cups Chicken or Beef Stock (page 39)

¼ cup packed dark brown sugar

¼ cup red wine vinegar, or more to taste

Freshly ground black pepper

**8 to 10 servings**

Return the meat to the pot, add the tomatoes with their liquid, the stock, brown sugar, and vinegar, and bring to a simmer. Simmer for 1 hour, uncovered. Season with salt and pepper to taste.

Add the cooked beans, drained, or canned beans and cook at a low simmer for 30 minutes. Add up to ¼ cup more vinegar to taste if desired. Discard the bay leaf. Serve hot.

# Side Dishes

*Baby artichokes,* which can be as small as a watch face or as big as an egg, are everything their larger relatives aren't: accommodating, low-maintenance, and, most important, chokeless, or very close to it. Here they're cut in half, roasted, tossed in a vinaigrette, and then decked out in a crunchy cheese and parsley coating and roasted a little bit more, until that coating turns golden brown.

# Roasted Baby Artichokes

12 baby artichokes (about 2 pounds)

½ cup olive oil

3 tablespoons fresh lemon juice

3 garlic cloves, finely chopped

¼ teaspoon red pepper flakes

Kosher salt and freshly ground pepper

⅔ cup grated Parmigiano-Reggiano

1 cup panko or dried bread crumbs, preferably homemade

⅓ cup coarsely chopped fresh Italian parsley

4 servings

Preheat the oven to 375 degrees.

Cut away the top ½ inch of each artichoke. With a paring knife, peel away 3 or 4 layers of tough outer leaves until you reach the tender light green leaves. Cut each artichoke in half lengthwise and remove the small choke, if any, at the center.

In a medium bowl, toss the artichokes with the olive oil, lemon juice, garlic, red pepper flakes, and salt and pepper to taste. Let stand for 10 minutes.

Using a slotted spoon, remove the artichokes from the vinaigrette and spread them on a baking sheet; reserve the vinaigrette. Roast the artichokes for 25 to 30 minutes, or until lightly browned and tender when pierced with a paring knife.

Meanwhile, mix together the Parmigiano, bread crumbs, and parsley in a small bowl. Stir in 2 tablespoons of the reserved vinaigrette.

When the artichokes are tender, sprinkle them with the crumb mixture, stir gently to combine, and roast for 10 to 15 minutes longer, until the bread crumbs are golden brown. Serve hot or at room temperature.

*Gramercy Tavern chef Michael Anthony* seems to speak "Produce" the way other people might speak Italian or Mandarin; it's as though he understands the aspirations of a stalk of asparagus that wants to be prepared and presented just so, or the desire a tomato has to be something more than a slice in a sandwich. This dish was inspired by a visit to his parents in rural Ohio, when he and his family picked the evening's asparagus just hours before they ate. The choice of fleur de sel, a hand-harvested sea salt, is a nod to the time he has spent in France over the years.

You can grill or broil the asparagus as well. Michael serves the asparagus and relish at room temperature.

# Roast Asparagus with Tomato Relish

1 bunch medium asparagus, tough ends snapped off

2 tablespoons olive oil

Juice of ½ lemon

Fleur de sel or other coarse sea salt

Tomato Relish (recipe follows)

4 servings

Preheat the oven to 375 degrees.

Toss the asparagus with the olive oil in a wide bowl. Spread the asparagus on a baking sheet and roast until browned and tender, 10 to 12 minutes, depending on the thickness.

Transfer the asparagus to a platter. Drizzle the lemon juice over the asparagus and season with a pinch of fleur de sel. Spoon the relish over the top and serve.

# Tomato Relish

6 large tomatoes (about 5 pounds)

2 tablespoons olive oil

2 celery stalks, finely chopped (about ¾ cup)

1 small onion, finely chopped (about ¾ cup)

1 large carrot, peeled and finely chopped (about ¾ cup)

2 garlic cloves, finely chopped

1 teaspoon ground coriander

4 teaspoons red wine vinegar

4 teaspoons balsamic vinegar

Kosher salt and freshly ground black pepper

1 quart

Bring a large saucepan of water to a boil. Cut a shallow X in the bottom of each tomato. Blanch the tomatoes for about 20 seconds, just until the skins start to loosen. Drain in a colander and cool under cold running water until cool enough to handle.

Peel the tomatoes. Cut them in half, squeeze out the seeds, and coarsely chop.

Heat the olive oil in a large saucepan over medium heat. Add the celery, onion, carrot, garlic, and coriander and cook, stirring occasionally, until the vegetables start to soften, about 5 minutes.

Add the vinegars and chopped tomatoes, season with salt, and bring to a simmer. Reduce the heat and simmer gently for 30 to 50 minutes, stirring occasionally, until the relish is concentrated and has a marmalade-like consistency (the cooking time will vary based on the ripeness of the tomatoes). Season with salt and pepper to taste. Let cool to room temperature. (*The relish can be made up to 7 days ahead and refrigerated, covered; bring to room temperature before serving.*)

*Asparagus usually makes its first appearance* at the Union Square Greenmarket in late April, at which point Danny Meyer's family embarks on an almost nightly celebration until the season ends about two months later. This simple asparagus gratin is a favorite in the Meyer household—it goes well with everything, especially grilled veal chops, salmon, chicken, or steak.

# Danny Meyer's Roasted Asparagus Gratin

1 pound medium asparagus, tough ends snapped off

2 tablespoons extra-virgin olive oil

3 tablespoons fresh lemon juice

Kosher salt and freshly ground black pepper

¼ cup mayonnaise

½ cup finely grated Parmigiano-Reggiano or Pecorino Romano

**4 to 6 servings**

Preheat the oven to 375 degrees.

Arrange the asparagus lengthwise, tips pointing in the same direction, in a 9-x-13-inch baking dish. Drizzle the oil and lemon juice over the asparagus and shake the dish to coat the stalks evenly. Season with salt and pepper and shake again.

Roast the asparagus, shaking the pan 2 or 3 times to redistribute the stalks, until crisp-tender, about 15 minutes (longer for thicker stalks). Remove from the oven and preheat the broiler.

Spread the mayonnaise evenly over the asparagus, then sprinkle with the cheese. Broil, watching closely, until the top has browned, 2 to 3 minutes. Serve.

*These slow-cooked beans are not pretty*, but that doesn't matter—what they lose in appearance, they gain in flavor. Spending quality time with garlic and olive oil softens them up and brings out their sweetness. Chopped tomatoes, crunchy homemade bread crumbs, and lemon juice complete the equation. This works at home for the same reason it works at family meal—the green beans, once started, get where they're going with nothing more than the occasional stir.

# Slow-Cooked Green Beans

1 cup plus 1 tablespoon olive oil

6 garlic cloves

1 pound green beans, trimmed

1 teaspoon kosher salt, or more to taste

1 cup bread crumbs from day-old country bread

½ teaspoon freshly ground black pepper

1 large beefsteak tomato, cored and coarsely chopped, juices reserved

2 tablespoons fresh lemon juice

**4 servings**

Heat 1 cup of the oil in a large skillet. Add the garlic and cook over medium-low heat, stirring, until it begins to brown, about 4 minutes. Add the green beans and salt and cook, uncovered, stirring frequently, until the beans are very soft and sweet, about 20 minutes.

Meanwhile, preheat the oven to 350 degrees.

Combine the bread crumbs in a food processor with the remaining 1 tablespoon olive oil and the pepper and pulse to mix. Spread the bread crumbs on a baking sheet and toast until lightly golden, 10 to 15 minutes. Set aside.

With a slotted spoon, transfer the beans to a serving bowl. Gently stir in the tomato and its juices. Add the lemon juice and some of the oil from the skillet, to taste. Season to taste with salt if necessary. Finish with a sprinkling of the bread crumbs and serve.

*Someone at Gramercy Tavern* put a tray of broccoli in the oven to roast, and it's not clear what happened next: Either that cook didn't notice the oven was very hot or someone else walked by and turned the heat way up without first peering inside. Ten minutes later, the broccoli came out slightly charred on top but crisp-tender at the stalk, and suddenly a misstep seemed a smart move. The two different flavors and textures in the vertically sliced stalks are enhanced by lemon, cheese, and bread crumbs.

Cutting the broccoli into top-to-bottom slices, each one looking like a little tree, provides variety in every bite. The half cup of oil makes this more an oven-fry than a roast. Then you remove the slightly crunchy broccoli with a slotted spatula or spoon, leaving the excess oil behind.

# Roasted Broccoli with Pecorino Romano & Lemon

2 heads broccoli (1½–2 pounds)

½ cup olive oil

¾ cup panko bread crumbs

1 tablespoon kosher salt

1½ teaspoons Aleppo pepper (see headnote, page 32) or red pepper flakes

2 lemons

1 cup finely grated Pecorino Romano

**4 to 6 servings**

Preheat the oven to 475 degrees. Line a large baking sheet with parchment.

Trim the broccoli stems to 2 inches and peel the remaining stem portions. Cut each stalk in half top to bottom, place the cut side flat on a cutting board, and cut top to bottom again into ½-inch-thick slices so that each slice contains both stem and floret.

In a bowl, toss the broccoli with the oil. Add the bread crumbs, salt, and Aleppo pepper and toss again. Place on the baking sheet in a single layer.

Zest both lemons with a Microplane grater. Cut 1 lemon in half for juicing later. Combine the zest and cheese in a large bowl and set aside.

Roast the broccoli for 10 to 15 minutes, until the florets are browned or slightly charred and the stems are just tender.

Using a slotted spatula or spoon, transfer the broccoli to the bowl with the cheese mixture and toss well. Squeeze the lemon juice from the halved lemon over the broccoli. Serve hot or at room temperature.

*A Gramercy Tavern cook,* considering the evening's supply of broccoli, reaches for rice wine vinegar, lime juice, sesame oil, and soy sauce, and an often all-too-familiar vegetable assumes an Asian profile. Toss roasted broccoli with a trio of fresh herbs, garlic, and spices for layers of flavors—the tasty whole is definitely more than the sum of its parts.

# Asian Broccoli

2 heads broccoli (1½–2 pounds), cut into florets, stems trimmed and cut into ¼-inch-thick slices

2 teaspoons kosher salt

¼ teaspoon freshly ground black pepper

1½ teaspoons ground ginger

Pinch of red pepper flakes

3 garlic cloves, smashed and peeled

¼ cup olive oil

2 scallions, chopped (about ½ cup)

¼ cup coarsely chopped fresh cilantro

5 large fresh basil leaves, torn

2 tablespoons coarsely chopped fresh mint

### For the vinaigrette

¼ cup rice wine vinegar

2 tablespoons fresh lime juice

2 tablespoons extra-virgin olive oil

2 teaspoons toasted sesame oil

1 teaspoon soy sauce

1 teaspoon fish sauce (optional)

1 teaspoon Sriracha hot sauce (optional)

4 to 6 servings

Preheat the oven to 450 degrees.

Put the broccoli in a large bowl and add the salt, black pepper, ginger, and red pepper flakes. Toss with the garlic and the oil.

Spread the broccoli on a baking sheet and roast for 15 to 20 minutes, until tender and lightly browned. Discard the garlic.

Meanwhile, combine the scallions, cilantro, basil, and mint in a large bowl.

TO MAKE THE VINAIGRETTE: In a small bowl, combine the rice wine vinegar, lime juice, olive oil, sesame oil, soy sauce, and, if you want a stronger-flavored dish, the fish sauce and Sriracha. Whisk until emulsified.

When the broccoli is done, add it to the bowl with the herbs and toss, then toss with the vinaigrette to taste. Serve warm or at room temperature.

*Using seasonal produce can mean temporary abundance,* and since cauliflower is inexpensive when it's plentiful, it's a frequent component of family meal. Arun Gupta, who works the fish station at dinner for Gramercy Tavern's tavern room, looks for a new idea when he contributes a vegetable dish, something that will make his coworkers look forward to dinner. His smoky roast cauliflower in a tart dressing is a popular offering.

# Roasted Cauliflower with Lemon-Caper Dressing

2 large or 3 small heads cauliflower, cored and cut into bite-sized florets

½ teaspoon red pepper flakes

1 teaspoon smoked paprika

Kosher salt and freshly ground black pepper

½ cup olive oil

### For the dressing

1 large egg yolk

½ cup fresh lemon juice

1 tablespoon capers, rinsed and drained

Pinch of salt

1 cup vegetable oil

½ cup finely chopped fresh Italian parsley

**4 to 6 servings**

Preheat the oven to 400 degrees.

Place the cauliflower florets in a large bowl and add the red pepper, smoked paprika, and salt and black pepper to taste. Toss with the olive oil.

Spread the cauliflower in a single layer on a large baking sheet and roast for 25 to 30 minutes, or until tender and lightly browned.

MEANWHILE, MAKE THE DRESSING: In a blender, combine the egg yolk, lemon juice, capers, and salt and blend. With the motor running, slowly drizzle in the oil, blending until the dressing is creamy.

In a large bowl, gently stir together the roasted cauliflower, dressing, and parsley. Serve.

*At the start, the red cabbage* will be swimming in what looks like too much liquid, but faith, patience, and a sustained simmer will change that. Almost all the liquid cooks off, concentrating the flavors and softening the cabbage's bite into a mellow, autumnal side dish. The caramelized roasted pears provide a sweet balance and are as versatile as your imagination allows. They can be just as happy served over vanilla ice cream as they are in this dish.

# Braised Red Cabbage with Roasted Pears

### For the braised cabbage

3 tablespoons unsalted butter

1 head red cabbage (about 2 pounds), quartered, cored, and thinly sliced

1½ cups thinly sliced onions

4 cups apple juice

1 cup dry white wine

¼ cup sugar

Kosher salt and freshly ground black pepper

¼ cup white vinegar

### For the roasted pears

6 tablespoons (¾ stick) unsalted butter

½ cup packed light brown sugar

4 Bosc pears, halved lengthwise, cored, and cut top to bottom into ¼-inch-thick slices

6 to 8 servings

TO MAKE THE BRAISED CABBAGE: Melt the butter in a large heavy skillet or Dutch oven over medium-low heat. Add the cabbage and onions and cook for 2 minutes, stirring to coat. Add the apple juice, white wine, and sugar, raise the heat to medium and simmer, uncovered, for about 1 hour, stirring occasionally, until the cabbage becomes tender and the liquid has reduced by three fourths.

MEANWHILE, MAKE THE ROASTED PEARS: Preheat the oven to 450 degrees. Line a baking sheet with parchment paper.

Melt the butter in a small saucepan. Add the brown sugar and stir until it dissolves. Remove from the heat.

In a bowl, gently toss the pear slices with the butter and sugar mixture, coating them well. Transfer to the baking sheet, spreading them out in a single layer, and roast them until they are caramelized and easily pierced with a toothpick, 12 to 15 minutes. Remove from the oven and keep warm.

Season the cabbage with salt and pepper to taste and stir in the white vinegar. Garnish with the roasted pears and serve.

*If plain roasted cauliflower is good,* roasted cauliflower with smoked paprika and Aleppo or red pepper, a favorite Gramercy Tavern combination, is even better. The vegetables for the sauce cook until they soften slightly and yield more flavor, and then they are combined with yogurt, lemon juice, and red wine vinegar. This Asian-inspired dish also works well as a vegetarian main course.

# Roasted Cauliflower with Yogurt & Vegetable Sauce

2 medium heads cauliflower (about 5 pounds), cored and cut into bite-sized florets

2 teaspoons smoked paprika

1 teaspoon Aleppo pepper (see headnote, page 32) or ½ teaspoon red pepper flakes

1 tablespoon kosher salt

1 teaspoon freshly ground black pepper

½ cup olive oil

### For the sauce

2 tablespoons olive oil

2 teaspoons ground cumin

2 medium onions, cut into 1-inch chunks

2 red bell peppers, cored, seeded, and cut into 1-inch pieces

1 medium carrot, peeled, halved lengthwise, and cut into ¼-inch-thick slices

1 jalapeño, halved, seeded, and minced

3 tomatoes, cored and cut into ½-inch pieces

2 tablespoons fresh lemon juice

1 tablespoon rice wine vinegar

3 cups low-fat plain yogurt

Kosher salt

½ cup coarsely chopped fresh cilantro

8 to 10 servings as a side dish or 4 to 6 servings as a main course

Preheat the oven to 400 degrees, with racks in the lower and upper thirds. Line two baking sheets with parchment paper.

In a large bowl, toss the cauliflower florets with the paprika, Aleppo pepper, salt, and black pepper. Add the oil and stir well to coat. Spread the cauliflower on the baking sheets and roast for 25 to 30 minutes, until golden brown.

MEANWHILE, MAKE THE SAUCE: Heat the oil in a large skillet over medium heat. Add the cumin and cook, stirring, for 1 minute. Add the onions, bell peppers, carrot, and jalapeño and cook for 12 to 15 minutes, until the vegetables soften.

Stir in the tomatoes, lemon juice, and vinegar and cook for 3 to 5 minutes, until the tomatoes soften.

Remove the pan from the heat and stir in the yogurt. When the cauliflower is done, return the pan to low heat and cook, stirring, for 1 to 2 minutes.

Add the cauliflower to the pan, cook for 1 minute, stirring to combine, and season to taste with salt. Garnish with the cilantro and serve.

# Breaking the Fast

Every night for a month, it happens: Nine Bengali waiters slip out of the dining room at Gramercy Tavern and head downstairs, and nine people with other jobs to do step in to take their place. A host refilled water glasses; the beverage manager held tongs poised over a big rectangular basket and asked a guest what kind of bread she wanted; a waiter cleared crumbs off a table. During Ramadan, the Bengalis must fast from dawn to sunset each day for a month and so cannot join in the family meal. Hours after the other staffers have eaten, they break their fast at a table set for them in the narrow hallway between the wine storage room and the basement prep kitchen.

The waiters' wives take turns dropping off home-cooked meals, but this year the restaurant cooks decided to help out by making a separate Ramadan family meal once a week, in addition to the main meal. Tonight, before they sat down, the Bengalis waited for Kamal Ahmed, the acknowledged head of the group, who has worked at the restaurant since 1995, to take his seat at the far end of the table. They raised their hands to their faces, quickly recited the evening prayer, and then helped themselves to fried fish, salad, and a stew of eggplant and cauliflower. They ate quickly—after all, coworkers were doing them a month of favors upstairs. Then they bused their dishes, thanked the sous chef who had come down to make sure the dinner was to their liking, and prepared to go back to work.

One of the younger men broke out in a dizzy sweat, either from too many hours without food or from eating too much food at once, and at the others' suggestion, he slipped into the temperature-controlled wine room to cool off. Everyone watched him through the glass wall, refusing to go upstairs without him.

When he emerged, embarrassed, they filed up the narrow stairs and silently slipped back into their positions. A hand at the beverage manager's elbow and she relinquished the basket of bread. One of the waiters adjusted each chair at an empty table, just so, while another walked the perimeter of his service area, checking.

Once the month was over, the Bengalis thanked the people who had helped them out, in kind, with a take-out meal from a favorite Indian restaurant in Brooklyn—over two dozen trays of food set on a table double the usual length of a family meal buffet. The waiters removed the lids on the containers with a flourish and retired to their usual table in a far back corner of the room, where they waited to serve themselves until everyone else had filled their plates.

*This dish allows for lots of options.* At Eleven Madison Park, the cooks make Swiss chard a component of what can be either a hearty side dish or a one-dish meal, cooking it with beans and fresh Mexican chorizo. You can substitute fresh sweet or hot Italian sausage, with or without fennel, if you prefer. The small amount of cooking liquid cooks down into a flavorful glaze.

# Chard & Chorizo

1 tablespoon olive oil

½ cup finely chopped onion

8 ounces fresh Mexican chorizo sausage (see headnote), casings removed, coarsely chopped

2 teaspoons tomato paste

1 bunch Swiss chard, stems removed, leaves washed well but not dried and coarsely chopped (about 8 cups)

2 15-ounce cans cannellini beans, drained and rinsed

½ cup dry red wine

Kosher salt and freshly ground black pepper

6 to 8 servings as a side dish or 3 to 4 servings as a main course

Heat the oil in a large deep skillet or Dutch oven over medium heat. Add the onion and cook until softened, 2 to 3 minutes, stirring once or twice. Add the sausage and cook, using a wooden spoon to break it up, for 5 minutes, or until lightly browned.

Add the tomato paste, stir to mix well, and cook for 1 to 2 minutes, until darkened in color. Add the Swiss chard. If there isn't much water still clinging to the chard, add a few tablespoons to create steam. Increase the heat to medium-high, cover, and cook for 2 minutes, or until the chard starts to wilt.

Add the beans and red wine and stir gently. Adjust the heat so that the liquid in the pan is bubbling slightly, cover, and cook for 10 to 15 minutes, until the chard is tender.

Season the chard to taste with salt and pepper and serve.

*Collard greens are one of Blue Smoke's building blocks,* both on the menu, where they accompany any and all of the restaurant's smoked and barbecued meats, and at family meal. This spicy version, bookended by the flavors of smoky bacon and cider vinegar, is a delicious side dish, served over rice to soak up the flavorful cooking liquid or with crusty bread.

Be sure to rinse the collards well to get rid of any grit that might be clinging to the leaves.

# Blue Smoke's Collard Greens

8 ounces sliced bacon, cut crosswise into ½-inch-wide strips

Kosher salt

2 large bunches collard greens (about 2 pounds), stalks trimmed and leaves coarsely chopped

2 cups Chicken Stock (page 39)

¼ cup apple cider vinegar

1 tablespoon jalapeño Tabasco sauce

2 tablespoons sugar

Freshly ground black pepper

**4 servings**

Fill a large pot with water and bring to a boil over high heat.

Meanwhile, cook the bacon in a large skillet over medium-low heat, stirring occasionally, until the fat has rendered and the bacon is crispy, 10 to 15 minutes. Using a slotted spoon, transfer the bacon to paper towels to drain; reserve 1 tablespoon of the bacon fat.

Prepare a bowl of ice water. Add 1 tablespoon salt to the boiling water and blanch the collard greens for 30 seconds. Drain and transfer to the ice water to stop the cooking. Drain again and squeeze out any excess water.

Bring the stock to a boil in the pot you used to blanch the collards. Add the vinegar, Tabasco, and sugar, then stir in the greens, bacon, and the reserved 1 tablespoon fat and reduce the heat to a simmer. Cook, covered, stirring occasionally, until the greens are tender, 20 to 25 minutes; there will still be some liquid left when the greens are ready.

Season to taste with salt and pepper and serve.

# Jack-of-All-Trades

If Peter Ducharme holds still for more than a minute, it's under duress, as he is now, stuck on a phone call that refuses to end. Clearly the person he is talking to doesn't appreciate how much Peter dislikes being tethered to his standing desk in the Blue Smoke basement kitchen, tapping his pen on the slanted metal desktop, turning to see who is taking what into the pantry or how the butcher is doing with the trolley full of meats he portions every day.

Peter is Blue Smoke's kitchen manager, a job that doesn't exist at any of the other Union Square Hospitality Group restaurants, a title that was invented for him when it became evident that he didn't fit into an existing job description. On any given morning, he may be outside the back door examining the steel smoker that vents into a tall chimney, or tallying incoming briskets, or subbing for a cook who is late or missing in action, or working on a catering order. He responds to downtime the way a kid thinks about a required afternoon nap.

He started as a line cook when Blue Smoke opened, in 2002, but the newer hires don't know that. One day after the lunch rush, Peter claimed a burner at the deserted far end of the line, and while everyone else readied their stations for dinner prep, he butchered a whole tuna and turned out a set of elegant, rectangular logs that he then coated in ancho chile, paprika, and Magic Dust, the signature seasonings that Blue Smoke uses on its ribs. He wanted to work through the recipe before a special party descended that night, and one by one, the younger cooks found an excuse to wander by to see what he was doing. They came away with a newfound respect for the resident jack-of-all-trades, who turned out to have knife skills, an eye for presentation, and the ability to work fast and keep his station neat.

"I worked my way up the line until I was in charge of purchasing and receiving," said Peter, "but it branched out from there." He likes it that way. "I can fill in for a sous chef, a line cook, or the physical-plant guy."

A couple of times, he tried leaving—he's been a mason, operated a crane, and worked for small restaurants and corporate kitchens—but now he prefers to make one job a bunch of jobs so that every day is up for grabs.

*In August, when the tables at the farmers' market* down the block from the Union Square Cafe are piled high with pyramids of fresh corn, the kitchen looks for new ways to prepare it. For this ten-minute dish, the kernels are cut off the cob and quick-cooked in a skillet in a single layer so that one side gets slightly caramelized, giving them another texture without drying them out. Then they're tossed with scallions and a pinch of smoked paprika to complement their sweetness.

# Caramelized Corn with Smoked Paprika

2 tablespoons olive oil

4 ears corn, husked and kernels removed

2 scallions, thinly sliced on a long bias

Pinch of smoked paprika

Kosher salt

**4 servings**

Heat the olive oil over medium heat in a skillet big enough to hold the corn kernels in a single layer or use two skillets if necessary. Add the kernels and cook until they are brown on the bottom, about 5 minutes; do not stir.

Add the scallions and toss. Season with the paprika and salt and serve.

*This eggplant goes into the oven whole* and emerges as an easygoing collaborator. There's no need to struggle with the high-maintenance preparation that makes some people hesitate to bother with eggplant—no salting, weighting, rinsing, drying, breading, or frying. The eggplant, an array of quick-toasted spices, and a tomato, bell pepper, and some cilantro cook up into a stew that works as a side dish or a vegetarian main course.

# Cumin-Spiced Eggplant with Tomato & Bell Pepper

1 large eggplant (1½–2 pounds)

2 tablespoons vegetable oil

1 tablespoon ground coriander

1 teaspoon turmeric

1 teaspoon ground cumin

1 teaspoon paprika

½ teaspoon cumin seeds

1 tablespoon finely chopped peeled fresh ginger

1 medium red onion, thinly sliced

Kosher salt and freshly ground black pepper

1 large tomato, cored, seeded, and coarsely chopped

1 small green bell pepper, cored, seeded, and cut into 1-inch pieces

¼ cup coarsely chopped fresh cilantro

4 servings

Preheat the oven to 400 degrees.

Pierce the eggplant all over with a fork. Place in a shallow baking dish and cook until very soft, 45 to 50 minutes. Let cool slightly.

Halve the eggplant lengthwise and scoop out the pulp in large chunks. Discard the big seed pockets and the stem and skin, and chop the eggplant into 1-inch pieces.

Heat the oil in a large skillet over medium heat. Add the coriander, turmeric, ground cumin, paprika, and cumin seeds and cook, stirring, for 2 minutes, until fragrant. Add the ginger, onion, 1 teaspoon salt, and ¼ teaspoon pepper and cook, stirring occasionally, until the onion is soft, about 5 minutes. Add the tomato and bell pepper and cook, stirring occasionally, for 5 minutes more.

Add ¼ cup water, raise the heat, and bring to a simmer. Reduce the heat to low and simmer for 5 minutes. Stir in the eggplant and cook for 8 to 10 minutes to heat the eggplant through and blend the flavors. Season to taste with salt and pepper.

Garnish with the chopped cilantro and serve.

*Faced with a bunch of baking potatoes,* North End Grill cook Jai Lakhwani turned them into herbed-and-peppered crisps simply by putting very thin slices coated with butter, Aleppo pepper, and herbs into a hot oven. A few minutes on each side is all it takes. Lining the baking sheet with parchment paper prevents burned edges.

# Oven-Roasted Potato Chips with Herbs

2 russet potatoes (1 pound), scrubbed

8 tablespoons (1 stick) unsalted butter, melted

1 tablespoon chopped fresh rosemary leaves

1 tablespoon fresh thyme leaves

1 teaspoon Aleppo pepper (see headnote, page 32) or red pepper flakes

2 teaspoons kosher salt

¼ teaspoon freshly ground black pepper

**4 to 6 servings**

Preheat the oven to 450 degrees, with racks in the upper and lower thirds. Line two baking sheets with parchment paper.

Using a mandoline or a sharp knife, slice the potatoes lengthwise ⅛ inch thick.

Mix together the butter, rosemary, thyme, Aleppo pepper, salt, and black pepper in a medium bowl. Add the potato slices to the bowl and mix gently, turning to coat the slices. Arrange the potato slices in a single layer on the baking sheets.

Bake for 15 minutes, until the chips are beginning to brown. Turn the slices and bake for 5 to 7 minutes, or until tender and golden brown. Serve hot.

*When are mashed potatoes not just mashed potatoes?* When you replace regular butter with brown butter, which gives them a deeper, nutty flavor. The result is a rich, silken dish that commands attention rather than being a carbohydrate afterthought.

# Brown Butter Mashed Potatoes

6 medium Yukon Gold potatoes (about 2 pounds), peeled and cut in half

Kosher salt

Brown Butter (recipe follows)

½ cup whole milk

½ cup heavy cream

Freshly ground black pepper

**4 to 6 servings**

Cover the potatoes with 2 inches of cold water in a large saucepan, add 2 tablespoons salt, and bring to a boil. Lower the heat to medium and cook until the potatoes are fork-tender, 15 to 20 minutes.

Transfer the potatoes to a colander and drain for 5 minutes, then pass them through a potato ricer or food mill into a clean saucepan.

Warm the brown butter, milk, and cream in a small saucepan. Using a wooden spoon or a heatproof silicone spatula, slowly stir the mixture into the potatoes over low heat until completely absorbed. Season with salt and pepper and serve immediately.

## *Brown Butter*

8 tablespoons (1 stick) unsalted butter

**About ½ cup**

Melt the butter in a small saucepan over medium heat. As it melts, the solids will separate and sink to the bottom. Skim the foam off the top.

Continue to cook the butter until it is dark brown—it always looks darker in the pan than it really is—but be careful not to let the butter get so hot that it starts to smoke, which will give it a burned taste. Remove from the heat and pour the brown butter through a fine-mesh strainer into a container. Cool to room temperature. (*The butter will keep, tightly covered and refrigerated, for up to 1 week.*)

*Chef Gabriel Kreuther of The Modern* takes bacon, fromage blanc, and potatoes and comes up with a dish reminiscent of his Alsatian boyhood. The bacon is roasted, not cooked on top of the stove. The potatoes are roasted, too, until they're nicely browned and have a crunchy exterior—in fact, Gabriel says that a slightly "burned" outside only contributes to the flavor. The fromage blanc is mixed with cream, herbs, and garlic, and everything is mounded into a little pyramid of taste synergy. Finish with a sprinkle of fleur de sel, the hand-harvested sea salt from France's Atlantic coast, and you'll have a sense of Gabriel's comfort food.

# Roasted Potatoes with Fromage Blanc & Bacon

1 8-ounce container low-fat fromage blanc or low-fat sour cream

2 tablespoons heavy cream or milk

2 tablespoons finely chopped fresh chives

2 tablespoons finely chopped shallots

1 garlic clove, finely chopped

Kosher salt and freshly ground white pepper

1 pound fingerling potatoes or small Yukon Golds

2 tablespoons olive oil

2 tablespoons unsalted butter

6 thick slices bacon, cut crosswise into ½-inch-wide pieces

Fleur de sel or other coarse sea salt

**4 to 6 servings**

Preheat the oven to 400 degrees. Line a baking sheet with parchment paper.

Using a whisk or wooden spoon, combine the fromage blanc, cream, chives, shallots, and garlic in a small bowl. Season to taste with salt and white pepper; cover and refrigerate.

Cut the fingerling potatoes in half or the Yukon Golds into thick slices, depending on their size, and then rinse to eliminate some of the starch. Dry well with paper towels.

Put the olive oil and butter in a large cast-iron skillet and heat briefly in the oven until the butter melts. Add the potatoes, stir to coat, and roast, turning once or twice, for 25 to 30 minutes, or until they are golden brown and tender when pierced with a knife. Transfer to a serving bowl.

While the potatoes are cooking, spread the bacon on the baking sheet and roast for 10 to 15 minutes, or until crispy. Remove from the oven.

Top the potatoes with the fromage blanc mixture, garnish with the bacon, and sprinkle with fleur de sel. Alternatively, mix the potatoes, fromage blanc mixture, and bacon together and garnish with the salt. Serve immediately.

# Hot-Dog Day

There's always a day, whether in a home kitchen or a state-of-the-art restaurant kitchen, that refuses to go the way it should, one that is so jam-packed that it leaves the cook without much chance to plan a meal. That's where hot dogs come in.

"I defy anyone to find a restaurant that doesn't occasionally have hot-dog night," said North End Grill sous chef Adam Harvey. "The question is, what do you do with it?" Union Square Cafe's fallback is hot dogs cooked with spicy beans. Eleven Madison Park's employees chose hot dogs with classic condiments and side dishes for an annual day-long meeting, but they shook things up by having the front-of-the-house and kitchen staffs swap jobs.

At North End Grill, the open kitchen boasts its share of New Jersey natives, so in anticipation of one numbingly busy Friday, the lunchtime family meal protein was "rippers," promoted by their fans as a New Jersey food tradition. Adam, who had spent his morning cutting whole octopus into exact portions, now turned that surgical precision to a new task—demonstrating the proper way to score a hot dog in a spiral pattern. A real ripper comes with a cheese sauce that nestles into those spiral grooves, but the spill quotient is too high for family meal, so staffers settled for beautifully scored hot dogs cooked on the charcoal grill, accompanied by oven-roasted potato chips flavored with smoky Aleppo pepper and fresh herbs, coleslaw, and lighter-than-air Rice Krispies treats.

Adam turned the scoring task over to one of the cooks in charge of family meal that day and returned to his portioning tasks—next up, a full tray of pork belly about to be divided into dozens of identical-sized servings. He picked up his knife, surveyed the pork as though it were a geometry problem, and marked off individual rectangles in his head.

Before he took the first cut, he rested his fists on the counter, knife at an angle, forearms outstretched, until someone commented on the tattoo that covered his left arm from the crook of his elbow to his wrist. With hairdos dictated by law and street clothes traded for white coats, chef's pants, and stand-all-day comfortable shoes, restaurant cooks don't have many chances to make a style statement beyond the choice of a baseball cap or jaunty beret or bandanna, so many of them decorate their skin. Tats are kitchen fashion—a collection of knives marching down a cook's arm, a barista's long-handled espresso filter, a sprinkling of stars, or the burning books Adam chose on the day he decided to cook instead of going to medical school.

He proudly fielded compliments until family meal came out, and then he filed into the dining room with the rest of the staff for what would be their last free moments until late afternoon. By the time everyone returned to the kitchen a half hour later, the mood was palpably different.

Zia Sheikh, a Tabla sous chef who'd reunited with chef Floyd Cardoz to open North End Grill, turned to Adam and the cooks. "Get your running shoes on, people," he said, and as if on cue, a stream of guests appeared for their noon reservations. It was the last thing anyone said that afternoon that didn't have to do with an order.

*Cube butternut squash,* toss it with oil and balsamic vinegar, and bake it, which is how Eleven Madison Park cooks prepare it for family meal. Each bite ends up tender in the middle and slightly caramelized on the outside. Sprinkle with Parmigiano, and a plain side dish steps forward to claim equal billing on the plate with the main course.

To make peeling the squash easy, first cut it in half crosswise so that each half will sit flat on a stable base, and work from top to bottom with a vegetable peeler or a small sturdy knife. Or pierce the whole squash a few times with a sharp knife and cook in a microwave oven for 2 minutes, which will loosen the skin without cooking the flesh.

# Roasted Butternut Squash with Balsamic & Rosemary

1 medium butternut squash (about 3 pounds), halved, peeled, seeded, and cut into 1-inch cubes

2 tablespoons olive oil

2 tablespoons finely chopped fresh rosemary

2 tablespoons plus 1 teaspoon balsamic vinegar

Kosher salt and freshly ground black pepper

½ cup grated Parmigiano-Reggiano

**4 to 6 servings**

Preheat the oven to 400 degrees.

In a large bowl, toss the squash with the oil, rosemary, the 2 tablespoons vinegar, and salt and pepper to taste. Spread the squash on a baking sheet or in a baking pan large enough to hold it in a single layer. Roast until the squash turns soft and lightly caramelized, about 40 minutes.

Transfer the squash to a bowl, toss with the Parmigiano and the remaining 1 teaspoon vinegar, and serve.

*From the moment these sweet potatoes* go into the oven, it's clear they're going to be more delicious than whole sweet potatoes, because the inside of each slice will be tender, while the outside will be just crisp enough for a pleasing contrast.

As they cook, make a butter-and-brown-sugar glaze that's seasoned with spices and pepper and balanced by apple cider vinegar. Then toss the roasted potatoes in the glaze, sprinkle with fresh thyme, and see how much tastier a sweet potato can be. The restaurants often grind their spices fresh, but this is fine with the ground spices you have on the pantry shelf.

# Spice-Glazed Sweet Potatoes

2 large sweet potatoes (about 2½ pounds), peeled and cut into ½-inch-thick rounds

2 tablespoons olive oil

Kosher salt

3 tablespoons unsalted butter

¼ cup packed dark brown sugar

1 star anise, ground in a spice grinder or left whole

½ teaspoon freshly ground black pepper

½ teaspoon ground cinnamon

⅛ teaspoon ground cloves

⅛ teaspoon ground allspice

3 fresh thyme sprigs, plus 2 teaspoons finely chopped fresh thyme for garnish

3 tablespoons apple cider vinegar

4 to 6 servings

Preheat the oven to 350 degrees. Line a baking sheet with parchment paper.

Toss the sweet potatoes with the oil and season with salt. Spread them on the baking sheet in a single layer and bake until golden brown and tender when pierced with a paring knife, about 30 minutes. Transfer to a serving bowl.

Meanwhile, melt the butter in a small skillet over low heat. Add the brown sugar and stir until it has melted. Add the spices and thyme sprigs, then add the vinegar, raise the heat to medium-high, and boil to reduce to a glaze, 1 to 2 minutes. Remove the piece of star anise if you used it and the thyme sprigs.

Pour the glaze over the potatoes and toss to coat evenly. Sprinkle with the chopped thyme and salt to taste and serve.

*In addition to sweet potatoes,* this creamy, vanilla-scented dish works with acorn, butternut, or Blue Hubbard squash. If you find a sweet little pumpkin, try that too. Think of this as mashed potatoes with a new cast of characters—with sweets or squash standing in for plain russet potatoes and mascarpone playing butter's part.

The safest way to cut a hard-rind squash in half is to pierce it with a big knife, steady the squash on the side away from the blade, and cut straight down, at a 90-degree angle. Or pierce it a few times with a sharp knife and soften it slightly in the microwave for about 2 minutes to make cutting it even easier.

# Mashed Sweet Potatoes (or Squash) with Vanilla & Mascarpone

4 pounds sweet potatoes or squash (see headnote), halved lengthwise, seeded if using squash

Olive oil

2 star anise

2 cinnamon sticks

1 vanilla bean

1 cup mascarpone

Kosher salt and freshly ground black pepper

**6 to 8 servings**

Preheat the oven to 350 degrees.

Rub the sweet potatoes or squash all over with olive oil. Put the sweet potato halves cut side down on a baking sheet, along with the star anise and cinnamon sticks. Or, if you're using squash, tuck the spices into the cavities and place the squash cut side up

Bake until tender, 40 minutes to 1 hour, depending on size, or until a fork pierces the flesh easily. Let the potatoes or squash cool slightly, until you can handle them easily. Discard the star anise and cinnamon sticks.

Use a large spoon to scoop the flesh into a large saucepan. Mash it with a fork, whisk, or potato masher. Split the vanilla bean, scrape the seeds into the pan, and stir to combine. Place the pan over medium-low heat, add the mascarpone, and stir well until it melts.

Season with salt and pepper to taste and serve.

*This may be the easiest and most versatile way* to inject some life into a simple vegetable side dish. A dose of tart and sweet pickled vegetables added to roasted broccoli or cauliflower gives them a boost.

This version works all year, with whatever vegetables are in season—red or yellow bell peppers, cucumbers, pearl onions, carrots, even jalapeños. The basic pickling liquid calls for vinegar, water, and sugar, but you can toss in any or all of the following: coriander, cumin, peppercorns, a cinnamon stick, or a pinch of red pepper flakes. Leave them in for a stronger flavor, or strain them out. Or tie up and add a bunch of fresh basil or dill, then pull out the herbs before you refrigerate the pickles.

# Year-Round Pickled Vegetables

10–12 cups of any of the following, alone or in combination:

Carrots, peeled and cut into ¼-inch slices

Red or yellow bell peppers, cored, seeded, and cut into whatever size pieces you like

Whole peeled pearl onions

Cucumbers (unpeeled), cut into ¼-inch slices

Jalapeños, pierced 4 or 5 times each with a sharp knife to help them absorb the liquid

### For the pickling liquid

4 cups white wine vinegar

2 cups sugar

½ cup kosher salt

Fresh herbs or spices of your choice (see headnote)

**Six 1-quart jars**

Place the vegetables in a nonreactive heatproof container, such as a stainless steel bowl or large saucepan; do not use cast iron or aluminum.

TO MAKE THE PICKLING LIQUID: Bring the vinegar, 4 cups water, the sugar, and salt to a boil in a large saucepan, stirring to dissolve the sugar and salt. Immediately pour the liquid over the vegetables. Add any fresh herbs or spices and cool to room temperature.

When the vegetables are cool, transfer them, with the liquid, to six 1-quart canning jars or other containers, making sure they are completely covered by liquid; you can leave the spices in, if you wish, for a stronger flavor over time, but remove the fresh herbs. Cover and refrigerate. (*Refrigerated, the vegetables will keep for a couple of months, given the off chance that no one finishes them before then.*)

*Because Maialino is in the Gramercy Park Hotel,* it stays open 365 days a year, unlike many other restaurants, which close on major holidays. For Thanksgiving dinner, the staff turns out a family meal that's a hybrid of American and Italian traditions. One favorite dish is cranberry sauce reborn as cranberry mostarda, a variation on the traditional Italian condiment that mixes candied fruits with a mustard-spiked sauce. Fresh cranberries replace the candied fruit, and the result is a spicy, surprising companion to any roast meat or fowl. Staffers like it so much that it hits the plate in servings much larger than dollops.

# Cranberry Mostarda

1 cup sugar

¾ cup packed light brown sugar

¼ cup plus 1 tablespoon dry mustard (such as Colman's)

1 tablespoon ground allspice

1 tablespoon ground ginger

1 teaspoon kosher salt

¼ teaspoon cayenne pepper

4 juniper berries

2 whole cloves

1 small cinnamon stick

1 piece star anise

1½ cups fresh orange juice

¼ cup fresh lemon juice

2 tablespoons light corn syrup

3 pounds (four 12-ounce bags) fresh cranberries

**8 to 10 servings**

Combine 1 cup water and all the ingredients except the cranberries in a medium saucepan. Bring to a simmer over medium heat, then cook over low heat, uncovered, stirring occasionally, for 45 minutes.

Put the cranberries in a large saucepan. Strain the spiced liquid over the cranberries, bring to a simmer, and cook, stirring occasionally, over low heat for 30 minutes, uncovered, or until the cranberries have popped and the mostarda has thickened. Remove from the heat and cool.

Serve the mostarda at room temperature or cold. (*The mostarda will keep, tightly covered and refrigerated, for up to 1 month.*)

# Eggs & Bread

*This egg sandwich, from Union Square Events,* the catering wing of the family, has gone through as many versions as there are ways to make eggs. Here is the one chosen to appear each summer at Shakespeare in the Park. It calls for a "wrecked" egg (with a broken yolk) and an easy-to-mix sauce.

Cheddar cheese curds are basically toddler cheese, irregular pieces of fresh young cheese that squeak when you bite into them. Curds, which you can find at cheese stores or large markets, are delicious, but grated regular cheddar is a perfectly suitable substitute.

# Egg, Bacon & Cheese Sandwich

### For the sauce

½ cup whole-milk Greek yogurt

3 tablespoons crème fraîche or sour cream

2 tablespoons ketchup

2 teaspoons chipotle chile sauce, such as Tabasco

Kosher salt and freshly ground black pepper

### For the sandwiches

8 slices bacon

8 slices hearty country bread or 4 soft rolls, split

6 tablespoons unsalted butter

4 large eggs

Kosher salt and freshly ground black pepper

⅓ cup fresh cheddar cheese curds or grated cheddar cheese

1 cup frisée or Bibb lettuce, torn into bite-sized pieces

8 thin tomato slices

4 sandwiches

TO MAKE THE SAUCE: Whisk together the yogurt and crème fraîche in a small bowl. Stir in the ketchup and chipotle sauce. Season with salt and pepper to taste. Set aside. (*The sauce can be refrigerated in a tightly covered container for up to 1 week.*)

TO MAKE THE SANDWICHES: Cook the bacon in a large heavy skillet over medium-high heat, turning once, until brown and crisp. Drain on a paper towel; set the pan aside.

Toast the bread (or rolls) and, using 2 tablespoons of the butter, spread butter on one side of each piece of toast (or the insides of the rolls).

Pour out the fat from the skillet and wipe out the pan with a paper towel; or, if you prefer a stronger bacon flavor, leave a small amount of the fat in the pan. Heat the remaining 4 tablespoons butter, or 3 tablespoons if you left some fat in the pan, over medium-low heat until it starts to foam. Crack the eggs into the pan, season with salt and pepper, and top with the cheese. Let cook until the eggs are barely set, about 30 seconds. Gently stir each egg with a heatproof silicone spatula to break up the yolks, then gently swirl the eggs and cheese together and finish cooking. You want "wrecked" eggs—broken fried eggs— not ones that are fully scrambled. Remove from the heat.

To assemble the sandwiches, spread some of the sauce on the buttered sides of the slices of toast (or the insides of the rolls). Layer the bacon slices, frisée, and tomato slices on 4 of the slices of toast (or the bottoms of the rolls). Place the eggs on top, cover with the remaining slices of toast (or roll tops), and serve immediately.

*What's a self-respecting zucchini to do* in the height of summer, when its tasty reputation has been put to the test by too much zucchini bread? Turn up instead in this easy frittata alongside mushrooms, scallions, and parsley. Accompanied by bread and a salad or fruit, it's a hot-weather meal made in a baking dish.

# Zucchini & Mushroom Frittata

Butter for the pan

¼ cup olive oil

2 cups thinly sliced zucchini (about 2 medium)

1½ cups sliced white or cremini mushrooms

⅓ cup finely chopped scallions

2 garlic cloves, finely chopped

7 large eggs

1 cup grated Parmigiano-Reggiano

⅓ cup finely chopped fresh Italian parsley

1 tablespoon finely chopped fresh basil

½ teaspoon kosher salt

Freshly ground black pepper

6 to 8 servings

Preheat the oven to 350 degrees. Butter a 9-inch square or round baking dish or a 10-inch ovenproof nonstick skillet.

Heat the oil in a large skillet over medium-high heat. Add the zucchini, mushrooms, scallions, and garlic and cook, stirring, until well softened, about 5 minutes. Remove from the heat and let cool slightly so that the heat doesn't precook the eggs.

In a medium bowl, beat the eggs. Stir in the cheese, parsley, basil, salt, and a dash of pepper. Then stir in the cooked vegetables.

Pour into the baking dish and bake until set, 25 to 30 minutes. Remove from the oven and turn out onto a large platter (or cut into squares or wedges in the pan). Serve hot, warm, or at room temperature.

*A frittata involves eggs and a filling,* but its resemblance to an omelet stops there. This one, loaded with an assortment of vegetables, fresh herbs, and cheese, is cooked first on the stovetop and then finished in the oven. An omelet requires the family to sit down "right this minute," which isn't always easy, but a frittata is a model of accommodation. Enjoy it out of the oven, or warm, or even at room temperature—it's a beautiful solution for dinner and an obvious excuse to have friends over for brunch.

# Springtime Frittata

### For the filling

1 medium russet potato, scrubbed

1 large artichoke, preferably with stem

2 tablespoons olive oil

1 heaping cup thinly sliced onion

1 teaspoon kosher salt

10 medium asparagus stalks, woody bottoms snapped off, peeled, and cut into ½-inch pieces

2 packed cups chopped Swiss chard leaves (from about 1 small bunch, trimmed)

### For the frittata

9 large eggs

3 large egg yolks

¼ cup heavy cream

½ cup grated Gruyère

¼ cup grated Parmigiano-Reggiano

2 tablespoons finely chopped mixed fresh basil, Italian parsley, and chives

2 tablespoons dried bread crumbs

1½ teaspoons kosher salt

Freshly ground black pepper

1 tablespoon olive oil, plus more for drizzling

6 to 8 servings

TO MAKE THE FILLING: Preheat the oven to 350 degrees.

Pierce the potato several times with a fork. Bake it directly on an oven rack for 1 hour, or until tender. Refrigerate until cool enough to handle.

Meanwhile, pull off the outer leaves of the artichoke, then pull out or cut away the pale green leaves in the center. Trim the stem to 1 to 2 inches. With a paring knife, trim away the dark green outer portion of the heart and the stem. Split the heart in half and use a spoon or small paring knife to carve out the prickly choke at its center. Cut the artichoke into ⅛-inch-thick slices. Set aside.

When the potato is cool enough to handle, peel it, quarter lengthwise, and cut crosswise into ⅛-inch-thick slices; it's OK if it crumbles. Set aside.

Warm the oil in a large skillet over medium heat until it is shimmering but not smoking. Add the onion, artichoke, and salt, reduce the heat to medium-low, and cook, stirring every few minutes, for 10 minutes, or until the vegetables are tender. Add the asparagus and Swiss chard and stir until the chard starts to wilt. After 2 to 3 minutes, increase the heat to medium-high and cook until the chard is tender and any water has evaporated, about 1 minute more. Set aside to cool slightly.

TO MAKE THE FRITTATA: Preheat the oven to 325 degrees.

Beat the eggs and yolks together in a large bowl. Stir in the cream, the Gruyère, 3 tablespoons of the Parmigiano, the herbs, bread crumbs, potato slices, asparagus-chard mixture, salt, and pepper to taste.

Heat the 1 tablespoon oil in a 10-inch ovenproof nonstick skillet over medium-high heat. Add the egg mixture and, with a rubber spatula or wooden spoon, stir to scramble the frittata for 30 seconds, scraping the bottom of the pan and breaking up any large egg curds. The frittata will still be mostly wet, with evenly dispersed cooked egg throughout. Remove the pan from the heat, smooth the top of the frittata, and gently tap the pan on the counter to settle it.

Slide the pan into the oven and bake for 20 to 30 minutes, or until the frittata is firm to the touch. Remove from the oven and turn out onto a large platter (or cut it into wedges in the pan using a nonabrasive spatula). Garnish with the remaining 1 tablespoon Parmigiano and a drizzle of olive oil. Serve hot, warm, or at room temperature.

*If you eat lunch at eleven in the morning* and dinner between four and five, as all the restaurant families do, breakfast food tends to lose out.

To fill the comfort gap, several of the restaurants serve up a breakfast-for-lunch meal. This frittata is ham and eggs taken uptown, baked with cheese and a little cream and potatoes and topped with sour cream and chives. It works as well for a light dinner or brunch as it does for breakfast.

# Ham & Cheese Frittata

8 extra-large eggs

2 tablespoons heavy cream

1 cup coarsely grated Gruyère

Kosher salt and freshly ground black pepper

2 tablespoons unsalted butter

¾ cup finely chopped onion

4 small red potatoes, scrubbed and cut into ¼-inch cubes (about 2 cups)

1 cup coarsely chopped cooked ham (such as prosciutto cotto or Black Forest; about 6 ounces)

1 cup grated Parmigiano-Reggiano

¼ cup sour cream

¼ cup finely chopped fresh chives

**6 to 8 servings**

Preheat the oven to 400 degrees.

Whisk together the eggs and cream in a large bowl. Whisk in the Gruyère and salt and pepper to taste until foamy.

Heat the butter in a 12-inch ovenproof nonstick skillet over medium heat until it foams. Add the onion and potatoes and cook for 8 to 10 minutes, stirring occasionally, until the potatoes are tender. Season with salt and pepper.

Pour the egg mixture over the onion and potatoes, reduce the heat to medium-low, and cook, pulling the edges away from the sides of the pan with a heatproof silicone spatula so that the uncooked egg flows to the bottom of the pan, until the frittata is half set but still liquid in the center. Sprinkle the chopped ham evenly over the top. Sprinkle with the Parmigiano.

Transfer the pan to the oven and bake for 10 to 12 minutes, or until puffed and golden.

Turn out the frittata onto a serving platter (or cut into wedges in the pan with a nonabrasive spatula). Garnish each serving with a spoonful of sour cream and a sprinkling of chives.

# The Best Life Imaginable

Last order of the night.

Word spread quickly through the kitchen at The Modern: The final table of the night had placed its order. One by one, people started to shut down sections of the kitchen, discarding ingredients that wouldn't keep, storing ones that would. Within minutes, a finished station had been stripped down to vacant stainless steel as runners ferried the remaining pans and utensils to the dishwashing station.

Twice a week, The Modern's kitchen is completely broken down and cleaned. Drawers come off of their sliders and shelves are pulled out of standing racks; anything that can be dismantled is. Cooks get on their hands and knees with big sponges dripping suds, climb up to reach into an exhaust hood, or tackle the insides of the pastry refrigerator doors.

The only one still cooking that Saturday night was chef de cuisine Sandro Romano, who was making the midnight family meal. Sandro came to New York for the first time as a tourist when he was twenty, and he liked the feeling that "nobody knows what you were before; you can just invent yourself." Nine years later he returned, but this time the city did not feel quite so welcoming. He was almost thirty, out of money, and out of time on his visa, down to single-digit days until he would have to return to Switzerland. Although he was a classically trained chef who had just spent ten years cooking and had a college degree in hospitality and business, he hadn't come back to New York to explore the possibility of a restaurant career. "I came," he said, "to explore Sandro."

He saw an ad for a job at Union Square Cafe, but he couldn't fill out an application because he couldn't read enough English to get beyond the word "waiter." He'd never been a waiter. Still, he had nothing else to do, so he walked over to the restaurant, expecting to get rejected.

That was what certainly would have happened if chef Michael Romano had not been at the Cafe and had not heard Sandro speaking French. Michael, who is fluent in the language, quickly discovered that he was talking to a cook with impressive credentials, one who was certainly worth an audition. One frantic shift and three hundred dinners later, Sandro had an unexpected solution to his visa problem.

With English, he could have started as chef de cuisine. Instead, he began at the pasta station, ten years older than his coworkers. Seven months later, his language skills had caught up with his cooking skills, and he became sous chef, then executive sous chef. He moved to another restaurant for a time but eventually returned to work at The Modern.

"I once tried to have a regular life, nine to five like other people," he said, "but I hated it. When you cook, you work hard, but it's what you do. It's like being an athlete—you're in your zone. You can't go out with your friends at night because you have to work the next morning, you have this discipline."

After readying everything for family meal, Sandro wandered through the kitchen, asking people how the night had gone and letting them know that it was time to eat. Cooks lined up to fill their plates, climbed up onto the empty counters, and balanced their plates on their knees. A case of beer appeared, along with some leftover chocolates from the private dining room. It was 1:30 in the morning before anyone even mentioned going home.

*For every traditional ethnic dish* that's been in a staffer's family forever, there's a novel invention like layered huevos rancheros, which is not quite a quesadilla, not quite by-the-book huevos, but inspired by both. This version, from Eleven Madison Park, is tasty enough to blot out any memories of its more familiar antecedents. Think of it as a quesadilla with an egg and beans on top, or as huevos rancheros with cheese, stacked. But don't overthink the dish; just enjoy the union.

Start with Cotija, a firm cow's-milk cheese from the Mexican town of the same name. You can find Cotija in gourmet or Latin specialty markets, or substitute Parmigiano-Reggiano.

# Layered Huevos Rancheros

### For the salsa

2 medium tomatoes, cored, seeded, and finely chopped

½ medium red onion, finely chopped

1 jalapeño, seeded and finely chopped

1 serrano chile, seeded and finely chopped

½ bunch fresh cilantro, finely chopped (about ½ cup)

Juice of 1 lime

Kosher salt and freshly ground black pepper to taste

### For the huevos rancheros

1 tablespoon olive oil

1 medium onion, finely chopped

2 garlic cloves, finely chopped

1 15-ounce can black beans, drained and rinsed

2 teaspoons ground cumin

1½ teaspoons cayenne pepper

1 teaspoon garlic salt

8 corn tortillas

2 cups grated Cotija (see headnote)

TO MAKE THE SALSA: Combine all the ingredients in a small bowl and stir well. Set aside. (*The salsa can be made up to 1 day ahead, covered, and refrigerated.*)

TO MAKE THE HUEVOS RANCHEROS: Preheat the oven to 350 degrees.

In a large skillet, heat the oil over medium heat. Add the onion and garlic and cook, stirring occasionally, until softened. Add the black beans, cumin, cayenne, and garlic salt and cook until heated through, about 5 minutes. Remove from the heat, and cover the skillet to keep the beans warm.

Meanwhile, arrange 4 of the tortillas on a baking sheet. Sprinkle about ¼ cup of the cheese over each tortilla and top with the remaining 4 tortillas. Bake for a few minutes, until the cheese has melted and the tortillas are crispy around the edges. Meanwhile, prepare the eggs.

4 large eggs, poached or fried, still warm

Kosher salt and freshly ground pepper

1 avocado, pitted, peeled, and mashed

Sour cream for serving

**4 servings**

As soon as the tortillas come out of the oven, layer the black beans, salsa, and eggs on top. Season the eggs with salt and pepper. Sprinkle with the remaining 1 cup cheese, garnish with the avocado and sour cream, and serve.

*The strong, salty flavors* of this one-skillet family meal from The Modern are spiked by kimchi, which adds a briny crunch. You can find jars of prepared kimchi in the international section of bigger markets.

# Eggs & Bacon with Spicy Fried Rice

4 slices thick-cut bacon, cut crosswise into ½-inch-wide pieces

2 cups store-bought cabbage kimchi, preferably red Napa, chopped; reserve (optional) some of the liquid from the jar

1 cup thinly sliced scallions

2 cups short-grain rice, cooked according to package instructions and cooled (about 5 cups)

2 tablespoons soy sauce

2 teaspoons toasted sesame oil

1 tablespoon sesame seeds

1 cup frozen peas (not thawed)

6 large eggs, fried, scrambled, or poached and still warm

Kosher salt and freshly ground black pepper

*4 to 6 servings*

Cook the bacon in a large skillet over medium heat, stirring occasionally, until lightly golden and crisp, 8 to 10 minutes. Remove the bacon with a slotted spoon and drain on paper towels. Pour off all but 1 tablespoon of the fat from the pan.

Add the kimchi to the bacon fat remaining in the skillet and cook over medium heat for 1 to 2 minutes, stirring occasionally. Remove from the pan with a slotted spoon and set aside.

Add the scallions to the skillet and cook for 3 minutes, or until wilted. Remove and set aside.

Wipe out the skillet. Add the rice and cook over high heat for 1 minute, stirring, to evaporate the excess moisture. Reduce the heat to medium-high, add the soy sauce, sesame oil, and sesame seeds, and cook, stirring, for 2 minutes. Add the frozen peas, kimchi, and scallions and cook, stirring, for 5 minutes, or until everything is warmed through. Remove from the heat and keep warm.

Season the eggs with salt and pepper to taste. Spoon the rice onto individual plates and top with the eggs. Sprinkle with the bacon. If you would like a spicier dish, drizzle on some of the reserved kimchi liquid. Serve.

*These simple biscuits are a marvel*—somehow each bite is moist and crumbly and rich and light all at the same time. They elevate the very notion of a biscuit.

How popular are they? Broken biscuits and any extras show up at the family meal buffet, and the biscuit pan is one of the first to turn up empty. All you have to do to achieve Gramercy Tavern pastry chef Nancy Olson's admirable results is to follow the directions, particularly the one about not overmixing the dough.

# Nancy Olson's Biscuits

1¾ cups all-purpose flour, plus more for the work surface

1 tablespoon baking powder

½ teaspoon salt

1 teaspoon sugar

8 tablespoons (1 stick) unsalted butter, cut into small cubes and chilled

1 cup heavy cream

2 tablespoons unsalted butter, melted (optional)

**12 biscuits**

Preheat the oven to 400 degrees. Line a baking sheet with parchment paper.

Mix all the dry ingredients in a large bowl. Cut in the chilled butter with two knives or your fingers until the mixture resembles coarse meal. Pour in the heavy cream, mixing with a wooden spoon just until the dough comes together. (Overmixing will result in tough biscuits.)

On a well-floured surface, roll out the dough to a thickness of 1 inch. Cut out the biscuits with a 2-inch round cutter or a drinking glass. Place the biscuits 2 inches apart on the baking sheet.

Bake for about 10 minutes, or until the biscuits are slightly puffed and the tops are lightly browned. If you're feeling self-indulgent, brush the biscuits with the melted butter when they come out of the oven. Serve hot.

*What a difference the addition of a single ingredient can make.* The molasses that sets this recipe apart is combined with butter to form a glaze. Unadorned, corn bread is a classic accompaniment to barbecued anything, but add this glaze, and it can cross the line into dessert.

# Molasses Corn Bread

Butter for the pan

1 cup all-purpose flour

1 cup yellow cornmeal

⅔ cup sugar

3½ teaspoons baking powder

1 teaspoon salt

6 tablespoons (¾ stick) unsalted butter

1 large egg, lightly beaten

1 cup buttermilk

### For the molasses glaze

8 tablespoons (1 stick) unsalted butter, melted

½ cup molasses

8 to 10 servings

Preheat the oven to 400 degrees. Lightly butter a 9-inch round cake pan.

In a large bowl, whisk together the flour, cornmeal, sugar, baking powder, and salt. Cut in the butter using two knives or your fingers until the mixture is the consistency of coarse meal; do not overwork it. Add the egg and buttermilk and stir well. Scrape the batter into the cake pan.

Bake for 20 to 25 minutes, or until a toothpick inserted into the center of the bread comes out clean.

MEANWHILE, MAKE THE MOLASSES GLAZE: In a small bowl, mix the butter and molasses together with a wooden spoon or rubber spatula until blended.

As soon as the corn bread comes out of the oven, pour the glaze over the top. Let it sit for 15 minutes while the glaze soaks in, then serve warm or at room temperature.

*Making brioche involves four basic steps,* two of which require you to do nothing but exercise patience. First you make a dough with instant yeast; second, you add the butter in little bits; third, you ignore the dough while it firms in the refrigerator; and finally, you ignore it again while it rises.

After you've made it, the horizon expands exponentially—use it for Gramercy Tavern's legendary Monkey Bread (page 264), for treats like French Toast Sticks (page 267), or for a slew of sandwiches. This brioche is dense without being heavy, rich without being cloying, tender but strong enough to stand up to sandwich fillings. It repays the baker's efforts in all sorts of ways.

You will need a stand mixer.

# Basic Brioche

2 cups bread flour

2 tablespoons sugar

1 tablespoon instant yeast

⅓ cup whole milk, at room temperature

2 large eggs

¼ teaspoon kosher salt

12 tablespoons (1½ sticks) unsalted butter, softened

1 loaf

Put the bread flour, sugar, and yeast in the bowl of a stand mixer fitted with the paddle attachment. With the mixer on low speed, add the milk and eggs. After 1 minute, add the salt, then mix and knead the dough until it forms a smooth ball, 8 to 10 minutes. To test for doneness, stretch the dough: If you can pull it until it forms little windowpane shapes without tearing, it's ready.

With the mixer running, add a tablespoon-sized glob of butter and wait for it to be absorbed before you add the next one. Continue in the same way until all the butter has been incorporated.

Transfer the dough to a bowl. Cover with plastic wrap and refrigerate for at least 2 hours, or as long as overnight, to firm it.

When the dough comes out of the refrigerator, it will be the consistency of Play-Doh. Press it into a 9-x-5-inch loaf pan and let it rise in a warm (80- to 85-degree) place for 2 to 3 hours, until it has doubled in size and bounces back when touched with a fingertip. At a lower temperature, the bread will take longer to rise.

Preheat the oven to 350 degrees.

Bake the brioche until golden brown, 25 to 30 minutes. Cool on a rack. (*Well wrapped, the brioche will keep for up to 2 days at room temperature; it can be frozen for up to 2 weeks.*)

*No one ever tires of Gramercy Tavern pastry chef Nancy Olson's* version of monkey bread, essentially sweet rolls the size of golf balls that expand while they're wading in toffee sauce and cinnamon sugar to become puffy, chewy, slightly crunchy, slightly gooey globes of happiness. Maialino chef Nick Anderer, who ate his share when he worked at Gramercy, couldn't bear to be without them, which is why there was a *brioche caramellato* on his opening-day menu—Nancy's monkey bread reimagined for a Roman trattoria.

When it's time to dip the dough into the melted butter and cinnamon sugar, use Nancy's efficient "wet hand, dry hand" method. Pick up each piece of dough in one hand and roll it in the melted butter, then place it on the plate of cinnamon sugar. Use your other hand to roll it in the cinnamon sugar and place it in the baking pan.

# Monkey Bread

### For the toffee sauce

⅔ cup plus ½ cup heavy cream

1 cup packed dark brown sugar

2 tablespoons light corn syrup

6 tablespoons (¾ stick) unsalted butter

1 vanilla bean, split, seeds scraped out, seeds and pod reserved

½ teaspoon salt

Basic Brioche dough (page 262), refrigerated as directed

4 tablespoons (½ stick) unsalted butter, melted and cooled

1 cup sugar

1 tablespoon ground cinnamon

One 9-x-13-inch pan (20 pieces)

TO MAKE THE TOFFEE SAUCE: In a medium saucepan, combine the ⅔ cup cream, the brown sugar, corn syrup, butter, vanilla seeds and pod, and salt, bring to a boil over medium-high heat, and cook for a few minutes, stirring, until the sauce thickens. Add the remaining ½ cup cream, stir well, and remove from the heat. Discard the vanilla pod. (*The toffee sauce can be made up to 1 day ahead and refrigerated; rewarm over low heat.*)

TO ASSEMBLE THE MONKEY BREAD: Pour the warm toffee sauce over the bottom of a 9-x-13-inch baking pan.

Divide the brioche dough into 20 pieces, each about the size of a ping-pong ball. Pour the melted butter into a shallow dish. Mix the sugar and cinnamon in another shallow dish. Roll each ball of brioche dough in the melted butter and then in the cinnamon sugar, placing them side by side in the baking pan. Reserve the remaining cinnamon sugar.

Place the pan in a warm (80- to 85-degree) place and let the rolls rise until they have doubled in size and spring back when you press them, 2 to 3 hours. At a lower room temperature, the bread will take longer to rise.

Preheat the oven to 350 degrees.

Sprinkle the monkey bread with the reserved cinnamon sugar. Bake until dark golden brown, about 40 minutes. Remove from the oven and let sit for 40 minutes, until the sauce sets on the brioche. Serve warm or at room temperature.

## VARIATION: JAM OR NUTELLA ROLLS

Omit the toffee sauce. Divide the dough as directed for Monkey Bread. Flatten each piece slightly and place a teaspoon of jam or Nutella in the middle of it. Lift the edges of the dough up over the filling and pinch them together with your fingers. Place the dough balls in muffin tins seam side down and let rise in a warm (80- to 85-degree) place for 2 to 3 hours, until doubled in size. At a lower room temperature, the bread will take longer to rise. Bake at 350 degrees for 15 to 20 minutes, until golden brown.

*One of the basic tenets of family meal is, no waste.* At Union Square Cafe, day-old bread is sliced and made into sweetened battered French Toast Sticks. Serve these on their own for breakfast or brunch or for dessert with ice cream.

You can substitute ordinary white bread, but the result will not be as rich.

# French Toast Sticks

8 slices (¾-inch-thick) day-old brioche, homemade (page 262) or store-bought, or challah (see headnote)

### *For the batter*

2 cups all-purpose flour

1½ cups sugar

1½ teaspoons baking powder

½ teaspoon baking soda

½ teaspoon ground cinnamon

¼ teaspoon freshly grated nutmeg

Pinch of ground cloves

2 cups buttermilk

2 large eggs

½ teaspoon vanilla extract

Vegetable oil for deep-frying

Confectioners' sugar for dusting

Pure maple syrup for drizzling

**4 to 6 servings**

Cut each bread slice into thirds to make sticks.

TO MAKE THE BATTER: Combine all the dry ingredients in a large bowl.

Stir together the buttermilk, eggs, and vanilla in another bowl. Pour into the dry ingredients and fold together 10 times. The batter may be a little lumpy, but that's OK—don't overmix. Working in batches, immerse the bread sticks in the batter and let them sit for 2 to 3 minutes. Transfer to a rack set over a baking sheet to drain while you heat the oil.

In a large deep skillet or pot, heat about 1½ inches of vegetable oil over high heat until it reaches 350 degrees on a deep-fat thermometer. Working in batches, fry the bread sticks for 3 minutes, turn, and fry on the second side until golden brown. Drain on paper towels. Sprinkle with confectioners' sugar, drizzle with maple syrup, and serve immediately.

*Blue Smoke pastry chef Jennifer Giblin* grew up on homemade whole wheat bread. Her mother used to make a half dozen loaves at a time, using bread flour that she ground herself from hard red winter wheat. These days many markets offer an array of flours, and while red whole wheat flour gives you more of the familiar wheat-bread flavor, this recipe also works with white whole wheat flour, which has the same whole-grain health benefits.

Vital wheat gluten, a wheat protein, is the secret to this bread's great texture—the loaf is neither dense nor heavy, because the protein gives it the extra boost it needs to rise properly. Look for it in the baking aisle of a well-stocked market or health-food store.

Serve warm with butter and honey or jam, or toasted, or use as a terrific sandwich bread.

# Jenn's Mom's Whole Wheat Bread

1 tablespoon active dry yeast

3½ cups whole wheat flour, from hard red winter wheat, hard red spring wheat, or hard white wheat, plus more if necessary

1 tablespoon kosher salt

6 tablespoons vegetable oil

½ cup honey

2 tablespoons vital wheat gluten (see headnote)

Butter for the bowl and pan

1 loaf

In a small bowl, whisk together the yeast, ½ cup warm water, and ¼ cup of the flour. Set aside until the yeast bubbles and the mixture is spongy, about 15 minutes.

Put the remaining ingredients, except the butter, in the bowl of a stand mixer fitted with the dough hook. Add the yeast mixture and knead at low speed, adding a little more flour early in the process if the dough is too wet, for about 15 minutes, until the dough is still slightly sticky but holds its shape.

Lightly butter a large bowl. Put the dough in the bowl, cover with a kitchen towel, and let rise in a warm (80- to 85-degree) place until doubled in size; this may take up to 2 hours if the room is cool.

Preheat the oven to 350 degrees. Butter a 9-x-5-inch loaf pan.

On a well-floured surface, shape the bread into a loaf by pulling the edges over toward the center, and place it in the loaf pan, seam side down. Bake for about 45 minutes, or until the internal temperature reaches 190 degrees on an instant-read thermometer and the loaf is browned and sounds hollow when tapped. Remove the loaf from the pan and cool on a rack before slicing.

*This bread pudding from Maialino* starts with a single step that makes all the difference—soaking the bread in a savory custard rather than in plain milk, which gives the pudding a velvety texture and infuses it with more flavor. Bread pudding is so popular at family meal that it's made in three varieties: one with ham and cheese, another for vegetarians (both given here), and a third for dessert (page 284).

# Savory Bread Pudding Two Ways

Butter for the baking dish

4 large eggs

3 cups half-and-half

2 cups whole milk

12 ounces day-old sourdough bread or baguette, cut into ½-inch cubes (about 12 cups)

1 teaspoon chopped fresh rosemary

1 teaspoon chopped fresh thyme

1 teaspoon kosher salt

¼ teaspoon freshly ground black pepper

1 cup grated Parmigiano-Reggiano or Grana Padano

3 cups chopped cooked ham, sausage, or bacon or 4 cups coarsely chopped mixed cooked vegetables (such as spinach or other greens, mushrooms, bell peppers, caramelized onions, and/or asparagus)

6 to 8 servings

Preheat the oven to 375 degrees. Butter a 9-x-13-inch baking dish.

In a large bowl, whisk together the eggs, half-and-half, and milk. Add the bread and let soak for 20 minutes, tossing occasionally.

When the bread is thoroughly soaked, add the herbs, salt, pepper, cheese, and meat or vegetables. Toss until combined.

Transfer the bread mixture to the baking dish. Bake for 50 to 60 minutes, until the custard has set and the bread is browned and crisp at the edges. Let cool for 10 minutes before serving.

# Desserts

*When Gramercy Tavern pastry chef Nancy Olson was growing up,* her family made sundaes with homemade ice cream and homemade hot fudge.

Cooking the sauce over low heat and using a wooden spoon or nonmetal spatula will ensure that it is silky smooth.

# Hot Fudge Sauce

2 ounces unsweetened chocolate, chopped

2 tablespoons unsalted butter

1 tablespoon light corn syrup

¾ cup heavy cream

1⅓ cups packed dark brown sugar

½ teaspoon vanilla extract

¼ teaspoon kosher salt

**1½ cups**

Combine the chocolate, butter, and corn syrup in a medium saucepan and cook over low heat, stirring with a wooden spoon or a heatproof silicone spatula, until the chocolate and butter have melted. Add the cream and sugar, increase the heat to medium, and bring to a boil, stirring constantly to dissolve the sugar and keep the mixture from sticking to the bottom of the pan. Remove from the heat, stir in the vanilla and salt, and cool slightly.

If the fudge seems a little too thin once it's cooled, return it to the stove and boil it, stirring, until it thickens slightly. Or, if it's too thick, reduce the heat to low and add a little hot water, stirring, to thin it to the consistency you prefer. (*Once cooled, the sauce will keep, covered and refrigerated, for up to 1 week; reheat over low heat.*)

# The Dessert Heiress

In the dead-cold winters of North Dakota, the Olson family ate a lot of homemade ice cream, because Napoleon, a town of barely a thousand residents, was the kind of place that prized frugality. Nancy Olson, Gramercy Tavern's pastry chef since 2006, remembers her mother, a resourceful homemaker who wasn't about to pay for a bag of ice, filling empty milk cartons with water and setting them outside to freeze, for hand-cranked ice cream. Vanilla ice cream sundaes made with a hot fudge recipe handed down—along with the ice cream freezer—by her mother's godmother were a family ritual.

Nancy, a small perpetual-motion machine with light blond hair and skin as pale as a Midwestern snowscape, gravitates toward cobblers, cakes, and pies rather than sculpted sweets, but her versions of these classic desserts reflect a pastry chef's discipline and skill, informed by an infectious delight in the process. Her family's influence shows up everywhere on the menu. She has been baking apple pie in one form or other for over half her life, since she was fifteen, and the current version uses seven kinds of apples to ensure that each bite is different. The streusel-topped rhubarb tart is a descendant of a kuchen that her mother and godmother always made.

Nancy likes to spend time with the next generation and pass on the traditions that matter to her. She has already taught her five-year-old nephew how to work the hand-cranked ice cream freezer. She adopts the students at a New York City public school as her trainees a couple of times a year. And she prides herself on having a young team of pastry cooks—her "guys and girls"—who balance her expertise with their sheer energy.

If there is a lull in the action, it must be time for Monkey Bread, which Nancy may prepare for no reason at all, or because the Ramadan feast marking the end of fasting needs a dessert, or simply because it has been too long since she last made it. When the aroma of the brioche rolls baking in toffee sauce wafts through the ventilation system into the upstairs tavern room, people who have no business being near the basement pastry kitchen suddenly come up with compelling reasons to walk by, slowly. Nancy has been known to post a sign in the kitchen window telling when the Monkey Bread will be ready and how much will be available, but the staff tends to ignore the signs.

When the latest batch emerged from the oven, a member of the prep team appeared in the doorway, a supplicating smile on her face, holding out a napkin and a plastic knife. If she could have one piece—just one—she wheedled, she would go back and share it with another woman. Just one piece to share, please?

Works every time.

*This silky vanilla-flavored Italian custard,* which uses buttermilk for a slightly tangy flavor, is the perfect companion to a sweet and tart rhubarb and strawberry compote. The compote, in turn, is excellent as well with yogurt or ice cream.

Cristina Nastasi, a pastry cook at the Museum of Modern Art cafes, came up with the combination because there was plenty of rhubarb on hand and she had a free moment. For someone who's been baking ever since she can remember and whose e-mail moniker includes the word "sugar," making a new dessert is more fun than taking a break.

# Buttermilk Panna Cotta with Rhubarb-Strawberry Compote

2 teaspoons unflavored gelatin

1 cup heavy cream

½ cup sugar

½ teaspoon vanilla extract

2 cups buttermilk

Rhubarb-Strawberry Compote (recipe follows)

**6 servings**

In a small bowl, sprinkle the gelatin over ½ cup of the cream. Let stand until softened, about 5 minutes.

Bring the remaining ½ cup cream, the sugar, and vanilla to a simmer in a saucepan over medium-high heat, whisking to dissolve the sugar. Remove from the heat and let cool for 1 minute, then whisk in the cream-gelatin mixture until the gelatin dissolves. Stir in the buttermilk.

Strain the mixture through a fine-mesh strainer into a large measuring cup. Divide the mixture among six 4-ounce ramekins or pour into a small serving bowl. Cover with plastic wrap and refrigerate for at least 5 hours, until set. (*Well-wrapped, the panna cotta will keep for up to 3 days in the refrigerator.*)

Run a sharp knife around the edges of the ramekins and unmold the panna cotta onto plates, or serve it right in the ramekins or scoop out of the bowl. Top with the fruit compote.

# Rhubarb-Strawberry Compote

½ cup sugar

4 cups thinly sliced rhubarb

2 cups quartered hulled strawberries

**About 3 cups**

Preheat the oven to 325 degrees.

Combine the sugar and ½ cup water in a small saucepan and bring to a boil, stirring to dissolve the sugar. Remove from the heat.

Combine the rhubarb and sugar syrup in a 9-x-13-inch baking dish. Bake, uncovered, until the rhubarb is tender, about 15 minutes.

Add the strawberries, stir, and bake for 5 minutes longer, until the strawberries have softened. Let cool to room temperature, then refrigerate until ready to use. (*The compote will keep, covered and refrigerated, for up to 1 week.*)

*For Gramercy Tavern chef Michael Anthony,* this is the perfect summer dessert, meant to be eaten out of doors as the sun goes down. The peaches macerated in sugar and rosé wine can be put right into your guests' empty wineglasses; the offhandedness is the point.

Superfine sugar will dissolve more completely than regular sugar in the lemon juice and wine, but you can substitute ordinary sugar.

# Drunken Peaches

6 medium peaches, as ripe as possible, quartered and pitted

1 cup superfine sugar (see headnote)

¼ cup fresh lemon juice

1 vanilla bean, split, seeds scraped out, and seeds and pod reserved

1 750-ml bottle rosé

**4 to 6 servings**

In a large bowl, toss the peaches with the sugar, lemon juice, and the vanilla seeds and pod. Pour the wine over the fruit and let sit for 30 minutes.

Remove the vanilla pod. Divide the peaches and liquid among wineglasses and serve.

*Union Square Events pastry chef Dan Keehner* uses a thin layer of almond cream as the base for this fruit crisp and adds almonds to the crumb topping as well.

The crisp works all year long with a rotating roster of seasonal fruits: blueberries and blackberries; peaches alongside the plums and apricots; rhubarb and strawberries; or sour cherries, if you're lucky enough to live in a part of the country where they grow.

The key is to taste and adjust the sugar for the filling depending on what you choose. Very tart fruit, like rhubarb or sour cherries, will require more than ripe peaches will. Very juicy fruit may need more bread crumbs—or a spoon instead of a fork when you dig in. It's delicious with whipped cream, crème fraîche, or even sour cream.

You will find almond flour, or the slightly coarser almond meal, at a well-stocked market or health-food store. Either one works for the almond cream base layer, which is almost like a thin layer of cake when baked. It's the best of both worlds—the smooth texture of a creamy layer with a bit more structural integrity to support the fruit and crumb topping.

# Plum & Apricot Crisp with Almond Cream

### For the fruit filling

1½ pounds plums, pitted and cut into ½-inch slices (about 4 cups)

3 cups coarsely chopped apricots (about 1 pound)

¾ cup sugar

½ cup fresh bread crumbs

### For the almond cream

7 tablespoons unsalted butter, softened

½ cup sugar

1 cup almond flour or almond meal (see headnote)

¼ cup all-purpose flour

2 large eggs

½ teaspoon light rum (optional)

Preheat the oven to 325 degrees, with a rack in the middle.

TO MAKE THE FRUIT FILLING: Toss the fruit with the sugar in a large bowl. Allow to sit for 10 minutes, or until the juices start to run. Stir in the bread crumbs.

TO MAKE THE ALMOND CREAM: In a large bowl, with an electric mixer on medium speed, beat the butter and sugar together until pale yellow and fluffy, 3 to 5 minutes. On low speed, beat in the flours. Add the eggs one at a time and then the rum, if using, mixing well after each addition. Set aside.

### For the crumb topping

1¼ cups all-purpose flour

1 cup almond flour or almond meal

¾ cup lightly packed light brown sugar

⅓ cup raw sliced almonds

½ teaspoon salt

7 tablespoons unsalted butter, melted and cooled

**12 to 15 servings**

TO MAKE THE CRUMB TOPPING: Combine all the ingredients except the butter in a large bowl. Pour the butter over the top and stir with a fork or your fingers until the mixture forms large crumbs.

TO ASSEMBLE AND BAKE THE CRISP: Spread the almond cream in a thin layer over the bottom of a 9-x-13-inch baking dish. Top with the fruit filling and cover the fruit with the topping.

Bake for 30 to 45 minutes, until the crumble is golden brown and fruit juices bubble up at the edges of the pan. Let cool on a rack for at least 15 minutes.

Serve warm or at room temperature.

*A quick pastry dough* is patted into a baking dish and prebaked, then topped with a layer of dried fruit compote made with orange juice and with an almond crumble spiked with black pepper. This is a most adaptable and unusual sweet—enjoy it with morning coffee or to give new meaning to a cup of tea.

# Tabla Dried Fruit Compote Crumble

### For the pastry

10 tablespoons (1¼ sticks) unsalted butter, softened

½ cup sugar

1 large egg, beaten

1½ cups all-purpose flour

### For the compote

1 cup golden raisins

1 cup coarsely chopped dried apricots

1 cup coarsely chopped pitted dates

¼ cup sugar

½ cup fresh orange juice

1 teaspoon vanilla extract

1 teaspoon ground cinnamon

½ teaspoon salt

### For the black pepper crumble

1⅓ cups all-purpose flour

⅓ cup lightly packed brown sugar

⅓ cup chopped skin-on raw almonds

⅓ cup sugar

½ teaspoon freshly ground black pepper

Pinch of salt

½ cup Brown Butter (page 233), melted

Butter for the pan

**12 to 15 servings**

TO MAKE THE PASTRY: In a large bowl, with an electric mixer on medium-high speed, beat the butter and sugar until pale yellow and fluffy, 3 to 5 minutes. Beat in the egg. Reduce the speed to low, add the flour, and mix just until combined.

Press the dough into a 1-inch-thick disk, wrap it in plastic wrap, and refrigerate for at least 1 hour, or up to 6 hours.

TO MAKE THE COMPOTE: Combine all the ingredients and 1½ cups water in a medium saucepan, and cook over medium-low heat, stirring occasionally, until the fruit is tender but not falling apart, 15 to 20 minutes. Set aside to cool. (*The compote can be made up to 1 day ahead, covered, and refrigerated.*)

TO MAKE THE BLACK PEPPER CRUMBLE: Combine all the ingredients except the butter in a small bowl. Add the brown butter and toss with a fork just until blended; the mixture should look like coarse meal.

TO ASSEMBLE AND BAKE THE CRUMBLE: Preheat the oven to 375 degrees, with a rack in the middle. Butter a 9-x-13-inch baking pan. Remove the dough from the refrigerator and allow to stand for 10 minutes so that it softens slightly.

Press the pastry dough into the bottom of the baking pan. Line the dough with aluminum foil, leaving an overhang, and fill with pie weights, dried beans, or rice.

Bake for 20 minutes, or until the pastry is just set. Remove the pan from the oven and gently remove the weights and foil. Bake the crust for another 15 to 20 minutes, until golden brown. Cool on a rack. Reduce the oven temperature to 325 degrees.

When the crust is cool, gently spread the fruit compote on top. Sprinkle the crumble topping evenly over the compote. Bake for 30 minutes, or until the top is golden brown. Let cool for at least 15 minutes. Serve warm or at room temperature.

*At Blue Smoke,* the cheddar that is classically perched on top of a piece of apple pie goes directly into an oatmeal crumb topping, melts in the oven, and complements the tart filling in every mouthful.

# Apple-Cheddar Crisp

### For the filling

6 Golden Delicious or Granny Smith apples, peeled

1 tablespoon fresh lemon juice

3 tablespoons unsalted butter

3 tablespoons packed light brown sugar

½ vanilla bean, split

½ teaspoon ground cinnamon

Apple cider or water if needed

### For the crumb topping

1 cup all-purpose flour

1 cup grated sharp white cheddar

6 tablespoons (¾ stick) cold unsalted butter, cut into small cubes

½ cup sugar

¼ cup packed light brown sugar

½ cup old-fashioned rolled oats (not quick-cooking)

**12 to 15 servings**

Preheat the oven to 350 degrees, with a rack in the middle.

FOR THE FILLING: Halve the apples, core them and cut into ¼-inch-thick slices. Toss with the lemon juice.

Melt the butter in a large skillet over medium-high heat. Add the sugar and scrape in the vanilla seeds, stirring to combine. Add the apples, sprinkle the cinnamon over them, stir to coat, and cook, stirring, until the apples just begin to soften, 5 to 7 minutes. If the apples seem too dry, add a little cider to keep the mixture juicy. Remove from the heat.

FOR THE CRUMB TOPPING: In a medium bowl, with an electric mixer on low speed, mix all the ingredients until combined. Increase the speed to medium and mix just until the topping begins to form clumps; do not overmix.

TO ASSEMBLE AND BAKE THE CRISP: Spoon the apples and juices into a 9-x-13-inch baking dish. Sprinkle the topping evenly over the apples.

Bake until the topping is toasty and golden brown and the juices are bubbly, 25 to 35 minutes. Serve hot, at room temperature, or cold.

*The cooked custard sauce* in this bread pudding inspires it, literally, to new heights, so it exists in the perfect space between dense and airy. It's one of a series of bread puddings that have become a mainstay at Maialino.

The traditional method for custard sauce involves stirring a bit of the heated milk mixture into the eggs to warm them so that they don't scramble when they're added to the rest of the milk. In the unlikely event that the custard does curdle, immediately pour the mixture into a blender and blend at high speed to smooth it out.

You can use golden raisins or dried cranberries in place of the dried cherries.

# Custard Bread Pudding with Dried Cherries & Citrus Zest

Butter for the baking dish

4 large eggs

2 large egg yolks

5 cups half-and-half

¾ cup sugar

2 tablespoons grated orange zest

1 tablespoon grated lemon zest

¾ teaspoon ground cinnamon

¼ teaspoon freshly grated nutmeg

1¼ cups dried cherries (see headnote)

1 pound day-old leftover brioche, challah, or rustic white bread, cut into ½-inch cubes (about 9 cups)

**12 to 15 servings**

Preheat the oven to 325 degrees, with a rack in the middle. Butter a 9-x-13-inch baking dish.

Whisk together the eggs and yolks in a large bowl.

Combine the half-and-half, sugar, zests, cinnamon, and nutmeg in a medium saucepan and heat over medium heat, stirring to dissolve the sugar. Immediately reduce the heat to low. Add 1 cup of the warm half-and-half mixture, a few tablespoons at a time, to the eggs, whisking constantly to warm them slowly and keep them from curdling. Gradually whisk the egg mixture into the saucepan and cook, whisking constantly, until the custard thickens slightly, about 5 minutes. Remove from the heat.

Combine the dried cherries and the bread in the baking dish. Pour the custard over the bread and let sit for 15 minutes.

Bake for 1 hour, or until the custard has set and the top is golden brown and crisp at the edges. Serve the bread pudding warm or at room temperature.

*A menu staple, Blue Smoke's signature oatmeal-raisin cookies* often make their way onto the family meal table—or out the door as staffers head home late at night. The dough includes a couple of unexpected ingredients: unsweetened coconut flakes (available in health-food stores) and cornflakes, which add crunch and new flavor to the standard equation. Golden raisins instead of the traditional dark ones change up the results as well. Regardless of what kind of oatmeal cookie you're accustomed to making, you will want to try this version.

# Blue Smoke's Oatmeal-Raisin Cookies

2 cups all-purpose flour

¾ teaspoon salt

½ teaspoon baking soda

¼ teaspoon ground cinnamon

1 cup old-fashioned rolled oats (not quick-cooking)

¾ cup cornflakes, lightly crushed with a rolling pin

⅓ cup chopped unsweetened coconut flakes

¾ cup golden raisins

1¾ cups loosely packed light brown sugar

⅓ cup sugar

1½ teaspoons vanilla extract

12 tablespoons (1½ sticks) unsalted butter, melted and cooled

1 large egg

1 large egg yolk

**About 24 large cookies**

Preheat the oven to 325 degrees, with racks in the upper and lower thirds. Line two baking sheets with parchment paper.

Stir the flour, salt, baking soda, cinnamon, oats, cornflakes, coconut, and raisins together in a medium bowl with a wooden spoon.

Combine the sugars and vanilla extract in a large bowl and whisk in the butter. Add the egg and yolk and whisk until smooth.

Stir the flour mixture into the butter mixture and mix well.

Using an ice cream scoop or a large spoon, scoop up about 3 tablespoons of dough for each cookie and place 2 inches apart on the baking sheets. Flatten the cookies slightly—they should still be mounded.

Bake for 12 to 15 minutes, until the edges are golden brown and the centers are set. Cool on a rack. (*Stored in an airtight container, the cookies will keep for 3 to 4 days.*)

*This Blue Smoke standby* is the perfect combination of easy-to-make and delicious. The cookies bake up slightly crisp, the crunchy peanut butter adds more texture, and the straightforward process will reassure even a beginning baker.

# Blue Smoke's Peanut Butter Cookies

1¼ cups all-purpose flour

¾ teaspoon baking soda

½ teaspoon baking powder

½ teaspoon salt

8 tablespoons (1 stick) unsalted butter

½ cup crunchy peanut butter

½ cup sugar

½ cup packed light brown sugar

1 large egg

**About 36 cookies**

In a bowl, combine the flour, baking soda, baking powder, and salt and stir together with a fork or whisk.

In a large bowl, with an electric mixer on medium-high speed, beat together the butter, peanut butter, and sugars until creamy. Beat in the egg.

Beating on low speed, add the dry ingredients to the butter mixture, mixing just until blended. Cover and refrigerate for 1 hour to firm the dough.

Preheat the oven to 375 degrees, with racks in the upper and lower thirds. Line two baking sheets with parchment paper.

Scoop up tablespoons of dough, roll into 1-inch balls, and place 2 inches apart on the baking sheets. Gently flatten each ball with a fork, making a crisscross pattern. If the dough sticks to the fork, rinse it occasionally in warm water and dry as you proceed.

Bake for 10 to 12 minutes, or just until the cookies begin to brown; do not overbake. Cool on a rack. (*Stored in an airtight container, the cookies will keep for 3 to 4 days.*)

*The striking pinwheel design* of these cookies is far simpler to achieve than you might think: Set a sheet of vanilla dough on top of a sheet of chocolate dough, roll up into a log that's 2 inches in diameter, and refrigerate, then slice. Turning the log in sugar before you slice it gives the cookies a crunchy edge.

# Chocolate & Vanilla Swirl Cookies

### For the chocolate dough

10 tablespoons (1¼ sticks) unsalted butter, softened

¾ cup sugar

2 tablespoons milk

1 large egg

2 cups all-purpose flour

⅓ cup unsweetened cocoa powder

½ teaspoon baking soda

Pinch of salt

### For the vanilla dough

½ pound (2 sticks) unsalted butter, softened

½ cup sugar

1 large egg yolk

1 teaspoon vanilla extract

2 cups all-purpose flour

Pinch of salt

TO MAKE THE CHOCOLATE DOUGH: In a large bowl, with an electric mixer on medium-high speed, beat the butter and sugar until pale yellow and fluffy, 3 to 5 minutes. Beat in the milk and then the egg until smooth.

Mix together all the dry ingredients in a small bowl. On low speed, beat the dry ingredients into the butter mixture, mixing just until blended. Wrap the dough in plastic wrap and refrigerate for at least 30 minutes, or until firm. (*The dough can be refrigerated, covered, for up to 1 day or frozen, well wrapped, for up to 1 month; thaw in the refrigerator.*)

MEANWHILE, MAKE THE VANILLA DOUGH: In a large bowl, with the mixer on medium-high speed, beat the butter and sugar until pale yellow and fluffy, 3 to 5 minutes. Beat in the egg yolk and vanilla.

On low speed, beat in the flour and salt, mixing just until blended. Wrap the dough in plastic wrap and refrigerate for 30 minutes, or until firm. (*The dough can be refrigerated, covered, for up to 1 day or frozen, well wrapped, for up to 1 month; thaw in the refrigerator.*)

1 large egg, beaten

½ cup sugar

**About 36 cookies**

TO SHAPE THE DOUGH: On a floured surface, roll each piece of dough into a rectangle 6 to 7 inches wide and ⅛ inch thick. Brush the top of the chocolate dough with some of the beaten egg. Place the vanilla dough on top. Roll up together from the long side into a log and brush with the remaining beaten egg.

Spread the sugar on a dry cutting board or a large plate and roll the log in it to coat. Wrap the log in plastic wrap and chill until firm, at least 1 hour, or up to 1 day.

TO BAKE THE COOKIES: Preheat the oven to 350 degrees, with racks in the upper and lower thirds. Line two baking sheets with parchment paper.

Cut the chilled dough log into ¼-inch-thick slices and arrange them about 2 inches apart on the baking sheets. Bake for 4 minutes, then switch the pans front to back and top to bottom and bake for 4 to 6 minutes more, until the vanilla dough is lightly golden brown. With a spatula, transfer the cookies to a rack to cool completely. (*Stored in an airtight container, the cookies will keep for 3 to 4 days.*)

*The perfect dessert for a night* when you're not ready to make a pie but want something special, these bars from Eleven Madison Park feature a shortbread crust topped with a lemon custard. Make the topping while the bottom layer bakes, smooth it over the crust, finish baking, and you have a lemony, buttery dessert in no time—think of it as a lemon tart made in a baking pan.

# Lemon Bars

### For the dough

2 cups all-purpose flour

½ cup sugar

Pinch of salt

½ pound (2 sticks) unsalted butter, softened

### For the lemon topping

1½ cups sugar

¼ cup all-purpose flour

4 large eggs, beaten

Juice of 2 lemons

Confectioners' sugar for dusting

**24 squares**

TO MAKE THE DOUGH: Preheat the oven to 350 degrees, with a rack in the middle.

Whisk together the flour, sugar, and salt in a bowl. With your fingers, work in the butter until just combined. Press the dough evenly into the bottom of an ungreased 9-x-13-inch baking pan.

Bake for 20 to 25 minutes, or until the dough is firm and golden. Remove from the oven; leave the oven on.

MEANWHILE, MAKE THE LEMON TOPPING: Combine the sugar and flour in a medium bowl. Whisk in the eggs and lemon juice until no lumps remain.

Pour the mixture over the baked crust. Bake for 25 minutes, until the lemon topping is just barely set. The lemon topping will not look entirely set, but it will firm up as the lemon bars cool. Transfer the pan to a rack to cool.

Dust the top of the lemon bars with confectioners' sugar. Cut into 2-inch squares and remove the bars from the pan with a metal spatula. (*The bars will keep, covered and refrigerated, for up to 2 days.*)

*These yeasty little first cousins of a doughnut* are crisp on the sugar-coated outside, dense on the inside. Yes, you need a stand mixer to make the dough. No, you do not need to be a lifelong baker. The beignets might not be quite symmetrical the first couple of times, but close your eyes, take a bite, and you won't care.

Marc Aumont, the pastry chef of The Modern, grew up in an apartment above his father's chocolate and pastry shop in Chamonix-Mont-Blanc, France, and at eleven he was already learning how to make beignets by turning sheets of dough into necktie-shaped pastries.

You need to make the dough a day ahead.

# Beignets

### For the dough

1½ teaspoons active dry yeast

2¾ cups all-purpose flour

⅓ cup sugar

¾ teaspoon salt

3 large eggs

½ vanilla bean, split, seeds scraped out and reserved

4 tablespoons unsalted butter (½ stick), softened

Peanut oil for deep-frying

Confectioners' or granulated sugar for finishing

**12 to 15 beignets**

TO MAKE THE DOUGH: Sprinkle the yeast over 2 tablespoons warm water in a small bowl and let stand for 10 minutes, or until foamy.

Sift all of the dry ingredients together.

In the bowl of a stand mixer fitted with the dough hook, combine the dry ingredients, eggs, yeast mixture, and vanilla seeds and mix on medium speed for 10 to 15 minutes. The dough will stick to the bowl at first and then it will come together around the dough hook. Reduce the speed to low, add the butter, and mix until it is incorporated, about 5 minutes. Put the dough on a floured plate, cover with plastic wrap, and refrigerate for 24 hours.

TO MAKE THE BEIGNETS: Line a baking sheet with parchment paper. On a floured surface, roll out the dough to a ¼-inch-thick rectangle. Cut the dough into 2-x-4-inch rectangles. Make a 1-inch vertical slit in the center of each piece and tuck one end of the rectangle through the opening to make a twist. Arrange the beignets on the baking sheet and let rest for at least 10 minutes in the refrigerator, or up to 1 hour.

In a large deep saucepan, heat 2 inches of peanut oil over high heat until it reaches 350 degrees on a deep-fat thermometer. Fry the beignets 2 or 3 at a time, to avoid crowding, for about 2 minutes on each side, until golden brown. Remove with a slotted spoon and drain briefly on paper towels.

Roll the warm beignets in confectioners' sugar and serve immediately.

# The Artist

Marc Aumont, the pastry chef at The Modern, likes to take visitors downstairs to a locked steel-mesh storage unit that houses, among other things, a tall, heavy steel cabinet. With a small flourish, he opens the door to show off the display on the bottom shelf—a rodent wearing a jaunty smile and a beret perched, legs crossed, atop a very large wheel of cheese, the whole thing made of pulled sugar.

Marc, a second-generation baker and sugar artist, can often be found in his cubicle office near midnight once his restaurant work is done, sketching ideas for sugar sculptures, or in the kitchen making prototypes like the rat and cheese and preparing for competitions. He has a notebook he's kept since he was a teenager, full of recipes written in a spidery, precise script, along with line drawings of dishes, parts of dishes, ideas for future dishes, and shapes for sculptures. Something he spilled a long time ago has turned the edges of some words into a soft-focus blur; another spill has made the paper brittle. Marc has recorded not only his own creations and recipes, but also those of his father, who ran the family's pastry shop in Chamonix-Mont-Blanc, in the French Alps.

For Marc, dessert is never simply a matter of ten seasonal sweets on a menu, but a seemingly endless space, ripe for exploring. The Modern has one dessert menu, and the adjacent Bar Room has another. Still, Marc undertook a new project—a chocolate cart for the restaurant, which is wheeled tableside after dinner. It includes three tiers of handmade chocolates: some with nuts and some without; chocolates with fruit; chocolate in cookies and in shards; chocolates with different textures—crunchy, soft, smooth, and brittle; comfortingly familiar chocolates; and some with unanticipated flavor surprises, like a chocolate ganache bonbon flavored with saffron honey. On the cart's top shelf stand three life-sized masks, inscrutable faces made of chocolate.

Marc prides himself on having a team of sixteen, and he defends the number vigorously even though he knows other restaurants get by with eight or ten people or far fewer. Too small a group would reduce their activities to mere production, not invention. He wants to be able to focus on ideas he hasn't thought of yet, the chance to create something new from the same basic tools he's worked with for most of his life: butter, sugar, flour, chocolate, fruits, and nuts.

*Eleven Madison Park is not open for lunch on Saturday,* so there's time for a late-morning treat in addition to the regular afternoon family meal. The pastry staff came up with what's known simply as "Saturday morning coffee cake," two layers of streusel swirled throughout what is basically a very moist vanilla cake made with Greek yogurt.

# Streusel-Swirl Coffee Cake

### For the streusel

½ cup packed dark brown sugar

½ cup coarsely chopped walnuts

1 tablespoon ground cinnamon

### For the coffee cake

8 tablespoons (1 stick) unsalted butter, softened, plus butter for the pan

1¾ cups sugar

1 vanilla bean, split, seeds scraped out and reserved

3 large eggs

1¼ cups all-purpose flour

1½ teaspoons baking powder

½ teaspoon baking soda

1 teaspoon kosher salt

1 cup low-fat Greek yogurt

**12 to 15 servings**

TO MAKE THE STREUSEL: Combine all of the ingredients in a small bowl. Set aside.

TO MAKE THE COFFEE CAKE: Preheat the oven to 350 degrees, with a rack in the middle. Lightly butter a 9-x-13-inch baking pan and line it with parchment paper.

In a large bowl, with an electric mixer on medium-high speed, beat the butter and sugar with the vanilla seeds until pale yellow and fluffy, 3 to 5 minutes. Beat in the eggs one at a time, mixing after each addition until the batter is smooth.

In a small bowl, whisk together the dry ingredients. On low speed, add one third of the yogurt to the butter mixture, followed by one third of the dry ingredients, and continue to alternate them, ending with the dry ingredients and scraping down the sides of the bowl after each addition.

Pour half of the batter into the baking pan and spread it evenly with a rubber spatula. Top with half of the streusel. Add the remaining batter, smooth again, and top with the remaining streusel. With a table knife, marble the streusel through the cake, starting at one end and weaving back and forth through the batter until you get to the other end.

Bake for 40 to 45 minutes, or until a toothpick or cake tester inserted into the center comes out clean. Cool for 10 to 15 minutes in the pan on a rack.

Serve the coffee cake directly from the pan. Or run a knife around the edges of the pan, turn the cake out onto the rack, and invert a large platter over the cake, then invert a second time so that it is right side up, and serve. (*The coffee cake will keep, covered, for 2 days at room temperature and up to 1 week in the refrigerator.*)

*Maialino chef Nick Anderer* says that he and his two brothers presented a daily challenge to his mother at the table. "*Gallons* of milk" every day is how he remembers their level of consumption. Mia Anderer's desire to keep her family happy and well fed yielded specialties like this simple apple cake, heavy on the fruit, made moist and slightly tart by the addition of orange juice. It became an instant tradition the first time she served it.

The batter goes into a tube pan in alternating layers with cinnamon-and-sugar-coated apples, and it rises around the apples as it bakes, leaving one golden layer of fruit in the middle of the cake and another at the top, with a bit of crust at the edges. The cake is the perfect accompaniment to an afternoon cup of tea and a great foundation for ice cream. It keeps well for days.

# Apple & Orange Cake

Butter for the pan

6 tart apples, such as Braeburn or Granny Smith, peeled, cored, and cut into 1-inch chunks

5 tablespoons sugar

2 teaspoons ground cinnamon

### For the batter

3 cups all-purpose flour

2 cups sugar

1 teaspoon baking powder

1 teaspoon kosher salt

4 large eggs

1 cup vegetable oil

¼ cup fresh orange juice

2½ teaspoons vanilla extract

**12 servings**

Preheat the oven to 350 degrees, with a rack in the middle. Butter a 10-inch tube pan and line the bottom with a ring of parchment paper.

In a large bowl, toss the apples with the sugar and cinnamon and set aside.

TO MAKE THE BATTER: In a medium bowl, whisk together the dry ingredients.

In a large bowl, whisk together the remaining ingredients. With an electric mixer on medium speed, gradually beat in the dry ingredients.

Spread half of the batter evenly in the prepared pan and scatter half of the apples over the top. Add the remaining batter, spreading it evenly, and finish with the rest of the apples. Bake for 1½ hours. Cool completely on a rack.

Run a knife around the sides and center tube of the pan and invert the cake onto the rack. Invert again onto a serving plate. (*The cake will keep, well wrapped and refrigerated, for several days.*)

*This chocolate sponge cake* filled with chocolate mousse and rolled up like a jelly roll offers the home baker lots of options. Serve it with berries or sprinkled with nuts. Or substitute softened ice cream for the mousse filling and freeze for an ice cream cake. Think of the cake layer as a delicious blank canvas.

The cake requires a methodical approach, but Maialino pastry chef Rachel Binder's recipe includes helpful tips to guide you to success, like rolling the cake up in a kitchen towel to prevent it from drying out while you make the filling.

# Double-Chocolate Mousse Cake

### For the cake

¼ cup all-purpose flour

¼ cup unsweetened cocoa powder

1 teaspoon baking powder

5 large eggs, separated

1 cup sugar

1 teaspoon vanilla extract

Confectioners' sugar for sprinkling

### For the chocolate mousse

12 ounces bittersweet chocolate, chopped

½ cup boiling water

5 large eggs, separated

3 tablespoons brandy or other liqueur, such as Grand Marnier or Cointreau

**8 to 12 servings**

TO MAKE THE CAKE: Preheat the oven to 350 degrees, with a rack in the center. Line an 11-x-17-inch baking sheet with parchment paper.

Whisk together the flour, cocoa, and baking powder in a bowl Put the egg whites in a large bowl and, with an electric mixer on medium speed, gradually beat in ½ cup of the sugar. Increase the speed to high and beat until stiff peaks form.

Put the egg yolks in another large bowl and, with the mixer on medium speed, gradually beat in the remaining ½ cup sugar. Increase the speed to high and beat until the mixture is thickened. Beat in 1½ tablespoons cold water and the vanilla.

Fold one third of the egg whites into the egg yolks. Sift one third of the dry ingredients over the yolks. Gently fold the remaining egg whites into the yolk mixture. Sift the remaining dry ingredients over the top and fold in gently.

Scrape the batter onto the baking sheet and spread it evenly. Bake for 20 minutes, or until the cake springs back when touched lightly. Cool the cake in the pan on a rack for 5 minutes.

Lightly sprinkle a clean kitchen towel with confectioners' sugar and turn the cake out onto it. Remove the parchment paper. Starting from a short end, roll up the cake in the towel. Refrigerate while you make the mousse.

TO MAKE THE CHOCOLATE MOUSSE: Process the chocolate in a food processor for 5 seconds, or until finely chopped. With the motor running, slowly add the boiling water and continue to process until the chocolate is completely melted. Add the egg yolks one at a time, blending well, and then add the brandy. Transfer to a large bowl.

# The Perfectionist

Rachel Binder's grandmothers did not cook like pastry chefs.

"Grandma, how long do you cook this?"

"Until you go to sleep."

"Grandma, how many cookies does this make?"

"Enough to fill the jar."

Rachel, the pastry chef of Maialino, inherited her grandmothers' enthusiasm but not their approach. She is all about precision, and she runs her spare, small pastry kitchen, a quiet oasis off to the side of the main kitchen, like a cross between a science lab and a temple of sweets.

She resembles nothing so much as a little girl playing dress-up: Her chef's pants are baggy and too long, even with the cuffs rolled up a couple of times, there is room to spare inside her white chef's jacket, and her clogs look like they belong to someone bigger. But she lets people know that any first impression based on size is way off; she is not a diminutive presence. Everyone here calls her Rocky, because the proper Hebrew pronunciation of "ch" is not so easy to master, and Rocky, who grew up in Israel, prefers the nickname to the softer and, to her, incorrect Americanized pronunciation.

She checks every item going into or out of the pastry kitchen, adjusting, suggesting, evaluating, refining. When a cook carried in a sheet pan of just-baked chocolate biscotti and carefully cut two cookies a half inch thick from one of the loaves, she consulted with Rocky about whether they were thick enough and done. Rocky tapped an expert finger along the top of the loaf, gauging the feel and the sound and pronounced judgment: one more minute.

As the breakfast rush started to subside, she went on the hunt for a sous chef who she'd been told had "borrowed" a flat of strawberries, with the air of someone who knows her cause is just and is determined to prevail. Rocky had been a pastry intern at Union Square Cafe when Michael Romano still ran the kitchen, and she recalled the level of perfection he demanded from his staff for items big and small.

"I'd be standing there when he came over to the pastry kitchen," she said, with an appreciative shiver. "He'd inspect the hamburger buns, the biscotti, and he'd want to know, 'Why is this like this?' The pastry chef said to me, 'I don't want to hear that Michael Romano is not satisfied.'" Ever since, Rocky has carried the same expectations with her, channeling that experience into everything from the proper way to slice bread to trial-and-error testings devoted to developing a perfect risotto ice cream.

In another large bowl, with an electric mixer on medium speed, beat the egg whites until stiff peaks form.

Stir about one quarter of the egg whites into the chocolate mixture to lighten. Fold in the remaining whites.

TO ASSEMBLE THE CAKE: Unroll the cake and spread the chocolate mousse over the top, leaving a ½-inch margin around the sides. Gently roll up the cake again. Wrap in plastic wrap and refrigerate for at least 4 hours, or as long as overnight.

Cut the cake into slices and serve.

*The winner of The Modern's first annual apple pie competition,* front-of-the-house division, is composed of a sweet crust flavored with lemon and ginger, an apple puree with spices and molasses, and a layer of pear slices caramelized with sugar and rum, topped with a sprinkling of sugared pecans. Its proud creator is general manager Dino Lavorini, who learned to make pastry during a restaurant apprenticeship in Florence, Italy, before he decided that the front of the house was where he really belonged.

# Prizewinning Apple & Pear Tart

### For the crust

2⅔ cups all-purpose flour

⅔ cup plus 2 tablespoons confectioners' sugar

12 tablespoons (1½ sticks) cold unsalted butter, diced

1 large egg

1 large egg yolk

Grated zest of 2 lemons

Heaping ½ teaspoon grated peeled fresh ginger

Butter and flour for the pan

1 large egg, beaten

TO MAKE THE CRUST: Sift together the flour and confectioners' sugar into a large bowl. Using two knives or your fingers, cut in the butter until the dough resembles coarse meal.

In a small bowl, beat the egg and yolk with the lemon zest and ginger. Mix the egg mixture with the flour-butter mixture using your fingers or a fork; do not overmix. Form the dough into a 1-inch-thick disk, wrap it in plastic wrap, and refrigerate for at least 1 hour, or as long as overnight.

TO BAKE THE TART SHELL: Butter and flour a 10-inch fluted tart pan with a removable bottom and put it in the refrigerator. Remove the dough from the refrigerator and let it rest, unwrapped, for 10 minutes.

Lightly flour a large cutting board or work surface. Working quickly, roll the dough out to a 12-inch round, ¼ inch thick. Roll the dough up around the rolling pin and carefully unroll it into the tart pan. Gently fit it into the pan, pressing the dough against the sides of the pan. Trim the excess dough and prick holes in the bottom of the crust in a few places with a fork. Cover the tart shell with plastic wrap and refrigerate for at least 30 minutes, or up to 1 day.

Preheat the oven to 375 degrees.

Line the tart shell with aluminum foil, leaving an overhang. Fill with pie weights, dried beans, or rice. Bake for 15 minutes, or until the dough is just set.

Remove from the oven and reduce the heat to 325 degrees. Carefully remove the weights and foil and bake the crust until golden, 15 to 20 minutes longer. Remove from the oven and brush the tart shell with the beaten egg. Set the pan on a rack to cool.

### For the apple filling

3 tart apples, such as Braeburn or Granny Smith, peeled, cored, and coarsely chopped

Juice of 1 lemon

2 tablespoons unsalted butter

¼ cup packed light brown sugar

½ teaspoon grated peeled fresh ginger

½ teaspoon ground cinnamon

¼ teaspoon freshly grated nutmeg

1 tablespoon molasses

### For the caramelized pears

2 tablespoons unsalted butter

¼ cup packed light brown sugar

2 tablespoons sugar

3 Bartlett pears, peeled, cored, and sliced top to bottom into ¼-inch-thick slices

3 tablespoons dark rum

### For the candied pecans

¼ cup sugar

1 cup coarsely chopped pecans

¼ cup quince or apricot jelly

**10 to 12 servings**

TO MAKE THE APPLE FILLING: Toss the apples with the lemon juice in a bowl.

Melt the butter in a medium skillet over medium heat. Stir in the brown sugar. When the butter and sugar are bubbling, add the apples, ginger, cinnamon, and nutmeg and cook, stirring frequently, until the apples are soft, 8 to 10 minutes. Stir in the molasses, remove from the heat, and cool.

Transfer the apple mixture to a food processor and pulse just until it is a coarse puree with some bits of fruit; be careful not to overprocess to applesauce. (*The puree can be made up to 2 days ahead, covered, and refrigerated.*)

TO MAKE THE CARAMELIZED PEARS: Melt the butter in a large skillet over high heat. Stir in both sugars and pears and cook, stirring gently, to soften the pears and evaporate any juice they may throw off, about 5 minutes. Add the rum and cook until the pears are caramelized, 3 to 5 minutes. Remove from the heat.

Line a baking sheet with parchment paper. Gently place the pear slices on the baking sheet to cool. Cover and refrigerate while you make the pecans. (*The pears can be made up to 1 day ahead.*)

TO MAKE THE CANDIED PECANS: Line a baking sheet with parchment paper. Bring the sugar and ¼ cup water to a boil in a small saucepan, stirring to dissolve the sugar, then boil to reduce by half, about 2 minutes. Reduce the heat to medium, add the pecans, and stir constantly with a wooden spoon until all the remaining liquid is gone and the pecans are glazed. Remove from the heat, spread the pecans on the baking sheet, separating clumps, and let cool.

TO ASSEMBLE THE TART: Spread the apple puree in the baked tart shell. Arrange the pear slices on top of the puree in concentric circles, overlapping them slightly, starting at the outer edge and working toward the center.

Heat the jelly in a small saucepan over low heat, stirring until melted and smooth. Carefully brush a thin layer of jelly over the pears. Sprinkle the pecans on top of the pears. Remove the sides of the pan and serve at room temperature.

# The Pie Contest

The first annual apple pie competition between the front-of-the-house and back-of-the-house staffs of The Modern was a serious affair. Eleven anonymous entries sat on a long display table in the restaurant's private dining room, each one identified only by a number and the pie's name, with the odd numbers assigned to desserts made by the dining room staff and the even numbers prepared by the cooks.

1. Betty Crocker's all-American apple pie
2. Spiced apple pie with Maker's Mark and spiced pecans
3. Pommes-pear with pecans
4. Apple pie with caramelized walnuts
5. Gâteau Mont-Michel
6. Apple-pear-rosemary galette
7. Napa Valley apple pie with Cabernet-caramel sauce and currants
8. Maker's Mark apple pie with caramelized almonds
9. Salted caramel and rum apple crisp
10. Apple-cranberry pie with marzipan almonds
11. Individual apple tart lattice cups

And at the number 12 spot, an empty space. A kitchen staffer rushed in at the last minute with a pie to fill it, but one of the contest organizers intercepted her at the door.

Anonymity was essential to avoid any hint of favoritism.

"It doesn't have a name," whispered the contestant.

"What's in it?"

"Brown butter and sage."

"OK, then," said the organizer as the pie was whisked away into place. "It's brown butter and sage apple pie."

The judging panel included chef Gabriel Kreuther and pastry chef Marc Aumont, both of The Modern, who stood at the back of the room chatting in French, trying to avoid overhearing who had made what.

A pastry staffer cut three sample slivers at a time for the judges, who tasted, stared into the far distance, considered, made notes, and moved on to the next one. Twelve samples later, the room was full of staffers lured by the promise of slices of leftover pie, the organizers had left the room to tally the judges' votes, and the judges were trying to rally themselves for the impending dinner service. A stand of toqued cooks huddled near the windows, while a group of dining room staffers eyed them from across the room.

When the organizers returned, they had three winners to announce—the best front-of-the-house entry, best kitchen-staff creation, and overall winner. The grand prize went to pie number 8, the Maker's Mark apple pie with caramelized almonds, made by a diminutive pastry chef who accepted the honor with a royal wave to the crowd.

*Sunny Raymond, the Union Square Cafe pastry chef,* puts this cake together in about 15 minutes, but figuring it out in the first place took several phone calls back and forth to her grandfather in Saint Lucia. He made the cake when Sunny was growing up but never used a recipe. "It was always a little bit of this and some of that," Sunny says. "The best part is the edges, which are a bit crunchy and taste like brown butter. West Indians love the crust on their cakes, but the center of this one stays moist and fluffy." Sunny's grandfather made his cake with coconuts that grew on the property.

# Quick Coconut Cake

¾ pound (3 sticks) unsalted butter, softened, plus butter for the pan

2 cups all-purpose flour, plus flour for the pan

2 cups sweetened shredded coconut

2 teaspoons baking powder

1 teaspoon salt

2 cups sugar

4 large eggs, at room temperature

2 teaspoons vanilla extract

1 teaspoon coconut extract

**8 to 12 servings**

Preheat the oven to 350 degrees, with a rack in the middle. Butter and flour a 9-inch cake pan, line it with parchment paper, and butter the parchment.

Put the coconut on a baking sheet and toast in the oven for 8 to 10 minutes, stirring once or twice, until light brown. Cool. Leave the oven on.

Whisk together the flour, baking powder, salt, and coconut in a bowl.

In a large bowl, with an electric mixer on medium-high speed, beat the butter and sugar until pale yellow and fluffy, about 5 minutes, stopping to scrape down the sides of the bowl. Add the eggs one at a time, beating for 1 minute after each one. Beat in the vanilla and coconut extracts. On low speed, add half the dry ingredients and mix briefly, then add the rest and mix just until combined.

Pour the batter into the cake pan and place the pan on a baking sheet. Bake for 1 hour to 1 hour and 15 minutes, or until a toothpick or cake tester inserted into the middle comes out clean (cover the cake with aluminum foil if it browns too quickly). Cool completely on a rack.

Run a knife around the sides of the pan to loosen the cake and invert it onto the rack. Invert again onto a serving plate. (*The cake will keep, covered, for up to 2 days.*)

# The Sisters

On a tough day around Thanksgiving, when Blue Smoke's whole-pie business can spike to 200 a day, or on Super Bowl Sunday, when a never-ending parade of take-out meals rolls out the door, the pastry kitchen is an endless workout. Bend, lift, stretch, ache a little bit, fill the tall standing racks with trays of sweets and breads, and begin again when someone empties them. But it's all dessert: By the time pastry chefs hit midlife, they are as likely to have memorized the Weight Watchers point system as they are to know a cookie recipe by heart.

Between them, Jennifer Giblin and Michiko Cinar have made desserts for decades, Jenn at Eleven Madison Park and Tabla, Michiko at Tabla, Union Square Cafe, and back at Tabla. They worked together there for four years and then both moved to Blue Smoke when it opened in 2002. They have in common a professional left turn often seen in kitchens: Jennifer had dreamed of being a police officer, while Michiko had done event planning for a nonprofit group before the desire to bake elbowed everything else out of the way.

Historically women gravitated toward pastry because the hours seemed less punishing than a cook's, since desserts were made during the day, leaving evenings free. Now that diners expect made-to-order desserts, only the senior members of the team get to go home at a more reasonable hour—and although they can, Jennifer and Michiko often linger anyhow, at least for a while. The pastry station is a quieter, more conversational wing of the large basement kitchen, where friendships form to the hum of a stand mixer and are defined by years of shared experience.

"I have a different relationship with each person here," Jennifer said. "I'm the mom to some. I'm sister to Michiko as well as friend. That transcends the place."

# Drinks

# The Expert

Juliette Pope stood before the Gramercy Tavern front-of-the-house staff and inhaled the scent of a glass of white wine. It was mystery-bottle night, a weekly exercise run by the restaurant's beverage director, who knows that endless lectures are not as engaging as the occasional well-informed guessing game.

The bottle stood on the sideboard, swathed in a black napkin. Staffers swirled, sniffed, and sipped their one-inch samples and tried to figure out what they were drinking. If they could analyze the elements, they'd be better able to describe it to a diner.

Juliette, a tall, slender woman who favors dark unadorned suits and a ponytail with a surgical center part, has been at Gramercy Tavern for more than fifteen years, in every capacity—line cook, pastry cook, waiter, captain, manager for ten years, beverage director for seven—and she was a cook at Union Square Cafe before that. She had arrived at the Cafe with a culinary school diploma and a single cooking entry on her résumé and moved up the ladder in the kitchen there and again at Gramercy Tavern—and then gave it up for front-of-the-house service, working her way up a second time. Now she can talk about all thirty of the wines by the glass and all five hundred bottles in Gramercy Tavern's inventory with enough familiarity to advise a server who wants to help a guest decide what to order.

When Juliette heard murmuring from a back table, she asked whether someone there had an idea as to the wine's identity.

"Sauvignon Blanc?" said one server, with great hesitation.

"A Gewürztraminer," someone else said, with more confidence.

"Possibly a very taut, austere Gewürztraminer," Juliette allowed, "in terms of taste. But not aromatically."

New or Old World? Everyone but two long-term servers said Old.

Minority ruled, as it turned out. Juliette unwrapped the bottle and held it aloft so that everyone could see. It was a Sauvignon Blanc from near the Russian River in northern California, an area that is unusually warm for the region, and so produces uncharacteristic wines.

The staffer who had guessed Sauvignon Blanc correctly was one of her "cellar rats," who show up at seven o'clock every morning to check and replenish the stock. This was his last night, because he was going back to college, and Juliette found herself feeling a little wistful—tomorrow she had to find a replacement who would be as willing to learn as he had been, the way she herself had been when she joined the company.

*Since family meal is an infinite opportunity for a staffer to shine,* it was inevitable that people would eventually get around to making beverages. Maialino staffers favor bright fruit drinks like this limeade as a refreshing accompaniment to the afternoon meal.

Thanks to frozen cherries and cherry juice, available in health-food stores, the cherry limeade works year-round, but fresh cherries in season add even more flavor, and you can drop some—or some pomegranate seeds, for that version—into the pitcher to make the drink even more beautiful to look at. Use these amounts as a template and adapt the proportions of fruit juice, sugar, and water to your taste preferences.

# Cherry or Pomegranate Limeade

2 limes, cut into eighths

1 cup fresh Bing cherries, crushed or cut in half and pits removed

2 cups sugar

2 cups fresh lime juice (from about 16 limes), or more to taste

2 cups cherry juice (see headnote) or pomegranate juice (such as POM)

**8 cups**

In a pitcher, using a wooden spoon, muddle (mash) the limes, cherries, and sugar together. Stir in the lime juice, 4 cups cold water, and the fruit juice. Taste and add more lime juice if you want to make the drink more tart or add more water to dilute.

Chill and serve over ice.

*Agua fresca (Spanish for "fresh water")* is a broad category that encompasses an array of cold drinks that incorporate fruit, or cereals, or seeds. Thanks to fresh pineapple and lemon juice, this one veers toward tart, while cucumber provides a cool vegetal note for contrast. Consider this recipe a starting point, and adjust the amount of simple syrup to your taste.

While family meal at the restaurants is nonalcoholic, this pairs nicely with rum.

# Pineapple-Cucumber Agua Fresca

5 tablespoons sugar

1 pineapple, peeled, quartered, cored, and cut into large chunks

2 seedless cucumbers, peeled and cut into large chunks

½ cup fresh lemon juice

1½ teaspoons salt

**About 6 cups**

To make the simple syrup, combine the sugar and 5 tablespoons water in a small saucepan and bring to a boil, stirring to dissolve the sugar. Remove from the heat and cool.

Working in batches, puree the pineapple and cucumbers with 4 cups cold water, the simple syrup, lemon juice, and salt in a blender or food processor until smooth. Strain through a fine-mesh strainer into a pitcher or bowl and refrigerate.

Serve over ice.

*Hibiscus flower petals,* which you can buy dried at health-food stores or Latin markets, are not the same thing as hibiscus tea. Known as *flor de Jamaica*, the flowers are used in Mexican, Caribbean, and North African cuisine. This recipe infuses hot water with the flower petals, cinnamon, and allspice. The refreshing result is brisk and sweet and a beautiful deep reddish purple. It mingles happily with either sparkling water or white wine.

# Hibiscus Cooler

2 ounces dried hibiscus flower petals (1 cup loosely packed; see headnote)

⅔ cup sugar

1 cinnamon stick

4 allspice berries

3 cups sparkling water or one 750-ml bottle white wine

1 small orange, cut into thin slices

1 lime, cut into thin slices

**8 to 10 cups**

Combine 4 cups water, the hibiscus petals, sugar, cinnamon, and allspice in a medium nonreactive saucepan and bring to a boil. Remove from the heat and let the ingredients steep for 20 minutes.

Strain the mixture through a fine-mesh strainer into a large pitcher. Add 4 cups cold water and chill until cold.

To serve, add the sparkling water and garnish with the orange and lime slices.

# Finding Home

The morning after Dino Lavorini, The Modern's general manager, got his MBA from the University of Pittsburgh, he woke up to a disconcerting thought: "I don't want to do any of the things I just studied. I just want to open a restaurant."

He had tried for years to leave behind the memories of a grandmother who tended a two-acre garden just blocks from his parents' home in Butler, Pennsylvania, of his father's smaller garden and of his mother's potpies and home-canned fruits and vegetables. His father was Italian, his mother Pennsylvania Dutch, and their cultures intersected in the kitchen. Dino's main childhood memory is of abundant food on the table. Like any child looking for autonomy, he set off to avoid what felt like destiny.

He decided to be a pediatrician but never got to pre-med, switching to international business and Italian studies. He headed for California and got a job driving the Oscar Mayer Wienermobile and was at the wheel when the vehicle made its New York City debut at Madison Square Garden. But being the official Wienermobile spokesperson, sitting in the midsection of a motorized promotional hot dog, did not feel like the start of anything big. So Dino took a job in financial services that lasted less than half a year, until he left for a two-week Italian vacation and didn't come back. He taught English to Italian businessmen in Florence to fund an unpaid apprenticeship at a little restaurant at the edge of the Piazza Santa Croce, which led to a James Beard Foundation scholarship to attend culinary school there.

Dino came home armed with a new ability to cook and a special love of pastry, but no idea what to do, so he tried a second time to become someone else. He enrolled in the University of Pittsburgh, got his graduate business degree, and then promptly turned his back on that version of the future. Finally he gave in to what had always been true—he wanted to work in restaurants.

When The Modern opened in 2005, Dino became its maître d', and then, several job leaps later, the general manager. The only link between this life and the one he discarded is his crisp white shirt, tie, and trim dark suit—it isn't hard to imagine him striding down the hallway of some financial outfit, minus the smile on his face. When he gathers his staff at The Modern for their morning meeting, it is clear that he enjoys talking about a new wine on the list more than explaining the details of a new clock-in policy. Business is part of his life, but it's no longer an end in itself.

Dino considers himself a restaurant marathoner, "not one of those people who works three months here, six months there," he says, "but a professional working with other professionals." Now he and his father trade joking e-mails about their respective cuisines, about his father's love of hearty pasta over the trendy ramps that diners at The Modern might prefer, and Dino has filled the small terrace outside his apartment with his own flourishing third-generation vegetable garden.

# The Next Chapter

Learning is in Sam Lipp's DNA—both his parents are science teachers—so when he started out at Maialino, he split his time between tutoring the front-of-the-house staff in beverage service and absorbing every lesson that came his way. During his tenure as assistant general manager, his style was not unlike that of a favorite high school teacher whose infectious energy eventually gets even the most reluctant member of the class involved.

For his efforts, he got a trickier assignment, a promotion to general manager at Union Square Cafe, the company's mother ship, which had opened around the time Sam started kindergarten. Union Square Cafe is a restaurant cozy with regulars, and part of his job was to satisfy those guests while attracting newcomers, a delicate exercise. He started out in a headlong blur, trying to learn everything he could firsthand, which meant that he might be stationed at the door at the bar in suit, dress shirt, and tie or found in his shirtsleeves running plates like any server on a busy night.

Sam dreamed of someday returning to Madison, Wisconsin, with his wife, to open his own place: great steaks, chops, and roasts, all of it elevated by what he'd learned in New York. But then the company made his mandate at Union Square Cafe official by naming him a managing partner, along with chef partner Carmen Quagliata. Together, they've embarked on a new project, figuring out what the next iteration of the venerable restaurant should be, as well as how to make it happen.

The curriculum in the coming years will include crash courses in economics, real estate, and kitchen design, as well as further studies in hospitality. Madison will be where Sam goes to visit on the rare occasions when he has time to take a trip.

# Saying Good-Bye

Sometimes, of course, family members leave home. A sous chef decides it might be better to be a private chef; a chef's assistant falls in love with a waiter who is accepted to graduate school in Pennsylvania. People burn out, or are offered jobs with a shorter commute, or leave simply because they have the sense that it is time. Real families watch their kids leave home assuming that they'll come back, at least to visit, but departures in a restaurant family can be permanent, so people say good-bye without knowing whether or when someone will return.

On these occasions, family meal is a send-off with its own set of rules, which usually involves allowing the departing staffer to choose the menu, a round of short speeches during which no one is supposed to cry, and, occasionally, the announcement of the name of the nearby bar where festivities will continue after the end of the shift.

Hoon Song started as a sous chef at Maialino on the day it opened, and he supervised the day shift until the Friday that was his last day. For a frenetic year and a half, he'd spent more time with his restaurant family than with his wife and toddler, and now he needed to catch his breath and figure out what was next. For his final family meal, he requested Cajun food, which kept sous chef Jean-Paul Bourgeois in the kitchen until the last minute, channeling his feelings into jambalaya, corn bread, and biscuits, while other cooks turned out fried green tomatoes and fresh fruit salad, and Rachel Binder's pastry team made three big pineapple upside-down cakes.

At four o'clock sharp, the line started to form in the back of the dining room—everyone but Hoon and Jean-Paul. The object of the celebration was downstairs, and theories about his absence ran from his practicing his speech to being too shy for all this attention. As for Jean-Paul, he never gets in line for his own meals until everyone else has been served.

When the two finally appeared and everyone sat down to eat, the official ceremony got under way. Chef Nick Anderer and then–general manager Terry Coughlin peppered their speeches with jokes about Hoon's food-without-borders notions of what ought to be on the menu; his breakneck, elliptical enthusiasms; and his creative relationship to English, his second language. Lena Ciardullo, who had worked with Hoon since Maialino opened, didn't break the rule about not crying when she spoke, but she bent it rather dramatically. Jean-Paul barely got a sentence out before his voice cracked, which he attributed to being nervous.

Hoon attempted to restore equilibrium. "I didn't hear anything any of you had to say," he began, "because I was thinking about my own speech." He got a big laugh, but his face crumpled. "I'm not crying," he insisted, wiping his eyes, before the room erupted in applause.

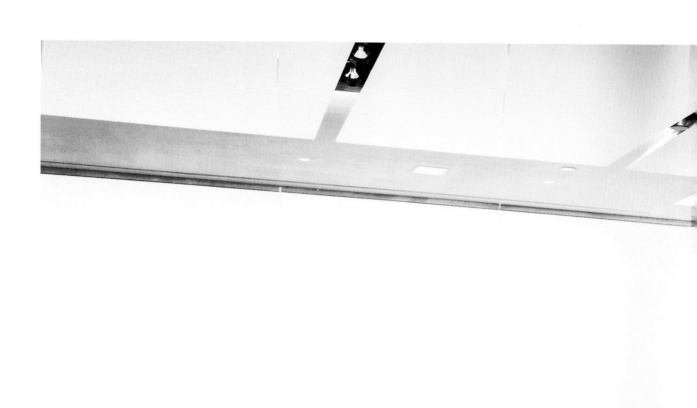

# Index

halibut:
  cornmeal-crusted fish tacos with black bean & peach salsa, 126–27
  grilled, with cherry tomatoes, sugar snap peas & lemon, 121–22
  summer fish sandwiches, 124–25
ham:
  & cheese frittata, 252
  savory bread pudding two ways, 270–71
ham hock, in brisket with red-eye gravy, 190–91
hanger steak:
  Dominican beef, 178–79
  Thai beef, 176–77
harissa paste, in Farro & Beans, 70
Harvey, Adam, 236
herb(s)(ed):
  baked fish with lemon & herb butter, 119
  Japanese eggplant & bulgur salad, 75
  orzo salad with zucchini, tomatoes & fresh herbs, 82–83
  oven-roasted potato chips with herbs, 232
  summer bean salad with tomatoes & herb dressing, 42
hibiscus cooler, 315-16
holiday roast pork, 194–95
hot dogs, 236
hot fudge sauce, 274
huevos rancheros, layered, 256–57
Humm, Daniel:
  Eleven Madison Park fried chicken, 155

I

Indian dishes:
  easy beef curry, 185
  Goan-spiced braised pork, 199
Italian & Italian-American dishes:
  baked ziti, 101-2
  buttermilk panna cotta with rhubarb-strawberry compote, 276–77
  chicken Parmigiano, less-is-more, 146-47

cioppino, 136–37
cranberry mostarda, 244–45
lamb Bolognese, 98–99
lasagna, Mama Romano's, 104-6
marinara, Maialino, 114
orecchiette with broccoli rabe, sausage & ricotta, 97-98
pappa al pomodoro, 30
pasta dough, fresh, 108-9
pasta e fagioli, 34–35
penne cacio e pepe, 91
penne with fennel, spinach & golden raisins, 90
spaghetti carbonara, 92
tomato panzanella, 52

J

jalapeños, in year-round pickled vegetables, 242–43
jam or Nutella rolls, 266
jerk shrimp, 132–33

K

Kalachnikoff, Howard:
  yellow bell pepper panzanella, 54-55
kale:
  lacinato kale & escarole salad with anchovy dressing, 53
  secret-ingredient soup, Michael Romano's, 32–33
Keehner, Dan:
  plum & apricot crisp with almond cream, 280-81
Kim, Sammy:
  paella, 138-39
kimchi:
  eggs & bacon with spicy fried rice, 258–59
  seared short rib wraps, 182–83
Knall, Kyle:
  couscous with carrot juice, 74
Korean dishes:
  Korean short ribs, 184
  seared short rib wraps, 182–83
Kotz, Ty, 151
Kreuther, Gabriel, 255, 306
  roasted potatoes with fromage blanc & bacon, 234-35

L

lacinato kale & escarole salad with anchovy dressing, 53
Lakhwani, Jai:
  oven-roasted potato chips with herbs, 232
lamb:
  black bean chili, 208–9
  Bolognese, 98–99
  meatballs with yogurt sauce, 204–5
lasagna, Mama Romano's, 104–6
Lavorini, Dino, 317, 319
  apple & pear tart, prizewinning, 304-5
layered huevos rancheros, 256–57
Lazlo, Geoff, 71, 74
  farro & beans, 70
  smoked fish & chopped egg salad, 118
leeks, with rice noodles & cabbage, 94
lemon(s):
  baked fish with lemon & herb butter, 119
  grilled halibut with cherry tomatoes, sugar snap peas & lemon, 121–22
  lemon bars, 290–91
  roasted broccoli with Pecorino Romano & lemon, 219
  roasted cauliflower with lemon-caper dressing, 221
lentil salad with summer squash & dried cherries, 68–69
lettuce:
  Bibb salad with green beans, radishes & rustic croutons, 43
  mussels with lettuce sauce, 134–35
  seared short rib wraps, 182–83
  Thai beef, 176-77
Levy, Doron:
  lamb meatballs with yogurt sauce, 204-5
Lilly, Robert:
  Tabla chicken with ginger & peppers, 154
limeade, cherry or pomegranate, 313
Lipp, Sam, 320